Welcome to East Anglia

CONTENTS

GW00546025

Pop into your nearest Tourist Information Centre for help and advice about places to visit, places to stay and other information about East Anglia and beyond. They are there to help both visitors and locals so do make use of their expert knowledge. See page 100 for details of where to find them.

Information for people with special needs relating to the places mentioned in this guide is contained in a free information sheet. For this and a list of other information sheets, available at 50p each, please contact the East Anglia Tourist Board.

Published by East Anglia Tourist Board, Toppesfield Hall, Hadleigh, Suffolk IP7 5DN
Telephone: (0473) 822922
Editors: Elizabeth Woolnough, Alison Smith
Advertising: Michael Penn, Simon Daykin

Printed in England, ISBN 1-873246-06-4   ■ Front Cover: Country Fair, Holkham Hall, Norfolk by Peter Miller

The Best Days Out Are Yesterdays

England's superb historical heritage is especially rich in East Anglia. Here you'll find splendid houses, elegant gardens, peaceful parks, lakes and country walks.

Often with restaurant meals, light refreshments, gift shops and many special events.

Blickling Hall
NORFOLK

Felbrigg Hall
NORFOLK

Oxburgh Hall
NORFOLK

Sheringham Park
NORFOLK

Ickworth
SUFFOLK

Lavenham Guildhall
SUFFOLK

Anglesey Abbey
CAMBRIDGESHIRE

Wimpole Hall & Home Farm
CAMBRIDGESHIRE

Free Visitors Guide to East Anglia

For further information on these and all other Trust properties in East Anglia, telephone 0263 733471 (9am–5pm) or write to The National Trust, Blickling, Norwich NR11 6NF.

The National Trust

Please mention East Anglia Guide when replying to advertisements

HISTORIC HOUSES

BEDFORDSHIRE

Luton Hoo, The Wernher Collection (signposted from J10 of M1): Set in parkland laid out by 'Capability' Brown, the house was originally built by Robert Adam in 1767. The Wernher collection comprises tapestries, porcelain, ceramics, ivories, bronzes and Renaissance jewellery. Works of Carl Fabergé, the Russian court jeweller and many personal possessions of the Russian Imperial family. *6 Apr-17 Oct, Fri, Sat & Sun 1.30-5 (last admission), gardens open 12. Tue, Wed & Thu for pre-booked parties only, Tel: (0582) 22955. House & gardens £4.50/£2/£4. Gardens only £2/75p/£1.75.*

Woburn Abbey, Woburn: Contains an impressive and important private collection of works including paintings by many of the World's Great Masters, furniture, porcelain and silver. Set in a beautifully landscaped 3,000 acre deer park. *1 Jan-28 Mar, Sat & Sun; 29 Mar-31 Oct, daily. 11-5 (last entry in winter 4). £6/£2/£5 (incl private apartments). £5/£2/£4 (excl private apartments).*

Ingatestone Hall, Essex

CAMBRIDGESHIRE

Anglesey Abbey (NT), Lode (6m NE Cambridge): 13c abbey, later Tudor house. Fairhaven collection of paintings and furniture. Outstanding 100-acre garden. Visitors centre includes a restaurant serving lunches and teas, shop and an exciting display showing how these unique gardens were developed. *House: 27 Mar-17 Oct, Wed-Sat, 1.30-5.20 (Sun & Bank Hol opens 1pm). £4.50/£2.25, Sun & Bank Hol Mon £5.50/£2.75 (includes House and Gardens). Gardens: 27 Mar-11 July, Wed-Sun & Bank Hol*

The Second George Room at Burghley House

Mon, 11-5.30; 12 July-7 Sept, daily, 11-5.30; 8 Sept-17 Oct, Wed-Sun, 11-5.30. £2.50/£1.25, Sun & Bank Hol Mon £3/£1.50. Closed Good Fri. Lode Mill also open (see Mills section).

Burghley House, Stamford: Built by William Cecil in 1587 and occupied by his descendants ever since: 18 treasure-filled State rooms are on view, including large art collection, wood carvings. Silver-decorated fireplaces and magnificent ceilings painted by Verrio. *9 Apr-early Oct, daily 11-5; closed 4 Sept. £3.80/£2.30/£3.50 (92).*

Elton Hall, Elton (8m W Peterborough, on A605): Historic house and gardens with fine collection of paintings, furniture and books. Afternoon teas and gift shop. *May, Spring and Aug Bank Hol Sun & Mons; July, Wed & Sun; Aug, Wed, Thur & Sun. 2-5. £3.30/£1.65. Garden only £1.50/75p.*

Hinchingbrooke House, Huntingdon (m W town centre on A604): 13c Benedictine nunnery, converted and added to in 16, 17 and 18c. Strong associations with Cromwells, Earls of Sandwich, Samuel Pepys. 60-acre park. Tea room. *1 May-30 Aug, Sun 2-5. Guided tours £1.50/£1/£1.*

Kimbolton Castle, Kimbolton (7m NW St Neots, on A45): Tudor house remodelled by Vanbrugh. Pellegrini mural paintings. Adam Gatehouse. *11 & 12 Apr, 30 & 31 May; 18 Jul-29 Aug, Suns; 30 Aug. 2-6 60p/20p/20p.*

Peckover House (NT), Wisbech: Merchant's house on North Brink of River Nene, c 1722. Fine plaster and wood rococo interior, notable and rare Victorian garden with unusual trees. Tearoom. *27 Mar-31 Oct. House & Garden, Sun, Wed & Bank Hol Mon. Garden, Sat-Wed. 2-5.30. House and Garden £2.30/£1.15. Garden only days £1/50p. Parties by appt.*

Wimpole Hall (NT), (off A603 near New Wimpole): Cambridgeshire's most spectacular mansion in a restrained 18c style. Rooms intimate and formal with work by Gibbs, Flitcroft and Soane. Park landscaped by Brigman, Brown and Repton. Re-creation of a formal Dutch garden. Picnic area. Lunches & Teas, 12-5. Shop. *27 Mar-31 Oct, daily (ex Mon & Fri), 1-5 (open Bank Hol Mon 11-5). 23 Jul-20 Aug, Fri also. Hall & gardens £4.50/£2. Farm (see Rare Breeds for details) £3.50/£1.50. Hall & Farm £6/£2.50.*

ENJOY 300 YEARS OF HISTORY IN A DAY

Holkham Hall is one of Britain's most majestic Stately homes, situated in a 3,000 acre deer park on the beautiful north Norfolk coast. This classic 18th Century Palladian style mansion is part of a great agricultural estate, and is a living treasure house of artistic and architectural history.

Attractions include: Holkham Hall, Bygones Museum, Pottery, Garden Centre, Gift Shop, Art Gallery, Tea Rooms, Deer Park, Lake and Beach.

OPENING TIMES & ADMISSION CHARGES
Daily (except Fridays & Saturdays) from 30th May to 30th September, 1.30 p.m.-5.00 p.m. Also Easter, May, Spring & Summer Bank Holiday Sundays & Mondays, 11.30 a.m.-5.00 p.m. Last admission 4.40 p.m.

Hall & Park:
Adults £2.70 Children £1.20
Bygones & Park:
Adults £2.70 Children £1.20
All Inclusive:
Adult £4.70 Children £2.00
10% reduction on pre-paid parties of 20 or more

**Holkham Hall,
Wells-next-the-Sea, Norfolk,
NR23 1AB.
Tel. (0328) 710227**

KENTWELL

Spend an hour or a day & share the magic of its spell

THE HALL *Magnificent mellow redbrick moated Tudor manor. Still a family home*
MOAT HOUSE *Remnant of 15th C. house, equipped as then*
GARDENS *Ancient Walled Garden, Moats, Herb Garden*
MAZE *Unique brick-paved mosaic Tudor Rose*
TUDOR FARM *Working Farm - traditional farmyard buildings, rare breeds, early tools & equipment*
FOR ADMISSION AND STANDARD OPENING TIMES SEE EDITORIAL ENTRY

DIARY OF SPECIAL EVENTS FOR 1993

Easter: Fri 9-Mon 12 Apr	**Great Easter Egg Quiz; Tudor Bakery and Dairy**
May Day: Sat 1-Mon 3	**Tudor May Day Celebrations**
Spring BH: Sat 29-Mon 31	**Re-Creation of Tudor Life**
June 20-July 18 (Sats, Suns & Fri 16 Jul only)	**Main Re-Creation** - *250 'Tudors' take the Manor back to a year in the 16th Century*
Aug BH: Fri 27-Mon 30	**Re-Creation of Tudor Life**
September 25-26	**Miichaelmas Re-Creation of Tudor Life**

KENTWELL HALL, LONG MELFORD, SUFFOLK. TEL 0787 310207

Elizabethan History started at

Historic Hatfield
SOMETHING FOR ALL THE FAMILY

- Historic Jacobean House 1611
- Old Palace 1497
- Formal, Knot, Scented and Wilderness Gardens
- Great Park with nature trails and venture play area
- Exhibition of William IV Kitchen and Model Soldiers
- Licensed Restaurant and Coffee Shop
- Gift and Garden Shops

21 miles north of London A1(M) 2 miles, M25 7 miles
Open 25 March to 10 October.
Tues-Sat: Noon-4.00pm Sundays: 1.30-5pm
Bank Holidays: 11am-5pm Park:10.30am-8pm

LIVING CRAFTS 6-9 May

FESTIVAL OF GARDENING 19 and 20 June

**Hatfield House, Hatfield, Herts. AL9 5NQ
Tel: Hatfield (0707) 262823**

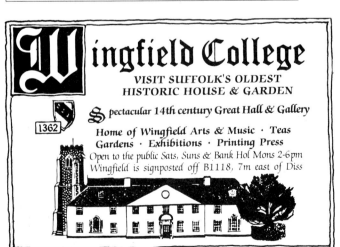

Wingfield College
VISIT SUFFOLK'S OLDEST HISTORIC HOUSE & GARDEN

Spectacular 14th century Great Hall & Gallery

1362

**Home of Wingfield Arts & Music · Teas
Gardens · Exhibitions · Printing Press**
Open to the public Sats, Suns & Bank Hol Mons 2-6pm
Wingfield is signposted off B1118, 7m east of Diss

Please mention East Anglia Guide when replying to advertisements

6

Layer Marney Tower

ESSEX

Audley End House (EH), Saffron Walden: Palatial Jacobean house with decorated interiors and collections of furniture and pictures. Remodelled in 18c and in 19c. Magnificent Great Hall, 17c plaster ceilings. Exhibition of family silver in the Butlers Pantry. Rooms and furniture designed by Robert Adams. Landscaped park by 'Capability' Brown. *1 Apr-30 Sept, Tue-Sun & Bank Hols, 1-6 (gardens from 12). £4.50/£2.30/£3.40 (92).*

Gosfield Hall, Gosfield, Halstead: Tudor house built around courtyard with later alterations. Old Well and pump house Elizabethan gallery with oak panelling, Queen Anne and Georgian rooms. *1 May-30 Sept, Wed & Thu, grounds 2-5, tours of house 2.30 & 3.15. Grounds free, tours of house £1.50/50p.*

Ingatestone Hall, Ingatestone: Tudor house and gardens, the home of the Petre family since 1540. Family portrait collection, furniture and other heirlooms on display. *10 Apr-26 Sept, Fri-Sun; 14 Jul-2 Sept, also Wed & Thu; Open Bank Hol Mons 12 Apr, 3 May, 31 May & 30 Aug. 1-6. £3/£2/£2.50.*

Layer Marney Tower (6m SW Colchester, on B1022): The highest Tudor gatetower in England, with early 16c Italianate decoration. Formal garden. Deer and Rare Breed Farm Park. Fine outbuildings. *1 Apr-3 Oct, Thu & Sun. Jul & Aug, also Mon, Tue, Wed & Fri, 2-6. Bank Hol Sun & Mons, also Good Fri 11-6. £3/£1.50.*

Paycocke's (NT), Coggeshall (6m E Braintree): Half-timbered merchant's house built c 1500. Richly carved interior. *28 Mar-10 Oct, Tue, Thu, Sun & Bank Hol Mon, 2-5.30. £1.40/65p.*

HERTFORDSHIRE

Hatfield House, Hatfield: Jacobean House, built 1611, containing famous portraits, rare tapestries, fine furniture and armour, and relics of Elizabeth I. Within the gardens stands the Old Palace (1497), childhood home of Elizabeth I. *25 Mar-10 Oct. House, Tue-Sat, guided tours only, 12-4; Sun, no guided tours, 1.30-5. Bank Hol Mon, no guided tours, 11-5. Park, daily ex Good Fri, 10.30-8. Gardens, daily ex Good Fri, 11-6. £4.50/£3/£3.70.*

Knebworth House, Knebworth: The home of the Lytton family since 1490, set in 250 acre park. Formal gardens. Extensive adventure playground. Miniature railway. Cafeteria in 400 year old tithe barn. *3 Apr-31 May, Sat, Sun, Bank Hols & school hols; 1 Jun-5 Sept, daily (closed Mon ex Bank Hols, also closed 16-19 Jul incl); 6 Sept-3 Oct, Sat & Sun. Park & playground 11-5.30, house & gardens 12-5. £4/£3.50/£3.50 (92), park & playground only £2.50 (92).*

Moor Park Mansion, Rickmansworth: Club house of Moor Park Golf Club, owned by District Council. Jacobean mansion built for James, Duke of Monmouth in 1678 and reconstructed in Palladian style in 1720. *All year, Mon-Fri ex Bank Hol, 10-12, 2-4. Free.*

LINCOLNSHIRE

Belvoir Castle, (off A607, nr Grantham): Home of the Duke and Duchess of Rutland with fine views over the Vale of Belvoir. The castle houses art treasures including works by Poussin and Rubens. Museum of the 17th/21st Lancers. Special events most Sunday and Bank Hols include medieval jousting. *1 Apr-30 Sept, Tue, Wed, Thu & Sat 11-5, Sun & Bank Hol Mon 11-6. Good Fri 11-5. Sun in Oct 11-5. £3.50/£2.50/£2.50.*

NORFOLK

Beeston Hall, Beeston St Lawrence (2m NE Wroxham, off A1151). Georgian country house in flintfaced "Gothic" style with classical interiors. Portraits, furniture, etc associated with the Preston family since 1640. Tea room in orangery, wine cellars and woodland walks. *11 Apr-19 Sept, Fri, Sun & Bank Hol Mons. Also Wed in Aug 2-5.30. £2.50/£1.*

Blickling Hall (NT) (1m NW Aylsham, off B1354): Jacobean red brick mansion, with fine plaster-work ceiling in great gallery, also tapestry. Notable garden, orangery, parkland and lake. Picnic area, shop, teas, lunches. Plant centre. *House: 27 Mar-31 Oct, daily ex Mon, Thu & Good Fri (open Bank Hol Mon); 1-5. Garden same days as house (daily in July & Aug), 12-5. House & Gardens £4.90/£2.40. Garden only £2.50/£1.20.*

Dragon Hall (King Street, Norwich): Magnificent medieval Merchant's Hall, with outstanding timber framed structure containing 15c Great Hall, superb crown post roof, carved and painted dragon, vaulted undercroft and 14c ogee doorways, screens passage and living hall. Shop. *1 Apr-30 Nov, Mon-Sat. 1 Dec-31 Mar, Mon-Fri. 10-4. Closed 19 Dec-2 Jan, also Bank Hol Mons & Good Fri. Open for groups at other times by appt. £1/free/50p.*

Felbrigg Hall (NT) (3m SW Cromer, near Felbrigg village): One of the finest 17c country houses in Norfolk, with orignal 18c furniture and pictures. Traditional walled garden, orangery with camellias, park, lakeside walk, woodland walk. Teas, lunches, picnic place, shop. *27 Mar-31 Oct, daily (ex Tue & Fri). House & Mon, 11-5. Gardens same days as house from 11. House & Gardens £4.30/£2.15. Gardens £1.70/85p.*

Holkham Hall (2m W Wells-next-the-Sea, off A149): 18c Palladian home of "Coke of Norfolk". Extensive collection of pictures, tapestries, statues and furnishings. Bygones collection. Pottery and garden centre. Tea rooms. *10-11 Apr; 2-3 May; 30 May-30 Sept, Sun-Thu. 1.30-5, Bank Hol Sun & Mon 11.30-5. Hall & Park £2.70/£1.20. Hall, Park & Bygones £4.70/£2. (see separate Bygones Collection in Museums section).*

Houghton Hall (14m E King's Lynn, off A148): Built for Sir Robert Walpole, the first Prime Minister of England, in the early 18c. Much of the original furnishings by William Kent remain in the superb State Rooms. Collection of approx 20,000 model soldiers and other militaria.

Knebworth House, set in a 250 acre park

The Priory Lavenham, Suffolk.

Visit the Priory and step into the magical atmosphere of the house and herb garden.

Enjoy coffee, home made lunches and teas **in the Refectory.**

Select from our range of unusual gifts & woven tapestries in **the Gift Shop.**

Also guided tours by appointment
Tel: 0787 247417.

House Open April to end of October
Daily 10.30 - 5.30.

SPRINGFIELDS

'One of Britain's Premier Show Gardens'

Open daily
April – September

Twenty five acres of landscaped gardens showing massed spring and summer bedding displays and roses. Indoor gardens, new restaurant and bar, shops, wheelchairs, etc.

Dates for your diary:

4-7 February	*Springfields Horticultural Exhibition and Forced Flower Show*
11-12 April	*Easter Craft Festival*
1-3 May	*Spaldling Flower Festival and Parade*
25 July	*Vintage and Classic Vehicle Show*
7-8 August	*Springfields Flower Show*

Send for illustrated brochure to: Springfields, Spalding, Lincs. Tel: 0775 724843

GARDENS & GROUNDS

Open Easter Sunday to 19th September, 1993
2 p.m. – 5.30 p.m. Wednesdays – Fridays – Sundays and Bank Holidays
Admission £1.75 Children 25p
Private parties by arrangement

Plant sales–tea rooms–gardening books.

These well established gardens offer a wide combination of plants, shrubs and trees. Featuring: Rare rhododrendrons – Azaleas – water plants and the herbaceous borders of the "Spider" walled garden.

Woodland and lakeside walks.

HOVETON HALL Wroxham, Norwich, NR12 8RJ Tel: (0603) 782798
1 mile north of Wroxham Bridge on A1151

BELVOIR CASTLE

NEAR GRANTHAM, LINCOLNSHIRE
Home of the Duke and Duchess of Rutland
The Castle commands a magnificent view over the vale of Belvoir,
and houses notable pictures, staterooms,
and the Museum of the 17th/21st Lancers.
Adventure Play Area, Gift Shop & Restaurant
Special events most Sundays and Bank Holidays
including Medieval Jousting Tournaments
For further details contact the Estate Office
FREEPOST, Belvoir Castle, Grantham, Lincs, NG31 6BR
Telephone 0476-870262
(The Castle is signposted from the A1, A52 & A607)

The house, set in a landscaped park, was built by Lord Arlington, whose son-in-law was the first Duke of Grafton (and a natural son of Charles II). Now the home of 11th Duke of Grafton, Euston Hall has a large collection of family portraits by Van Dyck, Lely and Stubbs. Home-made teas in Old Kitchen. Shop. 17th C. Church. Coach parties welcome. Thursdays, 3rd June – 30th September 2.30 – 5.00 pm. Also two Sundays (27th June and 5th September) 2.30 – 5.00 pm
All enquiries: Thetford (0842) 766366

EUSTON HALL 3m S. of Thetford on A1088
12m N. of Bury St. Edmunds

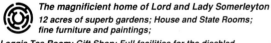

SOMERLEYTON HALL
with its gardens & famous maze

The magnificient home of Lord and Lady Somerleyton
12 acres of superb gardens; House and State Rooms;
fine furniture and paintings;

Loggia Tea Room; Gift Shop; Full facilities for the disabled.

**OPEN EASTER DAY
to SEPT 26th 1993**

12.30-5pm Details from the Administrator on Thursdays, Sundays and Bank Holidays
- plus
Tuesdays and Wednesdays in July and August only.
Gardens open and light lunches from 12.30pm

Special Rates for Parties

FREE PARKING Signposted from Great Yarmouth and Lowestoft
(No Dogs)

Fritton Lake
Country Park Tel 0493 488208

**250 acres of adventure
and relaxation for children and adults alike . . .**

2-mile Lake - with Angling, Boating & Guided Launch Trips

OPEN EVERY DAY
10am-6pm
April 1st-Sept 26th 1993
ask about disabled facilities . . .

SELF CATERING COTTAGES
with wood-burning stoves
& use of all Park facilities.

- 9-hole golf • putting
- beautiful gardens
- woodland walks • cafe
- wildfowl • gift shop
- adventure playground
- craft workshops etc. etc.

FREE PARKING Signposted from Great Yarmouth and Lowestoft
NO DOGS IN THE PARK

Please mention East Anglia Guide when replying to advertisements

Interior of Dragon Hall, Norwich

Stables with heavy horses and ponies. Facilities and lift for disabled. Picnic area, cafeteria, gift shop, children's playground. *11 Apr-26 Sept, Thu, Sun & Bank Hol Mons. Tel: (0485) 528569 for times and prices.*

Oxburgh Hall (NT) (7m SW Swaffham): 15c moated red brick fortified manor. Magnificent 80ft gatehouse. Henry VII visited. Mary Queen of Scots' needlework. Pugin chapel, notable French parterre garden, woodland walks. Lunches, teas, shop. *27 Mar-31 Oct, Sat-Wed, 1.30-5.30, gardens open at 12; Bank Hol Mon, 11-5.30. £3.60/£1.80.*

Sandringham House, Grounds and Museum (Open except when HM The Queen or any member of the Royal Family is in residence) (8m NE King's Lynn): Home of HM The Queen. Nature trail, museum of motor cars and dolls. Shop, cafeteria and restaurant. *11 Apr-3 Oct, Mon-Sat, 11-4.45, Sun opens 12. House closed 19 Jul-7 Aug incl. House and grounds closed 23 Jul-4 Aug incl. Admission House and Grounds £3/£1.50/£2. Grounds only £2/£1/£1.50.*

SUFFOLK

Christchurch Mansion, Ipswich: Extensive Tudor town house in park in town centre. Furnished period rooms. Decorative art collections of china, glass, etc. Attached art gallery (see Museums & Art Galleries section). *All year, Tue-Sat 10-5 (dusk in winter), Sun 2.30-4.30 (dusk in winter). Closed 24-27 Dec, 1 Jan & Good Fri. Free.*

Euston Hall, Euston (3m S Thetford, on A1088): 18c home of the Duke of Grafton, containing famous collection of 17c and 18c pictures by Van Dyck, Lely and Stubbs. Landscape by John Evelyn, William Kent and Capability Brown. 17c parish church in Wren style. Home-made teas and shop in Old Kitchen. *3 Jun-30 Sept, Thu. Also Suns 27 June & 5 Sept. 2.30-5. £2.25/50p/£1.50.*

Haughley Park, Stowmarket (3m W Stowmarket, signposted off A45, ignore Haughley signs): Jacobean manor house with lovely gardens, and woods set in parkland. *1 May-30 Sept, Tue, 3-6. £2/£1.*

Ickworth (NT). Horringer (3m SW Bury St Edmunds, on A143): Magnificent Palladian house with 106ft Rotunda connected to flanking wings by curving corridors. Staterooms with late Regency and 18c furniture, great family portrait collection, outstanding silver collection, orangery. Formal garden, park, woodland walks. Lunches, teas, shop. *House & Garden: 27 Mar-30 Apr, Sat, Sun and Bank Hol Mon; closed Good Fri. 1 May-30 Sept daily (ex Mon & Thur, open on Bank Hol Mons). Oct, Sat & Sun. 1.30-5.30. Park open all year, dawn-dusk. House, Garden & Park £4.30/£2. Garden & Park £1.50/50p.*

Kentwell Hall, Long Melford (N of Green in Long Melford): Romantic mellow red brick moated Tudor manor, in lovely setting. Still a family home. Unaltered 15c moat house, furnished and as equipped as then. Walled garden and large herb garden. Mosaic brick maze and Tudor farm. Home-made lunches and teas. *28 Mar-19 Jun, Suns only; 13-16 Apr, 1-4 Jun & 21 Jul-26 Sept, daily; 12-5. Historical Re-Creation: Easter, May, Spring & Aug Bank Hol weekends; Sat, Suns inc 16 Jul during 20 Jun-18 Jul; 25 & 26 Sept; 11-6 (16 Jul closes 5, Michaelmas weekend 12-5). House, gardens & farm £4/£2.50/£3.40 (92); Increased charges for Re-Creation days.*

Little Hall, Lavenham (6m NE Sudbury, on A1141): 15c hall house with crown post roof. Gayer-Anderson collection of furniture, pictures, sculptures and ceramics. Small walled garden. *9 Apr-10 Oct, Sat, Sun, Wed, Thu & Bank Hols, 2.30-5.30. £1/50p.*

Melford Hall (NT) Long Melford (3m N Sudbury, on A143): Turreted brick Tudor mansion, 18c and Regency interiors. Collection of Chinese porcelain. Beatrix Potter display. Interesting gardens. *27 Mar-30 Apr, Sat, Sun & Bank Hol Mon. 1 May-30 Sept, Wed, Thu, Sat, Sun & Bank Hol Mon. Oct, Sat & Sun. 2-5.30. £2.60/£1.30.*

The Priory, Water Street, Lavenham: Through the ages the home of Benedictine monks, medieval clothiers, an Elizabethan rector, and now of the Casey family who rescued the house from a derelict ruin. Beautiful timber-framed building (Grade 1) with stimulating interior design and stained glass by Ervin Bossanyi (1891-1975). Lovely herb garden of unique design. Work still continues on parts of the building. On display is an exhibition of photographs illustrating the restoration. Guided tours available. Coffees, lunches and teas served in the Refectory. *Easter-31 Oct daily 10.30-5.30. Open by appt for groups all year. £2.50/£1.*

Somerleyton Hall and Maze (5m NW Lowestoft, off B1074): The home of Lord and Lady Somerleyton. Rebuilt in Anglo-Italian style in 1846. Magnificent state rooms, furnishings, woodcarvings and paintings. Fine gardens; maze, garden trail and miniature railway. Shop, tea room. *Hall, gardens, maze and deer park: 11 Apr-26 Sept, Thu, Sun and Bank Hols; July & Aug also Tue & Wed, 2-5. Gardens open and refreshments available from 12.30. (Miniature railway runs Sun & Thu). Hall, gardens & maze £3.40/£1.65/£2.70.*

Wingfield College, Wingfield (7m SE Diss, on B1118): Founded by Sir John de Wingfield in 1362 incorporating earlier Wingfield Manor House. Fascinating Gothic timber-framed building hidden by 18c front. Great hall, cloister, lodgings range. Discovered and restored as private house 1971-81. Teas. Celebrated Arts and Music season *10 Apr-26 Sept, Sat, Sun & Bank Hol Mons, 2-6. Groups by appt all year. £2/£1.*

The Maze, Somerleyton Hall

Prices are in the order Adults/Children/Senior Citizens. Where prices are not available at the time of going to press, the 1992 (92) price is given. See Touring Maps on pages 104-108 for locations of places to visit.

GARDENS

BEDFORDSHIRE

Bedford Embankment Gardens, The Embankment, Bedford: The gardens, remaining much unchanged since their original layout, provide outstanding displays during the spring and summer months. Tree lined walkways and open parkland provide many opportunities for peaceful walks. *Open at all tines. Free.*

Stockwood Period Gardens, Stockwood Country Park, Farley Hill, Luton: Recreated examples of English horticulture from the medieval garden, to country garden to Elizabethan knot garden. Unusual plants from the National Plant Collection. *2 Jan-24 Dec; Apr-Oct Wed-Sun 10-5; Nov-Mar, Fri-Sun 10-4. Free.*

Swiss Garden, Biggleswade Road, Old Warden, Biggleswade: Romantic 19c landscaped garden with a fine collection of trees and shrubs, ornamental ironwork, ponds and a picnic area in adjoining lakeside woodland. *Jan-Mar, Sun & Bank Hol, Apr-Oct daily ex Tue. Sun & Bank Hol 11-6, other days 1.30-6. £1.50/75p/75p.*

Wrest Park House & Gardens, Silsoe (1/2m E Silsoe off A6): Louis XV style French chateau dominating almost 100 acres of landscaped gardens. *1 Apr-26 Sept, Sat, Sun & Bank Hols, 10-6. £1.50/75p/£1.10.*

CAMBRIDGESHIRE

Cambridge University Botanic Garden: Garden of great interest laid out by Henslow in 1846. Glasshouses, limestone rock garden. Picnic area. *All year (ex 25-26 Dec) Nov-Jan, Mon-Sat, 8-4; Feb-Apr & Oct, Mon-Sat 8-5; May-Sept, Mon-*

Dowcra's Manor Garden

Gardens of the Rose, St Albans

Sat, 8-6. Sundays 10-seasonal closing time. Guided tours by appt (fee). Mon-Sat free, Sun £1/50p.

Docwra's Manor, Shepreth (8m SW Cambridge, off A10, opposite the war memorial): Series of enclosed gardens containing choice plants. All the year round interest. 18c red brick house (not open). Barn. 20c folly. *All year, Mon, Wed & Fri 10-4 and first Suns of Apr-Oct 2-5. Bank Hol Mons, 10-4. Plants for sale. No dogs. Also open by appt Tel: (0763) 261473/261557. £1.50/Free.*

ESSEX

Bridge End Gardens, Saffron Walden: Victorian garden of great interest, garden ornaments, rose garden, Dutch garden and pavilions, fine trees. Garden being restored. Large Victorian maze, recently restored, is only open by appt through Tourist Information Centre. *All year, daily, 9-dusk. Free.*

The Fens, Old Mill Road, Langham: Small cottage garden – 2 acres in attractive surroundings. Interesting garden being established in conjunction with nursery selling hardy plants. *Mar-Oct, Thu & Sat. 10-5. By appt for other times Tel: (0206) 272259. £1 (to National Gardens Scheme and St Helena Hospice).*

Harborough Hall Garden, Messing: 5 acre garden, half of which is maintained. Unusual shrubs and trees, herbaceous borders, ponds, old fashioned roses. Many bulbs in spring. *Easter Sun and every Sun thereafter until end Sept, 2-6. By appt, Tel: (0621) 819853. £1/free/50p.*

Hyde Hall Garden, Rettendon

Hyde Hall Garden, Rettendon (Within 5m A12 Chelmsford by-pass. 3m NE Wickford, off A130): All year round garden of 8 acres set on a hill with fine views. Woodland garden, spring bulbs, large rose garden, ornamental ponds, herbaceous borders, glasshouses and national collections of Malus and Viburnum. Refreshments, plants for sale. *31 Mar-24 Oct, Wed, Thu, Sat, Sun & Bank Hol. Open Good Fri. 11-6. £2/75p.*

Mark Hall Gardens, Muskham Road, off First Avenue, Harlow (adjoins cycle museum): Three walled gardens developed as an ornamental fruit garden, a 17c style garden with parterre, and a large walled garden which demonstrates a number of gardening styles and techniques. *All year, daily ex Sat (closed 24-26 Dec), 10-4.45 Closes 3.45 in winter, Sun closed 12.45-2. Free.*

Saling Hall Garden, Great Saling, nr Braintree: 12-acre garden includes walled garden dating from 1698. Small park with emphasis on unusual trees, water gardens. *May-July, Wed, 2-5. Sun 27 June, 2-6. Other times for parties by written appt. £1.50/Free.*

Spains Hall, Finchingfield (8m NW Braintree, on B1053): Beautiful grounds including flower and kitchen gardens and large Cedar of Lebanon tree planted 1670. *May-July, Sun; also May Bank Hol Mons, 2-5 £1/50p.*

Bressingham Gardens near Diss

HERTFORDSHIRE

Capel Manor, Bullsmoor Lane, Enfield: The gardens include special themes: historical, modern, water, rock, sensory, disabled person's, amaze and new Japanese garden. Also visit the educational farm on the neighbouring estate. *Apr-Oct, daily; Nov-Mar, Mon-Fri. 10.30-5.30 (last ticket 4.30). £2/£1/£1.50.*

Cheslyn Gardens, Cheslyn House, Nascott Wood Road, Watford: Set in 3 1/2 acres, the gardens combine natural woodland and formal garden styles. *All year, daily ex 25 & 26 Dec, 10-4 (1 Apr-30 Sept until 8). Free.*

Gardens of the Rose, Chiswell Green, (1m S St Albans). Thousands of varieties of old, new and future roses displayed in the gardens of the Royal National Rose Society. Especially interesting are trial grounds where new varieties submitted by leading hybridists worldwide undergo a 3 year trial. *12 June-17 Oct, Mon-Sat, 9-5; Sun and Bank Hol Mon, 10-6. £3.50/free.*

NORFOLK

Alby Gardens, Cromer Road, Erpingham: 4 acres of gardens, grounds, wet areas and wild areas. Bee garden, observation hive and information centre. Large collection of interesting shrubs, plants and bulbs. Part of a large working craft complex on the A140 between Aylsham and Cromer. *8 Apr-end Sept, 10-5. Closed Mons including Bank Hol Mons. 50p/free.*

Bressingham Gardens, nr Diss: 6 acres of informal beds with over 5,000 kinds of hardy perennials, alpines, heathers and conifers. Adjoins a hardy plant nursery, which can be viewed from steam-hauled trains. *Gardens open daily, 1 Apr-31 Oct, 10-5.30. £3.50/£2.50).*

Congham Hall Herb, Lynn Road, Grimston (off A148, B1153 to Grimston): Formal herb gardens, wild flowers, potager, collection of over 200 labelled herbs and approx. 150 varieties of herbs for sale. *1 Apr-30 Sept, daily except Sat, 2-4. Other times by appt Tel: (0485) 600250. Free.*

Fairhaven Garden Trust, South Walsham (9m NE Norwich, off B1140): Woodland and water gardens beside the private South Walsham Broad with many rare and attractive shrubs and plants, particularly primulas and rhododendrons in early summer. Home-made teas. Parties catered for by arrangement. *11 Apr-3 May, Sun & Bank Hols. 5 May-26 Sept, Wed-Sun & Bank Hols. Special events: Primroses, 9-18 Apr. Candelabra Primula weekend, 29-31 May. 11-6, Sat 2-6. Walks with the warden each Sun in Jul, 2.30, ring to book, Tel: (060 549) 449. Autumn Colours, 31 Oct, 10-dusk. £2/£1/£1.50. Season ticket £7.*

Fritton Lake, nr Great Yarmouth: Lakeside gardens, woodland walks. Boating, windsurfing, fishing, wildfowl collection. Large adventure playground, craft workshops. Cafe and shop. See also countryside entry. *1 Apr-26 Sept, daily 10-6, last adm 4.15. £3/£2/£2.*

Gooderstone Water Gardens, Crow Hall Farm, Gooderstone (11m SE King's Lynn, off A47): Landscaped garden with flowers, shrubs, grassy walks, lake, pools and bridges. *1 Apr-31 Oct, daily 10.30-5.30. £1/30p.*

Hoveton Hall Gardens, Hoveton Hall (1m N Wroxham Bridge on A1151 Stalham Road): 10 acres of garden in a woodland setting. Large walled herbaceous garden, Victorian kitchen garden, woodland and lakeside walks. Daffodils, azaleas, rhododendrons and hydrangeas. *11 Apr-19 Sept, Wed, Fri, Sun & Bank Hols 2-5.30, £1.75/25p.*

Mannington Gardens and Walks nr Saxthorpe (18m N Norwich, off B1149): Gardens with lake, moat and woodland. Outstanding rose collection. Heritage rose exhibition. Saxon church and Victorian follies. Country walks and trails. Coffee, lunches, home-made teas and snacks. Manor house by prior arrangement for specialist groups. *Gardens open: 4 Apr-31 Oct, Sun 12-5; 5 May-27 Aug also Wed, Thu & Fri, 11-5. Gardens £2/free/£1.50. Walks & car park open daily from 9, £1 per car.* See also Countryside Section.

Natural Surroundings, Bayfield Estate, Holt: 8 acres of demonstration gardens, orchid meadow and woodland walk. Shop and sales area. *9 Apr-31 Oct, daily, 10-5.30. 1 Nov-8 Apr, Thu-Sun, 10-4.30. £1.50/free/£1.*

Norfolk Lavender, Caley Mill, Heacham (2m S Hunstanton, on A149): Lavender, Herb, Rose and River Gardens. During harvest (mid July-mid Aug) distillery and a lavender field can be

Fritton Lake Country Park

11

GARDENS

Norfolk Lavender fields

visited. Otherwise slide show (June and Sept). Gift shop with lavender products and other quality gifts with a Countryside theme. Lavender, herb and heather plants. Cottage tea room. *Shop, grounds and tea room open daily, 10-5. Closed for 2 weeks at Christmas and New Year. Tours and booked coach parties. Entrance to grounds free.*

Rainthorpe Hall Gardens, Tasburgh, nr Norwich (8m S Norwich, off A140): Large gardens of Elizabethan manor house (house open by appt Tel: (0508) 470618). Fine trees of botanical interest, includes a collection of bamboos. Conservation lake. Plants for sale. Access for wheelchairs to garden. *30 Mar-31 Oct. Wed, Sat, Sun & Bank Hols, 10-5. £1/50p/75p.*

Raveningham Gardens, Loddon (6m NW Beccles on A146): Gardens surrounding elegant

Georgian house. Variety of rare and variegated plants and shrubs. Nurseries open daily. Teas on Sundays and Bank Hols when gardens open. *28 Mar-12 Sept, Sun & Bank Hol 2-5.30, £1.70/senior citizen £1.20 (92).*

Sandringham Grounds (Open except when HM The Queen or any member of The Royal Family is in residence) (8m NE King's Lynn): Home of HM The Queen. Nature trail, museum of motor cars, teas, shop, cafeteria and restaurant. *11 Apr-3 Oct, Mon-Sat, 10.30-5, Sun 11.30-5. House and Grounds closed 23 July-4 Aug incl. House closed 19 July-7 Aug incl. Sandringham Flower Show 28 July. Grounds only £2/£1.50/£1.*

Willow Farm Dried Flowers, Neatishead, Norwich: Norfolk's Dried Flower Centre. Growers and suppliers of quality dried flowers and arrangements direct to the public. Shop and workshop open throughout the year for advice and help. Walk round show field in summer. Day classes for groups of 6, Oct-Mar, Tel: (0603) 783588. *Open all year Mon-Sat, 10-4; Sun 2-4. Closed 24-31 Dec. Free.*

SUFFOLK

Akenfield, 1 Park Lane, Charsfield (11m NE Ipswich, off B1078): 1/2 acre garden containing vegetables, many varieties of flowers including dried ones. Shown on "Gardeners' World", BBC TV. Home-made wines on view. *23 May-28 Sept, daily 10.30-dusk. £1/free/75p.*

Blakenham Woodland Garden, Little Blakenham (4m NW Ipswich, off the B1113): 5-acre woodland garden with many rare trees and shrubs. Lovely throughout the year with bluebells, camellias and magnolias being followed by azaleas, rhododendrons, roses, hydrangeas and fine autumn colouring. Free parking. No dogs. *1 Apr-30 Sept, Wed, Thur, Sun & Bank Hols, 1-5. £1.*

Bruisyard Vineyard & Herb Centre, Church Road, Bruisyard, Saxmundham: Vineyard, winery, herb and water gardens. *Full details see Vineyards entry.*

Craft at the Suffolk Barn, Fornham Road, Gt Barton, Bury St Edmunds: Traditional restored Suffolk Barn selling craft from East Anglia. Herb and wild flower garden with 200 plant

Conifers at Sandringham

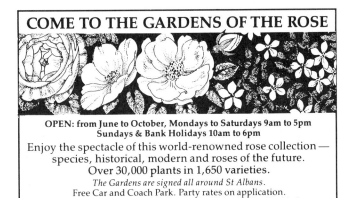

Please mention East Anglia Guide when replying to advertisements

species. Ornamental garden and plant sales. *Mid Mar-Christmas, Wed-Sat & Bank Hols, 10-5.30; Sun 12-5.30. Free, charity box.*

Gifford's Hall Hartest, nr Bury St Edmunds: 33 acre small country living with 12 acres of vines and a winery offering free tastings. Also rare breed sheep, pure breed free range chickens and an acre rose garden. There are wild flower meadows, cut flowers including sweet peas & chrysanthemums and a model organic vegetable garden. Tea rooms and shop. *9 Apr-31 Oct, daily, 12-6. £2.75/£1/£2.25. Coaches by appt.*

Helmingham Hall Gardens (between Ipswich and Debenham, on B1077): Lovely moated gardens little changed since Elizabethan times. Walled garden containing many rare roses, fine herbaceous borders and possibly the best kitchen garden in Britain. Also Highland cattle and safari rides in park to view Red and Fallow deer. Cream teas, stable craft shop. Home grown produce and plants for sale. *2 May-12 Sept, Suns, 2-6. Also coach parties on Suns and Weds by appt Tel: (0473) 890363. £2.20/£1.20/£2. Safari rides 80p/60p.*

Kentwell Hall, Long Melford (N of Green in Long Melford): Tranquil moated Gardens around 16c mansion with 17c walled gardens containing numerous espalier fruit trees. Moats, mature trees and hedges and much new planting. Lovely spring bulbs. Fine restored large dovecote and working farm with rare breed farm animals. *Separate admission to Gardens only when House open. Full opening times see Historic House entry. Gardens only £1.75/£1/£1.50 (92).*

Letheringham Watermill Gardens, Letheringham, 2m Wickham Market. Watermill (wheel newly restored).5 acres of gardens, riverside walk and water meadows. Home-made teas. Plants for sale. *28 Mar-31 May, 4 Jul-30 Aug, Sun & Bank Hol Mon, 2-6. £1.50/free/£1.*

The Priory, Water Street, Lavenham: Over a hundred varieties of herbs in garden of historic home (see Historic Houses section). *Easter-31 Oct, daily 10.30-5.30. £2.50/£1. Tel: (0787) 247417.*

Wyken Hall Gardens, Stanton (8m NE Bury St Edmunds off A143): Formal herb, knot, and woodland gardens. Walled garden with old fashioned roses. Woodland walk through ancient woodland to 7 acre vineyard. Large "Country Store" in converted 16c barn. Lunches, teas and wines from the vineyard. *1 May-30 Sept, Thu, Sun & Bamk Hol Mon. 11.30-5.30. Coaches by appt Tel: (0359) 50240. £1.50/free/£1.*

VINEYARDS

CAMBRIDGESHIRE

Chilford Hundred Vineyard, between Linton and Balsham: 18 acres of vines. Tours, tastings, interesting buildings. *1 May-30 Sept, daily, 11-5. Vineyard free, Winery Tour £3/free.*

ESSEX

Felsted Vineyard, The Vineyards, Crix Green, Felsted: Wine and cider making, vineyard work. Wines and vines may be bought. *All year, Sat 10-7, Sun 12-3; 1 Apr-30 Sept also Tue-Fri 10-7. 75p/free.*

New Hall Vineyards, Chelmsford Road, Purleigh, near Maldon: Vineyard trail and cellars open *Mon-Fri 10.30-5.30; Sat & Sun 10.30-1.30. Free. Special guided tours for pre-booked groups of 16+, 10 May-9 Sept, £3.50/free. 18th Annual English wine festival and craft fair 11 & 12 Sept £3.50/50p.*

Priory Vineyards, Priory Place, Little Dunmow: 10 acre vineyard and winery. Wine shop

Wild flowers at Gifford's Hall

with tourist items. *1 Apr-31 Oct, daily. Mon to Sat 11-5, Sun 12-5. £1.50/£1.*

HERTFORDSHIRE

Frithsden Vineyard, Roman Road, Frithsden, nr Hemel Hempstead: 3 acre vineyard planted in 1971 on a south facing slope in the foothills of the Chilterns. The grape variety is mainly Muller Thurgau. *Tours Jun-Oct, Sun 11.15-2, other times by appt. £2.50/free.*

NORFOLK

Elmham Vineyards, Elmham House, North Elmham, Dereham: Vineyards, winery, tastings and slide show. English wines and Norfolk Apple Wine for sale. *Conducted tours by appt Tel: (0362) 668571. £1.50.*

Pulham Vineyards, Mill Lane, Pulham Market, Diss: Vineyard, wine- making, bottling and tasting. *31 May-30 Sept, by appt only Tel: (0379) 676672.. £2.50/free/£2.*

SUFFOLK

Boyton Vineyards, Hill Farm, Boyton End, Stoke by Clare: Tour of vineyard, wine tastings & sales. *1 Apr-31 Oct, 10.30-6. Tours £1.50/free/£1.*

Bruisyard Vineyard & Herb Centre, Church Road, Bruisyard, Saxmundham: Vineyard, winery, herb and water gardens. Restaurant and picnic area. Free car park. Shop selling wines, vines, herbs and souvenirs. *Vineyard and gardens, all year, free. Guided winery tours, 2 Jan-24 Dec, daily 10.30-5, £3.20/£1/£2.90.*

Gifford's Hall, Hartest, nr Bury St Edmunds: 12 acres of wines and a winery offering free tastings. Tea rooms and shop. *Full details see Gardens entry.*

Shawsgate Vineyard, Badingham Road, Framlingham: 17 acre vineyard with modern winery making award winning English wines. Guided tours, vineyard walk, wine tastings, picnic area, children's play area, shop. *Open 1 Apr-31 Oct, daily, 10.30-5. All year for wine sales. Groups by appt. £2.75/free/£2.25.*

Helmingham Hall Gardens

Prices are in the order Adults/Children/Senior Citizens. Where prices are not available at the time of going to press, the 1992 (92) price is given. See Touring Maps on pages 104-108 for locations of places to visit.

NURSERIES AND GARDEN CENTRES

Stonham Barns, Pettaugh Road, (A1120), Stonham Aspal, Stowmarket, (just off A140). Interesting garden and leisure centre in the middle of the Suffolk countryside. Golf driving range, orchid centre, everything for the gardener and specialist advice and help. Original farm barns have been converted to house the Farmers Table restaurant, serving homemade lunches, cakes, teas, coffees all day to all manner of groups, parties and conferences. The Farm Shop offers a wide selection of home grown fruit, vegetables, gifts and crafts plus a selection of countrywear and our own range of preserves and chutneys, Stonham Hedgerow. The centre also houses many small businesses including pine furniture, pet foods, interior design, picture framing and glass engraving. *Open all year, 7 days a week, 10-5.30. Coaches & groups welcome by appointment. Talks and demonstrations on Orchids, Fruit Growing and Ribboncraft organised on request. Tel 0449 711755. Fax: 0449 711174*

LeGrice Roses, Norwich Road, North Walsham, Norfolk. Visit one of the UK's leading rose specialists. Acres of scent, an unbelievable range of colours (have you ever seen a grey, green or brown rose?) all to be enjoyed in our rose fields open July-Sept. Container grown roses available or book for November despatch or collection. Our spacious Garden Centre is open year round, offering one of the largest range of plants in East Anglia, mostly grown on our 45 acre nursery. Large display gardens, delightful garden shop with a wide range of gifts, house plants etc. Relax in Ramblers Restaurant and enjoy coffee, lunch or afternoon tea. Children, don't miss the aviary or Tom's mini-farm.
Easily found, 20 mins from Norwich (B1150), 30 mins from Gt Yarmouth (A149). Follow the Rose Centre signs. Open Mon-Sat 9-5. Sun & Bank Hols 10-5. Tel 0692 402591

Norfolk Lavender Ltd.,Caley Mill, Heacham, (on A149) Norfolk. Caley Mill is the home of the National Collection of Lavenders. See many varieties of lavender and a large miscellany of herbs. Hear about the harvest, and the ancient process of lavender distillation. The Countryside Gift Shop stocks the full range of Norfolk Lavender's famous products, together with a wide choice of other gifts to suit all pockets. The Herb Shop has many varieties of lavender and herb plants, together with unusual gifts for gardeners. The Cottage Tea Room specialises in cream teas, home made cakes and light lunches. Admission to car park and grounds free. *Open daily 10-5 (closed for Christmas holiday). Tea Room opening – Please see Afternoon Teas Section. Tel: Heacham (0485) 70384*

Taverham Garden Centre, Fir Covert Road, Taverham, Norwich (Situated 7 miles from Norwich on the A1067 Norwich/Fakenham road). Taverham Garden Centre is set in 15 acres of beautiful contryside in the pretty Wensum Valley to the west of the city of Norwich. The Garden Centre offers a riot of colour all year round, with acres of greenhouses packed with beautiful flowers and pot plants, all grown to the highest standards in the on-site propagating unit. For gardeners, there is an unrivalled choice of plants, shrubs and trees and an extensive range of bulbs and seeds, as well as attractive garden furniture and ornaments, terracotta pots and planters, paving slabs, pools and conservatories. Plus dried and silk flowers, books petfood, coffee bar, craft complex. Facilities for the disabled; coach parties welcome. Car parking for 1000 cars. *Open Mon-Sat, 9-5.30. Sun, 10- 5.30. Tel: (0603) 860522*

Notcutts Garden Centres: No visit to East Anglia is complete without a visit to Notcutts the nationally known and respected nursery and garden centres. Enjoy a stroll through the display grounds which include a children's playground, display borders and fine specimens of many interesting plants. Or browse through the pot plant centres, planterias or shops where attractive garden and house plants or garden tools and furniture are available. Whatever your interests, there will be plenty for you at:

Ipswich Road, Woodbridge, Tel: Woodbridge (0394) 383600. Also at

Station Road, Ardleigh, Essex, Tel: Colchester (0206) 230271.

Daniels Road (Ring Road), Norwich, Tel: (0603) 53155.

Oundle Road, Orton Waterville, Peterborough, Tel: (0733) 234600.

Fisk's Clematis Nursery, Westleton, nr Saxmundham, Suffolk IP17 3AJ (midway between Aldeburgh and Southwold on the B1125): Call and see many varieties of clematis in flower, on walls, pergola and in greenhouses, or send 75p for our colour catalogue. *Open Monday-Friday, 9-5; Sats and Suns in summer 10-1, 2-5. Tel: Westleton (072873) 263*

Bruisyard Vineyard and Herb Centre. One of the largest ornamental herb gardens in East Anglia. We have a wide variety of culinary, medicinal and pot-pourri herbs for sale as well as a good range of vines. We also offer vineyard and winery tours, a secluded picnic area, childrens play area, restaurant, a shop selling herb seeds, wines, herbal teas, local produce and crafts. Admission to the car park and gardens is free. *Open daily from 2nd January-24th December, 10.30-5, at Church Road, Bruisyard, Saxmundham, Suffolk IP17 2EF. Tel: Badingham (072875) 281.*

Peter Beales Roses, Attleborough. A large and world famous collection of roses featuring over 1100 rare, unusual and beautiful varieties. The National Collection of Rosa Species is held here with 250 unique varieties. Browse through 2 ½ acres of rose gardens or make a selection from thousands of container roses available in the summer months, or order for winter delivery. Experts are always on hand for advice or help in the selection of new varieties. *Open 9am to 5pm weekdays, 9am to 4.30pm Saturdays and 10am to 4pm Sundays. Catalogue available on request. Peter Beales Roses, London Road, Attleborough, Norfolk. Tel (0953) 454707*

Bawdeswell Garden Centre, Bawdeswell is situated 12 miles from Norwich on the A1067 which is the main Fakenham to Norwich road. We welcome you to our garden centre which stocks a wide range of plants and garden sundries, in fact absolutely everything for your garden. We also have a gift area for those special presents with a garden theme. Our childrens' playbus is unique and allows you to browse at leisure whilst your children amuse themselves in our play area. Round off your day with a visit to our coffee shop which serves light snacks throughout the day. *We are open 8-5.30 daily, Sundays and Bank Holidays 10-5. Tel: Bawdeswell (036288) 387.*

Frinton Road Nurseries Ltd, Kirby Cross, Frinton-on-Sea, Essex. On your way to the peaceful resort of Frinton-on-Sea call and inspect our wide range of top quality plants, shrubs and trees. Many of these are grown in our own nurseries, which you are invited to wander around at leisure. Our attractive shop and pot plant house stocks a wide range of sundries, tools and furniture and offers service from friendly and helpful staff. "The Applegarth", our new coffee shop is now open. *Open Monday-Saturday, 8.30-5.30. Tel: Frinton (02556) 74838.*

You will rarely find a Plant Centre quite like Bressingham. For one of Britain's largest ranges of finest quality plants, for efficient and personal service from trained horticulturalists, for a pleasant and relaxing environment with a comfortable Coffee Shop for light lunches and refreshments visit **Bressingham Plant Centre**. For the discerning gardener there is nothing like it! Bressingham Plant Centre is open every day 10am-5.30pm. Situated on the A1066 Thetford to Diss road. To be sure of plant availability and other details, telephone Bressingham (0379 88) 8133

Tony Clements' African Violet Centre, Terrington St Clement, King's Lynn, Norfolk. Wide variety of gold medal winning African Violets on show. Cultural advice given. Good selection of African Violets and other seasonal plants for sale. Attractive and inexpensive gift shop and tearoom for light refreshments. Ample parking, coach parties welcomed. Talk and demonstration to parties, by appointment. *Open daily throughout the year, 10-5 or dusk if earlier. Find us on the A17, near King's Lynn. Tel: King's Lynn (0553) 828374.*

Grow your own souvenir of East Anglia at Laurel Farm Herbs where you'll find a wide selection of top quality potted herb plants. They are attractive, fragrant, tasty, easy to grow and the ideal way to remember your holiday in East Anglia - every time you take a cutting. Meet local herb specialist Chris Seagon who will be glad to take you round the 160 herb varieties in his gardens. And remember to bring this advertisement with you for a 10% discount on all your purchases. Open every day (except Tuesday) from 10am to 5pm so come along and say hello. *Laurel Farm Herbs, main A12 at Kelsale between Saxmundham and Yoxford. Tel (0728) 77223.*

Thorncroft Clematis is a small family run nursery specialising in growing clematis, they have a large sales area displaying around 200 varieties, as well as a display garden showing different ways to grow them. There is always someone available to give advice on selecting and planting. *Open from Easter Saturday until the last Sunday in October from 10-5 daily except Wednesdays when it is closed all day. Directions are – ON the B1135 exactly halfway between Wymondham and East Dereham, Norfolk. Tel: Attleborough (0953) 850407.*

Please mention East Anglia Guide when replying to advertisements

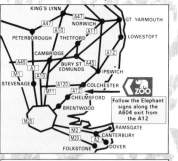

ANIMAL COLLECTIONS

BEDFORDSHIRE

Stagsden Bird Gardens, Stagsden (5m W Bedford on A422): Bird gardens and breeding centre set in 8 acres of countryside. Specialising in cranes, owls, rare pheasants, waterfowl and old breeds of poultry. Souvenir shop, light refreshments and picnic area. *All year, daily 11-6 (dusk if earlier). £2.50/£1/£2.*

Whipsnade Wild Animal Park, Dunstable: Set in 600 acres of beautiful parkland with over 3,000 animals. All the family favourites as well as rare and endangered species. Daily demonstations. Ride on the Great Whipsnade Railway. Childrens run wild playcentre, bear maze and childrens farm. *All year, daily ex 25 Dec. 10-6 (closes earlier in winter). £6.95/£4.95/£5.60 (92).*

Woburn Wild Animal Kingdom, Woburn Park: Britain's largest drive through safari park. Attractions include sea lion display, parrot demonstration, elephant encounter, boating lake, pets corner. Restaurant, gift shop and picnic area. *20 Mar-31 Oct, 10-5. £7/£4.50/£4.50 (92).*

Woodside Farm & Wildfowl Park, Farm Shop Mancroft Road, Aley Green (just off J9 of M1, follow brown tourist signs): Large selection of farm animals and wild fowl. Picnic and adventure play areas, traditional farm shop, crafts and gift centre. Programme of childrens entertainment. Cafe. *All year, daily ex Sun & Christmas period. 8-5.30. £1.40/£1.10/£1.10.*

CAMBRIDGESHIRE

Grays Honey Farm, Cross Drove, Warboys (12m NE Huntingdon, on A141): Bee and honey display and pictorial exhibition. Watch bees at work in an observation hive. Make your own beeswax candles. Black forest model railway layout. Aviary and picnic area. Shop with range of honey products. *31 Mar-24 Dec, Mon-Sat, Bank Hols, 10.30-6.30. 70p/35p.*

White-naped cranes, Stagsden Bird Gardens

Hamerton Wildlife Centre, Hamerton, Huntingdon: Set in 15 acres of parkland the Wildlife centre has lemurs, marmosets, meerkats, wallabies and unique bird collection (one of the largest in eastern England) of rare and exotic species from around the world. Coffee shop, children's adventure playground and gift shop. *All year, daily (closed Christmas Day), summer 10.30-6, winter 10.30-4 (last admission 1hr before closing). £3/£1.50/£2.50.*

Linton Zoo, Cambridge's Wildlife Breeding Centre, Hadstock Rd, Linton, Cambs (10m SE Cambridge along B1952, just off A604): Interesting collection of wildlife set in 10 acres of gardens. Collection includes lions, leopards, tapir, lynx, binturongs, owls, vultures, parrots, snakes, insects. Children's play area, picnic areas, shop, cafe. Free car park. *All year (ex 25 Dec), summer 10-6 (dusk in winter). £3.50/£2.50/2.50/£2.*

Peakirk Waterfowl Gardens, Peakirk, nr Peterborough, Cambs (7m N Peterborough, on B1443): Flock of Chilean flamingos and 107 species of duck, geese and swans in 17 acres of water gardens. Tea room (Mar-Oct), gift shop. *All year, daily (ex 24 & 25 Dec), 9.30-5.30 (dusk in winter). Monthly meetings with talks and slide shows Sept to Apr in the foyer. £2.50/£1.25/£1.50. Family ticket £5.*

Stags Holt Farm Park, Stags Holt, March: Victorian farm buildings set in ancient parkland. Visitors can see Suffolk Punches and farming bygones. Tea room. *9 Apr-end Sept, daily (closed Mons, ex Bank Hols) 10.30-5. £2.30/£1.20/£1.50.*

Wildfowl & Wetlands Trust Centre, Welney, Wisbech. A wetland nature reserve of 850 acres attracting large numbers of ducks/swans in winter, waders in spring/summer plus a range of wild plants, butterflies and insects. Information hall, gift shop and tea room. Car park and picnic site. *All year, daily (ex 24 & 25 Dec), 10-5. £2.70/£1.35/£2 (92).*

Willersmill Wildlife Park/Sanctuary and Fish Farm, Shepreth nr Royston. Set in natural grounds and lakes with a large collection of birds, animals and fish. *All year, daily 10.30-6 (closes at 5 in winter). £3.25/£1.75/£2.50 (Mon-Sat). £3.75/£2/£3 (Sun & Bank Hols).*

Wimpole Home Farm, (NT) Wimpole Hall, nr New Wimpole: Restored farm buildings, exhibition of farming in restored barn. Rare breeds of cattle. Light refreshments. *27 Mar-31 Oct, daily (ex Mon & Fri, open on Bank Hol Mons). 23 Jul-20 Aug, also Fri. 10.30-5. £3.50/£1.50. Joint ticket with Hall £6/£2.50.*

Wood Green Animal Shelter, Godmanchester: Europe's most progressive animal charity with over 1,000 animals - from llamas and pot bellied pigs to dogs and cats. The shelter is set in 50 acres with a restaurant and lake. *All year, daily 9-3. Free.*

Dedham Rare Breeds Centre

18

ESSEX

Ada Cole Memorial Stables, Broadlands, Broadley Common (2m SW Harlow): Home for rescued horses, ponies, donkeys and mules. Gift shop. *All year, daily (ex 25 Dec) 2-5, free.*

Basildon Zoo, London Rd, Vange, Basildon, Essex (10m from Dartford Tunnel. Junct. 30 from M25): Mammals, big cats and numerous birds. Children's play area and patting area. Cafe and picnic area. *Daily, (ex 25-26 Dec), 10-5 (or dusk in winter). £2.50/£1.25.*

Colchester Zoo, nr Colchester, Essex: Worldwide collection of animals and birds, 150 species in 40 acres of parkland. The daily events include Parrot Shows, Sealion Shows, Falconry Displays, Meet the Elephants, Penguin Parade and Snake Handling. *All year (ex 25 Dec), 9.30-5.30 (or 1 hour before dusk in off season). £5/£3/£4.*

Dedham Rare Breeds Centre, Mill Lane, Dedham: A farm park of 16 acres, specialising in the preservation of rare British farm animals. The animals are displayed in open paddocks and in buildings. There is a children's paddock where they can stroke the animals. *All year, daily (ex 25 Dec), 1 Apr-30 Sept, 10-5.30; 1 Oct-31 Mar, 10-3.30. £3/£1.80/£2.50.*

White headed duck, Peakirk

Epping Bury Farm Centre, Upland Road, Epping Upland: Open farm centre with rare breeds of pigs, sheep, goats, cattle and poultry. Nature trail with lake and stream. Picnic sites and play areas. *All year, daily (ex 25 & 26 Dec), 9.30-8. £2/£1.25/£1.25. Childrens adventure barn £2.*

Hayes Hill Farm, Stubbins Hall Lane, Crooked Mile, Waltham Abbey, Essex: Hayes Hill and

Touching a snake, Colchester Zoo

Holyfield Hall. Hayes Hill is a traditional show farm with mainly British farm animals. Holyfield Hall is a dairy and arable farm. Milking 2.45 daily. Guided tours available. *All year, Mon-Fri 10-4.30; Sat, Sun & Bank Hol 10-6. £2/£1.20/£1.20.*

Hobbs Cross Open Farm, Theydon Garnon (2m E Theydon Bois): Modern working farm with 180 breeding sows, beef cattle, sheep, hens and chicks. Farm trail, adventure playground, straw jump, picnic area, blacksmith's forge. Licensed restaurant and farm shop. *All year, daily, 9-6 inc Bank Hols. Closed 25 Dec-2 Jan. £2.50/£2/£2.*

Marsh Farm Country Park, South Woodham Ferrers (12m S Chelmsford, off A130): Working farm centre (under cover) with cattle, sheep and pigs. Pets corner, hand milking demonstrations and free range chickens. Visitor services barn with displays and farm tea room. Adventure play area. Country walks by river and through nature reserve. *13 Feb-end Nov, Mon-Fri 10-4.30 (Sat, Sun & Bank Hol Mon closes 5.30). £1.75/£1.25/£1.25 (92).*

Mistley Place Park, Environmental & Animal Rescue Centre, New Road, Mistley: 25 acres of woodland, lake and grassland overlooking the

River Stour. Horses, goats, lambs, peacocks, turkeys, ducks, geese and ornamental hens. Nature trail with maze. Tearooms and gift shop. *All year, daily 10.30-dusk. £2/£1/£1.*

Mole Hall Wildlife Park, Widdington, Newport, Essex. Deer, otters, chimps, guanaco, wallabies etc; birds, butterfly pavilion, attractive gardens, picnic & play areas. *All year, daily, 10.30-6 or dusk if earlier. Butterfly pavilion and pets corner closed in winter. Closed 25 Dec. £3.50/£2.25/£2.75.*

Southend Sea Life Centre, Eastern Esplanade: Featuring over 30 displays of British sea creatures, ranging from shrimps and starfish to stingrays and octopus. Walkthrough tunnel surrounded by sharks, rays and other native fish species. *Scheduled to open June. Daily, 10-6 (later in summer). £4.35/£3.25/£3.45.*

HERTFORDSHIRE

Bowmans Open Farm, Coursers Road, London Colney, St Albans: Large commercial farm with 380 milking cows, 250 sow pig herd and a large variety of arable crops. Shop and refectory facilities available. *All year, daily 9-5.30. £2.75/£1.75/£1.75.*

Longford Childrens Farm, St Margarets, Great Gaddesden (off A4146 at Great Gaddesden): Family run farm of small animals to pet and feed. Animals include rabbits, guinea pigs, pygmy goats, Vietnamese pot bellied pigs and many others. *All year, daily 9-5. 90p.*

Paradise Wildlife Park, White Stubbs Lane, Broxbourne: Leisure and wildlife park set in picturesque Broxbourne woods. 17 acre complex suitable for all ages. Animal park has lions, monkeys, zebras, camels and domestic animals. Woodland railway, crazy golf, childrens adventure playground. Restaurant, cafeteria, picnic area, shop. *All year, daily, summer 10-6, winter 10-dusk. £3.50/£2.50/£3.*

Standalone Farm, Wilbury Road, Letchworth Garden City: A small working farm. Cattle, sheep, pigs and poultry. Daily milking demonstration. Shire horses, goats, ducks and bees. Indoor and outdoor picnic areas. Refreshments, shop. *1 Mar-30 Sept, daily 11-5 (last adm 4). £2.20/£1.10/£1.10 (92).*

Mole Hall Wildlife Park

Please mention East Anglia Guide when replying to advertisements

Zebras at Banham Zoo

LINCOLNSHIRE

Butterfly and Falconry Park, Long Sutton, Lincs, (off A17): One of the largest walkthrough Butterfly Houses in Great Britain. Hundreds of exotic free winged butterflies in a tropical paradise, with ponds and waterfalls. Outdoors see falcons, eagles and owls with live displays twice a day. Insectarium, wildflower meadows, farm animals, pets corner. Tea room, gift shop, adventure playground, large picnic area, school room and country fayre shop. Ample parking. *13 Mar-31 Oct, daily, 10-6 (closes 5 in Oct). £3.20/£2/£2.80. Guided tours by appt.*

NORFOLK

Banham Zoo and Appleyard Craft Court Banham, nr Diss, Norfolk (6m NW Diss on B1113): Set in over 20 acres of landscaped countryside, the zoo is the ideal setting for the care and conservation of a wide selection of rare and endangered species. Snow leopards, ocelots, maned wolves and many primates including chimpanzees, gibbons, lemurs and marmosets. World of Penguins, reptile house, monkey jungle island and owl collection. Activity and information centre featuring a soft play area and Perky Parrots themed storyroom. Appleyard Craft Court featuring Bakery, Craft Barn, Caneware, Bistro and Cidery. Licensed catering and free parking. *All year, daily, (ex 25-26 Dec) 10-6.30 or dusk if earlier. Tel: (095 387) 771 for adm prices.*

Cranes Watering Farm, Starston, Nr Harleston: See a real working farm (wellingtons required!) with pigs, sheep and cows. Watch the cows being milked 4-5pm approx. Please note there is more variety of animals between Sept & March. Farm shop, picnic on the farmhouse lawn. *1 Feb-31 Dec, Tue-Sat 10-5; Sun 10-12 (open until 5 on Suns Jun-Aug). Easter, May & Spring Bank Hols, 10-5. Closed over Christmas period. Free to shop customers.*

Equine Rest and Rehabilitation Centre, Overa House Farm, Larling: Stable yard & paddocks. Horses, ponies and donkeys can be seen at this centre run by the International League for the Protection of Horses. *All year, Wed & Sun (ex 25 & 26 Dec), 2.30-4 or by appt Tel: (0953) 717114. Free.*

Equine Rest and Rehabilitation Centre, Anne Colvin House, Snetterton: On view are stables and paddocks with the horses, ponies and donkeys looked after by the International League for the Protection of Horses. *All year, Wed & Sun (ex 25 & 26 Dec), 2.30-4 or by appt Tel: (0953) 498682. Free.*

Kingdom of the Sea, Southern Promenade, Hunstanton: Watch sealife on a breathtaking scale in over 20 natural settings. Walk under water, an experience unlike any other as the mystery of the ocean unfolds in a real life adventure. In the Ocean Tunnel you are surrounded by tens of thousands of gallons of water with the creatures of the deep all round, only inches away. Seal observatory and Captain Nemo's 'Hands-on' interactive centre. *All year (ex 25 & 26 Dec), daily. 10-dusk. £3.99/£2.99/£2.99.*

Kingdom of the Sea, Marine Parade, Great Yarmouth. Over 25 natural British marine life displays themed on Norfolk's coastline, including Breydon Water estuary and Winterton dunes. Tropical reef sharks in the underwater ocean tunnel walk and tropical reef fish in the 'Amazing Green Submarine' will grip the imagination of old and young alike. *All year, (ex 25 & 26 Dec), 10-dusk. £3.99/£2.99/£2.99.*

Norfolk Rare Breeds Centre, Decoy Farm House, Ormesby St Michael, Great Yarmouth: Rare breeds centre of domestic farm animals with cattle, sheep, pigs and poultry. Also donkeys, goats, heavy horses rabbits and waterfowl. Information area, crafts, shop. Farm museum. *9 Apr-end Sept, daily ex Sat, 11-5. 1 Oct-8 Apr, Sun only, 11-4. £2/£1.25/£1.75.*

Norfolk Shire Horse Centre, West Runton (2m E Sheringham, off A149): Shire horses demonstrated working at 11.15am and 3pm. Native ponies, bygone collection of horse drawn machinery. Picnic area. Shop and teas. *4 Apr-end Oct, daily (ex Sat unless it is a Bank Hol weekend), 10-5. £3/£1.50/£2.*

Norfolk Wildlife Centre & Country Park, Gt. Witchingham, nr. Norwich, Norfolk (12m NW Norwich, off A1067). Large collection of British and European wildlife exhibited in spacious natural enclosures in 40 acres of parkland. Unique team of trained reindeer, pull their wheeled sledge or cart round the Park most afternoons giving free rides to children. Commando and adventure play areas. Clear-water trout pool. Mystery rides on the woodland steam railway. Model farm with rare domestic breeds, where many of the animals are tame enough to be stroked. Attractive tea room, gift shop, picnic areas, peacock lawn, and free car park. This is not a zoo. *1 Apr-31 Oct, daily 10.30-6. £3.50/£2/£3.*

Otter Trust, Earsham, nr Bungay, (1m W Bungay, off A143): World's largest collection of otters exhibited under near natural conditions. Trust specialises in breeding European Otters in captivity for re-introduction into the wild and its collection of British Otters is unique. Set in beautiful surroundings on banks of the river Waveney, riverside walks, picnic areas, copses with Muntjac Deer and Chinese Water-deer, three lakes with large collection of European wildfowl, attractive Visitor Centre, including tea room and gift shop. *1 Apr-31 Oct, daily, 10.30-6. £3.50/£2/£3.*

Park Farm Visitor Centre, Snettisham (4m S Hunstanton): See farming in action on a genuine working farm. Unique sheep show in the sheep

Kingdom of the Sea, Hunstanton

The East of England Birds of Prey and Conservation Centre is situated on the B1117, just South of the village of Laxfield.

Here we have many different types of birds of prey including hawks, falcons, eagles, buzzards and owls.

We have three flying displays per day as well as birds in aviaries.

We also have a tea shop offering home made food for lunches and snacks as well as a gift and souvenir shop and lecture room. Some of our aviaries also have close circuit television in order that we can watch those birds who have raised young.

We are open all year round opening at 10.00 am until 5.30 pm.

East of England

BIRDS OF PREY
&
CONSERVATION
CENTRE

The East of England Birds of Prey and Conservation Centre
St Jacobs Hall, Laxfield,
Suffolk IP13 8HY
Telephone: 0986 798844

The OTTER TRUST
Earsham, Norfolk

A unique wonderland of waterfowl, Otters, Night herons and Muntjac Deer on the banks of the beautiful river Waveney. See the world's largest collection of otters in natural enclosures where the British Otter is bred for re-introduction to the wild.

OPEN DAILY, 1 APRIL – 31 OCTOBER, 10.30am – 6pm

Come on Safari to...

SUFFOLK WILDLIFE PARK

...and enjoy the thrill of an African Wildlife Experience, with over 100 acres of beautiful Suffolk coastal countryside and wonderous wildlife to explore in the tradition of the great African explorers of the Victorian era.

PLUS

* *Get close to Lions, Cheetahs, Camels and Antelope*
* *African Owls and exotic Parrots*
* *Wildfowl in a natural lakeside setting*
* *Ride in style on our Safari Roadtrain*
* *Large Children's Play Area (for letting off steam)*
* *Relax in the Explorer's Cafeteria or Picnic in the park*

OPEN DAILY from 10.00a.m. - 6.30 pm or dusk if earlier (except Christmas and boxing Day.)

SUFFOLK WILDLIFE PARK, KESSINGLAND, SUFFOLK. Tel: LOWESTOFT (0702) 740291

Please mention East Anglia Guide when replying to advertisements

22

Pensthorpe Waterfowl Park

theatre and a shearing demonstration (30 mins). Safari ride by Land Rover or tractor and covered trailer to see the red deer herd (45 mins). Farm trails, picnic area, tea room, gift shop, wool room, gigantic adventure playground. Meet all the animals: cattle, calves, pigs, piglets, hens, lambs, rabbits, horses, ducks, turkeys and more. Pets corner, pedal tractors, sheep centre with over 40 different breeds on display. Eggs 'n' all exhibition. Free parking. *21 Mar-31 Oct, daily 10.30-5. £3.50/£2.50/£3. Admission & safari £6.50/£4.50/£6.*

Pensthorpe Waterfowl Park, Fakenham, Norfolk. (Clearly signposted off the A1067 Norwich – Fakenham road): Explore a world of colourful waterbirds and enjoy the 200 acre Park with lakeside, riverside, woodland and meadow walks. Water gardens. Restaurant, wildlife exhibitions, countryside gift shop and children's adventure playground. *Jan-Mar, Sat & Sun. Apr-Dec, daily (closed 25 Dec). 11-5. £3.50/£1.60/£3 (92).*

Pettitts Animal Adventure Park, Camp Hill, Reedham, Norfolk (6m S Acle, off A47): Feathercraft shop. Tame deer enclosure. Amusement rides. Santa Fe train and vintage car ride. 1/2 mile miniature train rides. Remote control boat marina. Adventure assault course. Children's paradise area with many tame animals and birds to feed, large areas of mown grass for picnics. Live entertainment in high season, Animal costume characters. Free use of barbecue, cresta toboggan ride, snake slides. Cafe, pizza bar. *11 Apr-29 Oct, daily ex Sat, 10-5.30. £4.50/£3.50/£3.*

Redwings Horse Sanctuary, Frettenham (6m N Norwich): Visitors are able to meet the rescued horses, ponies and donkeys. Gift shop and refreshments. *11 Apr-12 Dec, Sun & Bank Hol Mon 2-5, also Mon in Jul & Aug. £1.50/75p/75p.*

Thrigby Hall Wildlife Gardens, nr Filby, Gt Yarmouth, Norfolk (5m NW Gt Yarmouth, between Caister and Acle, off A1064): Selection of Asian mammals, birds and reptiles in 250 year old landscaped gardens. Tropical house, snow leopards, bird house, deer paddocks and lake. Large willow-pattern garden. Children's play area. Cafeteria (1 Apr-31 Oct), gift shop in Hall. *All year, daily, 10-6 or dusk if earlier. £3.70/£2.30/£3.20.*

Wroxham Barns, Tunstead Road, Hoveton: Junior Farm, home to a collection of calves, sheep, pigs, chickens, kids, rabbits, orphan lambs and shetland ponies. All weather walkways enable all year round opening. Visitors can take part in feeding times and egg collection as well as stroke the animals. *All year, daily 10-5. £1.50.*

SUFFOLK

Cow Wise, Meadow Farm, West Stow, Bury St Edmunds (1 mile from West Stow Anglo-Saxon Village): A modern working dairy farm with Friesian and Jersey cows, calves, goats, free-range hens and lambs. Visitors can see the cows milked from a specially constructed gallery. Touch table, freshwater life, sense boxes. Milking starts 3pm. Bottle feed the baby animals 2.30 & 4. *1 Mar-11 Jul, Sun & Bank Hols. 22-30 Aug, daily. 2-5. Groups by appt on other days, Tel: (0284) 728862. £1.70/£1.20.*

East of England Birds of Prey and Conservation Centre, Laxfield (on the B1117 between Stradbroke and Halesworth): Large selection of birds of prey in aviaries. Three flying displays a day. Tea, gift and souvenir shop. *All year, daily ex 25 Dec. 10-5.30. £3/£2.*

Easton Farm Park, Wickham Market, Suffolk (outside Wickham Market, turn off A12 onto B1116 and follow Easton signs): Victorian farm setting for many species of farm animals including rare breeds. Modern milking unit with viewing area. Unique Victorian dairy. Large collection of early farm machinery, rural bygones. Green trail, pets paddock, food and farming exhibition, adventure playground, gift shop, tea room. *21 Mar-30 Sept, daily, 10.30-6. £3.70/£2/£3.*

Kentwell Hall, Long Melford (N of Green in Long Melford): Rare breed domestic farm animals in lovely tranquil setting around timber framed farm buildings. *Separate admission to farm only when house open. Farm only £1.75/£1/£1.50 (92). Full opening times see Historic House entry.*

Pentlow Farm, nr Cavendish: Childrens farm with lots of farm and baby animals easily accessible. Feeding time can be shared by all visitors. *1 Mar-31 Aug, Sun & Bank Hol Mon 12-5; school hols 2.30-4.30. Free.*

Suffolk Wildlife and Rare Breeds Park, Kessingland, nr Lowestoft, (on main A12): The African wildlife experience! Take the Safari Road-Train to experience over 100 acres of African wildlife or follow one of the African Explorer Trails to discover, on foot, lions, cheetahs, leopards, zebra, camels, African owls and parrots. Panoramic lake with an abundance of waterfowl. Farmyard corner and large childrens play area. Cafeteria and shop. *Daily (ex 25 & 26 Dec), 10-6.30 (dusk if earlier). Tel: (0502) 740021 for adm prices.*

Red Poll Cow, Easton Farm Park

Prices are in the order Adults/Children/Senior Citizens. Where prices are not available at the time of going to press the 1992 (92) price is given.
See Touring Maps on pages 104-108 for locations of places to visit.

ANCIENT MONUMENTS

BEDFORDSHIRE

Bushmead Priory, (on unclassified road near Colmworth 2m E of B660): A rare survival of the medieval refectory of an Augustinian Priory, with its original timber-framed roof almost intact and containing interesting wall paintings and stained glass. *3 Apr-26 Sept, Sat 10-6, Sun 2-6. £1.10/55p/85p (92).*

De Grey Mausoleum (EH), Flitton, nr Silsoe: Remarkable treasure house of sculpted tombs and monuments from 16c to 19c, dedicated to the de Grey family of nearby Wrest Park. *Weekends only. Keykeeper. Access through Flitton Church. Free*

Houghton House, (1m NE Ampthill off A418): Reputedly the inspiration for 'House Beautiful' in Bunyan's 'Pilgrim's Progress', the remains of this early 17c mansion still convey elements which justify the description, including work attributed to Inigo Jones. *Any reasonable time. Free.*

Someries Castle, East Hyde, Luton (signed off the A6129 Luton-Harpenden Road): Late medieval fortified manor house, one of the earliest brick buildings in England. Now a ruin with chapel, gateway and porters lodge still standing. *Open at all times. Free.*

CAMBRIDGESHIRE

Bridge Chapel, St Ives. 15c bridge with chapel attached in midstream, one of only four in England. Basement with oven built into thickness of wall and balcony over river. *Open all year, key available from Town Hall, Norris Library and Museum (see Museums entry) or local shops.*

Buckden Towers, Buckden, Huntingdon: Complex of mainly Tudor buildings on a 12c foundation, formerly an Ecclesiastical Palace of the Bishops of Lincoln, recent extensive restoration. Access for wheelchair visitors. Car Park. *Exterior courtyard open all year during daylight hours. Guided tours of the interiors by appt. Donations to the Restoration Fund welcome.*

Cambridge American Military Cemetery & Memorial, Coton (on A1303 Madingley Rise, 1m W Cambridge): Cemetery for military personnel killed during WWII. Visitors reception building, information area, graves area and Memorial Chapel. *16 Apr-1 Oct, 8-6. 1 Oct-15 Apr, 8-5.*

Denny Abbey (EH), Ely Rd, Waterbeach (6m NE Cambridge): Remains of 12c church and 14c dining hall of religious house. Run as a hospital by Knights Templar after being a Benedictine priory, and in 1342 became a Franciscan nunnery. Later became a farmhouse until WWII. *1 Apr-30 Sept, daily 10-6. 1 Oct-31 Mar, Suns only 10-4. (Closed 24-26 Dec & 1 Jan). £1.10/85p/55p (92).*

Duxford Chapel (EH), Duxford (5m SE Cambridge, off A505): 14c chapel. *Admission any reasonable time. Key keeper. Free.*

Ely Cathedral, Ely: One of England's finest cathedrals. The Octagon is the crowning glory. Beautiful medieval buildings. Guided tours, Brass Rubbing Centre and Stained Glass Museum in summer season. *Open daily 7-7 during the summer; Mon-Sat 7.30-6.30, Sun 7.30-5 during the winter. £2.50/£2 (2 children admitted free with every adult).*

Flag Fen Bronze Age Excavation, Peterborough: Unique in Britain – Bronze Age remains on timber platform. Reconstruction at one tenth life size of Flag Fen 3,000 years ago. Accurate reconstruction of Bronze Age countryside – with fields, live animals and buildings. Play area for under 8 year olds. New Visitor Centre – housing hundreds of splendid bronzes and other fascinating finds. *All year, daily (ex 25 & 26 Dec), 11-4. Site tours 4 Apr-31 Oct. £2.85/£1.95/£2.55.*

Isleham Priory (EH) (4m W Mildenhall on B1104): Remains of Norman church. *Admission any reasonable time. Free.*

King's College Chapel, Cambridge (College is in the centre of the city in King's Parade): The exhibition, which is contained in the northern side chapels of King's College Chapel, shows why and how the chapel was built, in pictures, works of art and models. *University Term, Mon-Sat 10-3.30. Vacations, daily, 10-4.30. (Closed 23 Dec-1 Jan & 9-11 Apr). Chapel free, exhibition £1/50p/50p. Groups by prior appt Tel: (0223) 350411.*

Longthorpe Tower (EH), nr Peterborough: 14c three storey tower of fortified manor house. 14c biblical and instructive wall paintings, most complete set of such paintings in England. Also, art exhibitions by local artists held periodically. *1 Apr-30 Sept, daily 10-6. 1 Oct-31 Mar, daily (ex Mons) 10-4. Closed 24-26 Dec, 1 Jan. £1.10/85p/55p (92).*

Peterborough Cathedral

Colchester Priory

Peterborough Cathedral, Peterborough: The present cathedral was built between 1118 and 1238 and is said by some to have the finest West Front in Europe. It is built of local Barnack Limestone and contains a magnificent 13th century hand-painted wooden ceiling in the nave. See also the Hedda Stone (early Saxon sculpture), the superb fan vaulting in the Retrochoir, the tomb of Katherine of Aragon and the former burial place of Mary, Queen of Scots. *Jan-Apr & Oct-Dec, Mon-Sat 7- 6.15; May-Sept, Mon-Sat 7-8. Suns all year 8-5. Donations welcome. Almoners Hall Visitor Centre Mon-Sat 11-3, £1/75p/50p.*

Ramsey Abbey, Ramsey (12m NE Huntingdon, on B1040): Early 17c house (now a school) on ruins of Benedictine monastery: altered in 19c by Sir John Soane and Edward Blore. *1 Apr-31 Oct, Suns 2-5 & Thu during term time 3-5. Free.*

Ramsey Abbey Gatehouse, Ramsey (NT): Ruins of 15c gatehouse. *1 Apr-end Oct, daily, 10-5. Free.*

Thorney Abbey Church, Thorney (7m NE Peterborough): Abbey church dating from c 1100, with a fine church organ originally built 1787- 1790. Guided tours by arrangement. *All year, daily. Free.*

ESSEX

Chelmsford Cathedral, Chelmsford: Medieval church with perpendicular architecture. Reordered in 1984 blending old with new. Modern tapestry and sculpture. *Open daily, 8-5. Free.*

Coggeshall Grange Barn, (NT) Coggeshall: Restored 12c barn. Earliest surviving timber framed barn in Europe. *28 Mar-10 Oct, Tue, Thu, Sun & Bank Hol Mon, 1-5. £1.10/55p.*

Castle Acre Castle

Cressing Temple, Witham Road, Cressing, near Braintree: Site of Knights Templar settlement. Wheat Barn and Barley Barn, early 13c. Walled garden, archaeological work in progress. *2 May-30 Sept, Mon-Fri 9-4.30, Sun 2-5.30. £1/50p/50p (Sun £2/£1/£1).*

Hadleigh Castle, Hadleigh, nr Southend (EH): Familiar from Constable's picture, the castle stands on a bluff overlooking the Leigh Marshes. Single large bailey 50ft high. 13c and 14c remains. *Admission any reasonable time. Free.*

Harwich Redoubt, Opposite 42 Main Road Harwich: Circular fort built 1808 as part of the East Coast defences against Napoleon. Moat, cells, cannon, museum of local finds. *All year, Sun 10-12, 2-5 (ex 30 May & 26 Dec). Jul & Aug, daily 2-5. £1/Free.*

Hedingham Castle, Castle Hedingham, nr Halstead: Magnificent Norman Keep, Garrison Chamber, Banqueting Hall, Minstrels Gallery. Lake and Woodland walks. *Easter-31 Oct, daily 10-5. £2.25/£1.25/£2. Family ticket £6 (2 adults & 3 children).*

Moot Hall, High Street, Maldon: Built in 15c for the d'Arcy family. The Millenium embroidery is on display which was made to commemorate the area's 1,000 years of war and peace. *The embroidery will be in the Moot Hall until 30 June, after which time contact the Town Council for further information. Mon-Sat, 10-3.45. £1/50p/50p. Appointment with the Town Council necessary to see the rest of the Moot Hall. Tel: (0621) 857373.*

Mistley Towers (EH), Mistley (on B1352, 1 1/2m E of A137 at Lawford): Two towers designed by Robert Adam in 1776. *All year, Mon only in winter. Keykeeper. Free.*

Mountfitchet Castle and Norman Village of 1066, Stansted (3m NE Bishop's Stortford): Award winning reconstructed Norman motte and bailey castle and village, only one in the world, on the original site. Walk back in time to 1066 and see how the Normans lived. *14 Mar-14 Nov, daily, 10-5. £3.50/£2.50/£3.*

Priors Hall Barn (EH), Widdington (4m S Saffron Walden): One of the finest surviving medieval barns in SE England. Representative of a type of aisled barn in NW Essex. 124 x 30 ft by 33 ft high. Little altered. *1 Apr-30 Sept, any reasonable time at weekends. Free.*

St Botolph's Priory (EH), Colchester: Remains of 12c priory near town centre. *Admission at any reasonable time. Free.*

Saffron Walden Turf Maze, Saffron Walden: *All year, daily. Free.*

Tilbury Fort (EH), Tilbury: One of Henry VIII's coastal forts. Remodelled and extended in the 17c in French style. *1 Apr-30 Sept, daily 10-6. 1 Oct-31 Mar, daily (ex Mon) 10-4. Closed 24-26 Dec, 1 Jan. £1.80/90p/£1.40 (92).*

Waltham Abbey Church, Highbridge St, Waltham Abbey. Fine Norman church founded in 1060 by King Harold, who is reputedly buried here. The Crypt Centre houses an exhibition about the history of the town and abbey. Visitor centre and shop. *All year, 10-4. Sun, open at 12; Wed open at 11. Summer until 6. Free.*

HERTFORDSHIRE

Berkhamsted Castle, Adjacent to Berkhamsted station: The extensive remains of a large 11c Motte and Bailey castle which held a strategic position on the road to London. *Any reasonable time. Free.*

Cathedral and Abbey Church of St Alban, St Albans: Norman abbey, built 1077 with the use of Roman bricks from Verulamium. It became the premier Abbey of medieval England until its monastic life ended in 1539. After Victorian restoration, it became a cathedral in 1539. Bookshop, giftshop and refectory. *All year, winter 9-5.45, summer 9-6.45. £1 donation.*

Hertford Castle, Castle Steet, Hertford: Used for defence, prison and palace with a fascinating history of royal links including Henrys V and VIII and Elizabeth Tudor. 15c gatehouse, Norman walls and mounds remain in riverside gardens. *May-Sept, 1st Sun in the month, 2.30-4.30. Free*

St Albans Clock Tower, Market Cross, St Albans: Early 15c curfew tower. Exhibition of local history. See the 1866 clock mechanism, the belfry housing the original curfew bell and the 18c market bell. Superb views from the roof. *9 Apr-mid Sept, Sat, Sun & Bank Hol 10.30-5. 25p/10p.*

Scott's Grotto, Scotts's Road, off Hertford Road, Ware: 18c underground complex decorated with minerals and shells. Built by Quaker poet John Scott. *Apr-Sept, Sat & Bank Hols 2-4.30. £1 donation.*

Hertford Castle

NORFOLK

Baconsthorpe Castle (EH) (6m SW Cromer): 15c moated semi-fortified house. *Admission any reasonable time. Free.*

Beeston Regis Priory, Beeston Regis Common, near Sheringham: Extensive ruins of priory with interpretation on site. *Admission any reasonable time. Free.*

Binham Priory (EH), Binham (5m SE Wells off B1105): Early English west front with unique tracery window. *Admission any reasonable time. Free.*

Blakeney Guildhall (EH), Blakeney (5m NW Holt on A149): Remains of 14c Guildhall. *Dawn to dusk. Free.*

Burgh Castle, Great Yarmouth (EH): Remains of Roman fort, overlooking River Waveney. Tea room, Easter to Oct. *Admission any reasonable time. Free.*

Burnham Norton Friary (1m N Burnham Market): Gatehouse of Carmelite Friary founded 1241. Two storeys with flushwork panelling. Early 14c moulding and vaulted ceiling. *All year, daily. Free.*

Caister Roman Site (EH), nr Gt Yarmouth: Remains of Roman commercial port. *Admission any reasonable time. Free.*

Castle Acre Castle (EH), near Swaffham: The remains of a Norman manor house, which became a castle, with earthworks, set on a hill by the side of the village. *Any reasonable time. Free.*

Castle Acre Priory (EH), nr Swaffham: Impressive ruins of Cluniac priory founded c. 1090 by William de Warenne, second Earl of Surrey. Remains include church and decorated 12c West front, monastic buildings, 15c gatehouse and prior's lodging (still roofed). *1 Apr-30 Sept, daily 10-6. 1 Oct-31 Mar, daily (ex Mons) 10-4. Closed 24-26 Dec, 1 Jan. £1.80/90p/£1.40 (92).*

Castle Rising Castle (EH), Castle Rising: Fine mid 12c keep with notable history. Set in centre of massive earthworks. Originally seat of Earls of Sussex, 1544-1693 owned by Dukes of Norfolk. Remains include bridge and gatehouse. *1 Apr-30 Sept, daily 10-6. 1 Oct-31 Mar, daily (ex Mons) 10-4. Closed 24-26 Dec, 1 Jan. £1.10/55p/85p (92).*

Cockley Cley Iceni Village and Museums (3m SW Swaffham): Iceni encampment reconstruction believed on original site. Saxon church c630 A.D., Folk and East Anglian museum in historic cottage. Agricultural implement, vintage engine and carriage museums. Nature trail. Gift shop and light refreshments. Picnic area. *1 Apr-31 Oct daily, 12-5.30. 1 Jul-30 Sept, daily, 11-5.30. Group bookings, inc. schools by appt 10-8. Tel: (0760) 721339. £2.50/£1/£1.50/students £1.50 (92).*

Creake Abbey (EH), nr Burnham Market: Remains of an abbey church dating from 13c, including presbytery and north transept with chapels. *Admission any reasonable time. Free.*

Grimes Graves, Weeting (EH) (1m N Brandon on B1108): Neolithic flint mines 4,000 yrs old. First excavated in 1870s. Intricate network of over 300 pits and shafts. One pit open to the public – 30 ft deep with 7 radiating galleries. *1 Apr-30 Sept, daily 10-6. 1 Oct-31 Mar, daily (ex Mons) 10-4. Closed 24-26 Dec, 1 Jan. £1.10/55p/85p (92).*

Nelson's Monument, Gt Yarmouth: Monument erected in honour of Nelson in 1819. 144ft high. 217 steps to top. *Jul & Aug, Tel (0493) 855746 for details. Adm charge.*

New Buckenham Castle, New Buckenham, Norfolk: Norman Mott and Bailey Castle plus chapel. Keep said to be the largest in England (diameter). Stocks in village centre and fine church. *All year, Mon-Fri 8-5.30; Sat 8.30-4. £1/30p.*

North Elmham Saxon Cathedral and Bishop's Castle (EH), nr Dereham: Saxon cathedral later converted to hunting lodge. *Admission any reasonable time. Free.*

North West Tower, North Quay, Great Yarmouth: Medieval tower which was originally part of the town walls. Displays about Great Yarmouth's history, trading wherries and the Norfolk Broads. *9 Apr-30 Sept, daily. 1-31 Oct, Sat & Sun, also daily during half term week. 9-5. Free.*

Norwich Cathedral, Norwich: The cathedral was founded in 1096 AD. Features include 15c carvings depicting stories from the Bible, a 14c reredos, Norman style architecture, chapels and cloisters. It is also the place where Edith Cavell is buried. *Open daily, 7.30-6. Tours arranged between 9 & 4, and by arrangement with the Visitors' Officer Tel: (0603) 626290.*

St Benet's Abbey, nr Ludham: Ruins of monastery founded by King Canute in 1020 AD. Access from River Bure or by farm track from minor road (signposted Hall Common) off A1062 1/3m NE of Ludham Bridge. *Admission any reasonable time. Free.*

Please mention East Anglia Guide when replying to advertisements

St John's Roman Catholic Cathedral, Norwich: 19c Gothic style building. Tower tours provide excellent view of city. *All year, daily. Tower tours May-Sept, Sat, 2.30-4.30. 50p. Cathedral shop open daily, 1 May-30 Sept, 10.30-3.45.*

St Olaves Priory, (EH), nr Great Yarmouth: Early 14c undercroft with brick-vaulted ceiling. (See also nearby windmill). *Admission any reasonable time (ex 25 Dec & 1 Jan). Keykeeper. Free.*

St Peter Mancroft Church, Market Place, Norwich: Fine 15c parish church but with Norman foundations and magnificent wooden roof. Perpendicular font. Flemish tapestry created in 1573, Treasury with plate, paintings and 1190 manuscript. *All year, Mon-Fri 9.30-4.30, Sat 10.30-12.30. Free.*

Shrine of Our Lady of Walsingham, Holt Rd, Walsingham: *Open all year, 6.30am-dusk. National Pilgrimage 31 May; Pilgrimage for Sick & Handicapped, 30 Aug.*

Slipper Chapel, nr Houghton St Giles (1m W Little Walsingham, on B1105): Now RC National Shrine of Our Lady. Small 14c Chapel connected with ancient shrine in Walsingham (latter now destroyed). New shrine complex including tea room, repository and chapel of reconciliation. *All year, daily, 9-dusk. Parties please advise.*

Thetford Priory (EH), Thetford: Founded by Norman warrior Roger Bigod. Henry VIII's natural son Duke of Richmond formerly buried here (now see Framlingham Church, Suffolk). *Admission any reasonable time. Free.*

Thetford Warren Lodge (EH): Ruins of a small two-storey hunting lodge. Built c 1400 for the Prior of Thetford's gamekeeper. Can only be viewed from the outside. *Admission any reasonable time (ex 25 Dec & 1 Jan). Free.*

Weeting Castle, Weeting (EH) (1m N Brandon on B1106): Ruins of an early medieval Manor house within a rectangular moated enclosure. *Admission any reasonable time (ex 25 Dec & 1 Jan). Free.*

SUFFOLK

Bungay Castle Ruins, Bungay: Castle site situated at the centre of fine market town. Twin towers and massive flint walls are all that remain of original Norman Castle. Saxon mounds. *All year, daily, 9-6. Keyholders listed at site. Free. Printed guide available locally.*

Bury St Edmunds Abbey (EH): Enough remains of the abbey church to give an idea of its large scale. The two great gateways are the best preserved buildings and the Abbey gardens are attractive. *Open during gardens opening times, contact Borough Council. Tel: (0284) 763233. Admission free.*

Clare Castle: Earthworks and ruins. *Daily.*

Clare Priory Ancient Ruins, the ruins of Augustinian Friary. *All year, daily ex Jan 1 & 2, 10-6. Donations welcome.*

Framlingham Castle (EH), Framlingham: Impressive 12c curtain walls with 13 towers and Tudor brick chimneys. Built by Bigod family, Earls of Norfolk. Wall walk. 17c almshouses built by Pembroke College, Cambridge on site of Great Hall. Home of Mary Tudor in 1553. *1*

Walsingham Roman Catholic Shrine

Apr-30 Sept, daily 10-6. 1 Oct-31 Mar, daily (ex Mon) 10-4. Closed 24-26 Dec, 1 Jan. £1.50/75p/£1.10 (92).

Guildhall of Corpus Christi (NT), Lavenham: Impressive 16c timber-framed building. Its 9 rooms display items of local history which give an insight into the past of Lavenham, with an exhibition about the woollen cloth industry over the centuries. *27 Mar-31 Oct, daily, 11-5. Closed 9 Apr. £2.30/60p.*

Leiston Abbey (EH): Remains of 14c abbey including transepts of church and range of cloisters. *Admission any reasonable time. Free.*

Orford Castle (EH), Orford: Magnificent 90 ft high keep with views across River Alde to Orford Ness. Built by Henry II for coastal defence in 12c with polygonal keep (18 sided) but cylindrical inside. Local topographical display. *1 Apr-30 Sept, daily 10-6. 1 Oct-31 Mar, daily (ex Mon) 10-4. Closed 24-26 Dec, 1 Jan. £1.50/75p/£1.10 (92).*

St Edmundsbury Cathedral, Angel Hill, Bury St Edmunds: Originally St James' Church which was made a cathedral in 1914. 16c nave, east end added post-war, north side built 1990. Cloister gallery exhibition series, April to October. Many concerts and musical events. *1 Jun-31 Aug, daily 8.30-8. Winter 8-5.30. Free.*

St James's Chapel (EH), Lindsey: Medieval chapel once attached to nearby castle. *1 Apr-30 Sept, daily 10-6. 1 Oct-31 Mar, daily (ex Mon) 10-4. Closed 24-26 Dec & 1 Jan. Free.*

Snape Concert Hall, Snape (5m NW Aldeburgh on A1094): Concert Hall, home of the Aldeburgh Festival (11-27 June), the Snape Proms in

August, Aldeburgh Showcase Concerts in September and Britten Festival in October. Other concerts throughout the year. Master classes at the Britten-Pears School Apr-Oct. Tours with slide show arranged for parties by appt. *View from outside daily, all year.*

Sutton Hoo, nr Woodbridge: The treasure from this famous Anglo-Saxon cemetery is on display in the British Museum, and an 8 year archaeological research project at the site has recently been completed. Guided tours are run by the Sutton Hoo Society: *11 & 12 Apr; May-mid Sept, Sat & Sun; 2 & 3pm. Tel for information, (0394) 460309.*

Theatre Royal (NT), Bury St Edmunds: Rare example of late Georgian playhouse, built by William Wilkins in 1819. A working theatre with fine pit, boxes and gallery. *Daily ex Sun and Bank Hols, 10-6 (no access while theatrical activity). Free.*

West Stow Anglo-Saxon Village (in West Stow Country Park), West Stow (7m NW Bury St Edmunds off A1101): Thoroughly researched site, six complete reconstructions of buildings, taped guides, information point and visitor centre, an Anglo-Saxon house being built. Contact: *Alan Baxter, The Visitor Centre, West Stow Country Park, Tel: (0284) 728718. All year daily (ex 24-27 Dec), 10-4.15. £2.50/£1.80/£1.80. (Groups by appt).*

English Heritage (EH) Historic Buildings & Monuments Commission for England.

Prices are in the order Adults/Children/Senior Citizens. Where prices are not available at the time of going to press, the 1992 (92) price is given. See Touring Maps on pages 104-108 for locations of places to visit.

EAST ANGLIA FOR THE CHILDREN

By Caroline Putus

Where to take the children? It's a perennial problem whether you're on holiday, or just looking for something to do one weekend afternoon. East Anglia has lots of attractions that will keep the kids amused. This is just a personal selection, tried and tested by one energetic four year old and assorted friends aged up to seventy. Some of the best we've visited recently include **Sacrewell Farm and Country Centre** near Peterborough, with a lovely nature trail and where children are, almost uniquely these days, encouraged to use, handle and examine the exhibits;

ing to Aladdin's Cave (scarily dark until I remembered to take off my sunglasses!), embellished with a fluorescent growling monster, flying carpet scent and a jolly genie. We thundered through tunnels in the miniature Am-Trak train, swooped above the boating lake on the chairlift, watched Harry's heartstopping acrobatics in the Fort Fun adventure playground, and ate Southern Fried chicken to the accompaniment of a brass band. We just didn't have time for the live shows like the circus or the parrot show, but we did watch the sealions. The loos are clean and plentiful with clever nappy chang-

the beach, so that young members of the family could play in the sand, while the older ones prepare to be amazed, amused, and disgusted!

The **Kingdom of the Sea** has two sites in East Anglia: one at Hunstanton, which we visited, and one at Great Yarmouth. I thought this a very impressive attraction, and one that will appeal to all ages. A series of well-interpreted underwater scenes explains marine life off the British coast. Fish native to our waters can clearly be seen in a natural environment. Our party, which ranged in age from 3 to 70, were all captivated. As well as lobsters, crabs, eels, dogfish, rays, plaice and all the other fish, at Hunstanton you can see seals recovering from injury or illness at the Seal Hospital. There were three there when we visited; sleek, fat torpedoes whizzing through the water with such consumate grace that one of them didn't even bother to open its eyes! The children liked the Touch Pools best. Here, starfish, mussels, sea anemones, and crabs patiently allowed eager fingers to pluck them out of the water and discover their secrets. Have you ever seen a starfish's legs? The Kingdom of the Sea has a good quality and clean fast-food restaurant, nice clean loos, a baby-changing room, and a really good gift shop stocked with a wide range of good-quality and affordable "fishy" gifts. All in all, we thought it one of the best attractions we've visited.

Easton Farm Park, deep in the Suffolk countryside, is another good attraction for smaller children. Combining a working dairy herd with displays in a Victorian model farm setting, there are lots of animals to see and touch and plenty of open space for letting off steam. We took a picnic, although there is a tearoom serving light food. You can see the cows being milked, stroke the gleaming golden coats of the Suffolk horses (some of which had foals when we visited), pet the pygmy goats and look at the poultry and peacocks. There's a lovely nature trail through woods and meadows and along by the river, and lots of shady places to sit while the children run about. We enjoyed looking at the vintage farm machinery and rural bygones, and loved the pretty little octagonal Victorian dairy with its cool blue and white tiles and marble counters. There's an adventure playground for those with any energy left over (guaranteed not to be adults), and a gift shop with lots of affordable souvenirs and some nice posters.

Make friends with a crab at the Kingdom of the Sea!

Mountfitchet Castle at Stansted, an imaginative and realistic recreation of a Norman motte and Bailey castle and village on its original site; **Colne Valley Railway** at Castle Hedingham, where you can picnic and play in the woods and then take a steam train ride through the pretty Colne Valley (scrumptious food here, too!); and the **Dinosaur Natural History Park** at Weston Longville, where realistic dinosaurs stalk the wooded parkland, and there's a maze, adventure playground, interpretative centre, clean loos and baby-changing room, and a good shop stocked with blood-curdling dinosaur souvenirs! Here are some others that we particularly enjoyed.

Pleasurewood Hills is one of the region's best known children's attractions. Although it's not cheap to get in, it is good value for money, as all the rides are included in the entrance price. There's a good range of attractions for smaller children and enough to keep you interested for a whole day. Harry (4, but brave!) liked the Rattlesnake, a small but viciously snakey switch-back ride; the t-shirt soaking Wild Water Falls; and, best of all, the gondola ride along a stream lead-

ing shelf units. The little pull-along trolleys for tired toddlers are a nice touch. There's a barbecue area, a wide range of fast food, and an arcade of gift shops. There is a lot to see and do, so go for the day. Our only criticism: not enough shade on a very hot day. And Harry hasn't stopped pestering to go back.

Ripley's Believe It or Not is Great Yarmouth's newest attraction and is fascinating for adults and older children. Making clever use of models, video, holograms, and the genuine thing, it is a collection of the weird, wonderful, and just plain unbelievable. There's a section on ghastly foods, where the menu includes real caterpillars and soup made of cremated human bones; there's a real shrunken head, a handbag made of chewing gum wrappers, and handpainted crisps. There's a cinema showing film of stomach-churning feats like the man who could pull his girlfriend along on a trolley - with his eyelids! - or the man (why were they all men?) who blew up balloons through his eyes. There's a real live talking leprechaun, and a tantalisingly disappearing naked lady. An unusual attraction, right opposite

MACHINERY AND TRANSPORT

Leighton Buzzard Railway

BEDFORDSHIRE

Leighton Buzzard Railway, Page's Park Station, Billington Road: A preserved narrow gauge railway operating rare steam and diesel engines on passenger trains through varied scenery around the historic market town of Leighton Buzzard. *28 Mar-3 Oct, Sun & Bank Hol Mon; 4-26 Aug, Wed & Thu. 11-4.30 (until 3.10 Wed & Thu). £3.50/£1.75/£2.75.*

Shuttleworth Collection, Old Warden Aerodrome (2m W Biggleswade, signposted off A1): 7 hangars providing close-up viewing of historic aeroplanes and road vehicles, maintained in full working order, which evolved between 1870 and 1945, with their associated memorabilia. Flying displays May-Sept. *4 Jan-23 Dec, daily 10-5, Nov-Mar closes 4. £4/£2.50/£2.50 (92).*

CAMBRIDGESHIRE

Fenland Aviation Museum, Bambers Garden Centre, Old Lynn Rd, West Walton, Wisbech. Exhibits Vampirt T11, aircraft engines, Merlin engines, aircraft components, ejector seats, radio equipment, World War II memorabilia and uniforms. *6 Mar-26 Sept, Sat, Sun, Bank Hol, 9.30-5. Other times by arrangement Tel: (0945) 585808. 50p/25p/25p.*

Imperial War Museum, Duxford Airfield (8m S Cambridge, on A505 at Junction 10 on M11). Former Battle of Britain fighter station, with hangars dating from the First World War. It houses an extensive collection of preserved military and civil aircraft including Concorde 01, and a wide range of tanks, artillery and military vehicles. Special exhibitions include a furnished 1940's prefab, the reconstructed Battle of Britain Operations Room and Dawn Patrol, which features lifesize animated figures and dramatic sound and lighting effects to depict a First World War airfield scene. Adventure playground, ride simulator, souvenir shops and refreshments. *All year (closed 24-26 Dec & 1 Jan); Mar-Oct 10-6; Oct-Mar 10-4. £5.50/£2.75/3.80. Dogs not admitted.*

Nene Valley Railway, Stibbington (7m W Peterborough, off A1): Regular steam trains operate over the line to Peterborough, a return trip of 15 miles. Many steam locomotives are kept on this line including both British and Continental types. The railway has featured in television series including Hannay, London's Burning, Christobel etc and as the site for breathtaking stunts in the James Bond film "Octopussy". *Services operate Mar & Nov, Suns; Apr-Oct, Sat, Sun & Bank Hol Mon; Jun-Aug, also Wed & some Tue, Thu & Fri. Santa specials operate on Sat, Sun & Wed in Dec. Dates subject to change Tel: (0780) 782854. Special train hire available at other times. Fares £5/£3/£3.50. Talking timetable Tel: (0780) 782921.*

Prickwillow Engine Museum, Main Street, Prickwillow (4m E Ely): Mirrlees, Bickerton & Day Diesel engine. 5-cylinder, blast injection, 250 bhp working unit. Vickers-Petter two cylinder two-stroke diesel engine and others. *1 Apr-30 Sept, daily, 9-dusk. Working days 9 May, 20 Jun, 25 Jul, 5 Sept, 3 Oct, 2-5. Other times by appt. Tel: (035388) 230. Free, donations welcome.*

Stretham Drainage Engine, Stretham, nr Ely: Giant steam beam engine and scoop wheel erected 1831 to drain surrounding fens. *10 Apr-31 Oct, Sat, Sun & Bank Hol 10.30-5.30. Weekday opening hours and adm charge under revision, Tel: (0353) 649210 or (0954) 780415 for further information.*

Wisbech Stadium, South Brink, Wisbech, Cambs: The best in short circuit motor racing from Spedeworth International. Featuring stock cars, hot rods and bangers. See all the action, walk round the pits and chat to the drivers. Good coach and car parking, covered stands, catering, licensed bar. *Mar-Nov, most Sats 7pm - to check Tel: (0945) 584736. £5/£2.50/£2.50. Special rates for premier events.*

ESSEX

Audley End Miniature Railway, Audley End, nr Saffron Walden: Miniature railway one mile long. Three diesel and three steam trains run through beautiful woodland over River Cam. *28 Mar-17 Oct, Sat, Sun & Bank Hol Mon; 9-18 Apr, 22-30 May & 17 Jul-5 Sept, daily. From 2pm. Santa specials, 12 & 19 Dec, from 11am. £1.50/£1.*

Castle Point Transport Museum, The Old Bus Garage, Canvey Island: 1930 bus garage housing a collection of old buses and coaches. Some restored others awaiting restoration, some examples are unique. *Apr-Sept, last Sat in month 10-5. Open Day 10 Oct. Donations welcome.*

Colne Valley Railway, Castle Hedingham Station (4m NW Halstead, on A604): Running through one of the prettiest parts of the Colne Valley, this tourist steam operated railway offers facilities for all the family; Restaurant & Buffet carriages (Egon Ronay approved) 5 acre woodland riverside picnic area, vintage steam and diesel locomotives and carriages. Booked parties, educational visits & tours by appt anytime. Wine and Dine Pullman evenings Easter-Christmas, most Sats (must be pre-booked). Many special events for schools and diners. *Static display open daily (ex Mons & 24 Dec-31 Jan) 11-5. Steam days: Easter-Oct, Sun, School summer hol Wed and Bank hol weekends (ex Christmas & New Year). £4/£2/£3/£10 family for steam days (includes free rides). £2/£1/£2/£5 family for non steam days. For timetable and further information Tel: (0787) 61174.*

East Anglian Railway Museum, Chappel Station, (off A604 6m west of Colchester and A12): Not just a collection spanning 100 years of railway history – it actually takes you behind the scenes of an important part of heritage. Find out how signals work, how steam engines operate and admire the Victorian building skills. On special days the trains operate to give visitors that nostalgic taste of rail travel in a more leisurely age. Free parking, picnic area, refreshments, souvenir and bookshop. Heritage centre. *All year, daily. Mon-Fri, 10-5. Sat & Sun 10-5.30. Steamdays: 1 Jan; 7 Mar; 4, 9-12 Apr; 2-3 & 30-31 May; 6, 20 June; 4, 18 July; 1, 4, 11, 18, 25, 30 Aug; 5 Sept; 2-3 Oct. Steam days £3.50/£2/£2/family £10. Non steam days £2/£1/family £5.50. Tel: (0206) 242524 for details of special events inc Santa steamings & special schools programme.*

Mangapps Farm Railway Museum, Burnham-on-Crouch: Extensive collection of all kinds of railway relics, including steam and diesel locos, carriages and wagons, historic buildings and one of the largest collections of signalling equipment open to the public. Most of collection housed under cover. 400 metre demo line. *All year, Sat, Sun & Bank Hol (ex 25 & 26 Dec). Easter-30 Sept, also Wed. Daily in Jul, Aug & school hols. 1-6. £3/£2/£2.50. Surcharge on steam and some special event days.*

Mark Hall Cycle Museum, Muskham Road, off First Avenue, Harlow: A unique collection of over 60 cycles and accessories illustrating the history of the bicycle from 1818 to the 1980s. Housed in converted 19c stable block of Mark Hall Estate. Wheelchair access to all galleries and toilets. *All year (ex 24-26 Dec), daily ex Fri & Sat, 10-1, 2-5; Free.*

HERTFORDSHIRE

Mosquito Aircraft Museum, Salisbury Hall, St Albans: Salisbury Hall was chosen by the deHavilland Aircraft Company in 1939 to develop in secret the wooden high speed unarmed bomber, the 'Mosquito'. 20 types of de Havilland aircraft on display, deHavilland and other engine types and a collection of memorabilia. *1 Mar-31 Oct, Thu 2-5.30, Sat & Sun 10.30-5.30. £2/£1/£1.*

NORFOLK

Barton House Railway, Hartwell Rd, Wroxham (8m N Norwich, on A1151): 3 1/2 inch gauge miniature steam railway and 7 1/4 inch gauge riverside railway with full-size accessories. Train rides. *Apr-Oct, third Sun each month, 2.30-5.30. 30p/10p.*

Bressingham Steam Museum and Gardens (2 1/2m W Diss, on A1066): Over 50 steam engines of various types. 5 miles of narrow gauge railway rides. 6 acres of internationally famous gardens. Steam-driven roundabout. Norfolk fire museum with a collection of fire engines and equipment. Exhibition hall. Childrens play area. Shop and restaurant. *1 Apr-31 Oct, daily. 10-5.30. £3.50/£2.50. Steam days, Sun, Thu, Bank Hol Mon, also Wed in Jul and Aug. Tel: (037988) 386/382 for details of Christmas events (booking essential).*

Bure Valley Railway, Wroxham to Aylsham: This narrow gauge steam railway runs for nine miles through the Broadland countryside from the bustling Broads capital of Wroxham to the ancient market town of Aylsham. Trains connect with the National Trust's Blickling Hall and there is a boat train service at 10.15. *Open Easter; May-Jun, Sun-Thu; Jul-Sept, daily; Oct, Sat-Wed; Dec, Sat & Sun. Return trip £6/£3.50/£5/family £16.50. Tel: (0263) 733858 for timetable details.*

Caister Castle Car Collection, West Caister, Gt Yarmouth. Largest private collection of motor vehicles in Gt. Britain, dating from 1893 to present day, housed in Caister Castle. No coaches. Accompanied children only. *Mid May-27 Sept, daily except Sats, 10.30-5. Adm charge.*

Charles Burrell Museum, Minstergate, Thetford: Museum displays of restored Burrell traction engines and other machinery. Recreated workshops, offices and displays of the life and work of this famous Thetford firm. *1 Apr-30 Sept; Sat, Sun & Bank Hols; 10-5. For details of*

additional weekday opening Tel: (0842) 752599 (Thetford Tourist Information). £1.20/60p/60p.

City of Norwich Aviation Museum, Old Norwich Rd., Horsham St Faith (off A140 Norwich to Cromer road): Exhibition building containing Norfolk aeronautical history, aero engines, Vulcan bomber from the Falklands Task Force (cockpit open to visitors) plus other aircraft. Souvenir shop. *All year (ex Christmas and New Year), Sun & Bank Hol 10-5; Open Easter Sat; May-Aug also Tue & Thu 7.30-dusk; Jul & Aug also Wed 2-5. By appt at other times Tel: (0603) 625309. £1/35p/75p.*

County School Station, North Elmham (5m N of East Dereham): Restored country station. Exhibitions about the railway, the county school and the Wensum valley. Small length of track with working diesel train and brake-van. Small tea room providing light refreshments. Picnic area and way-marked circular walks (4 1/2 and 6 miles) with free leaflet. *All year, Sat, Sun & Bank Hols; 10-6 (picnic area and circular walks open at all times). Free.*

Forncett Industrial Steam Museum, Forncett St Mary (10m SW Norwich, off A140): Museum housing unusual collection of large industrial stationary steam engines including the one that used to open Tower Bridge. Seven of the largest can be seen working on steam days. *Steam days 2 May, 6 Jun, 4 Jul, 1 Aug, 5 Sept, 3 Oct, 7 Nov & 5 Dec. 10-5. Steam day £2.50/2 children free with each paying adult/£1.75.*

North Norfolk Railway, The Station, Sheringham: Full size preserved steam railway, five miles in length. Steam trains run from Sheringham

There's plenty to see and do all year round at the Shuttleworth Collection. Five decades of transport history fill seven floodlit hangars displaying unique aeroplanes: a 1909 Bleriot, a pioneering 1930s Gloster Gladiator and victorious machines from two world wars. As well as Richard Shuttleworth's magnificent road vehicles like the 1898 Panhard Levassor and a Railton Straight 8.

Time *always* flies at Old Warden

Our flying displays take place from May to September; during the winter months too there is much to see.

Whatever the weather time will fly!

- **Restaurant & shop**
- **Free parking**

Open daily from 10am. Last admission 4pm (3pm Nov-Mar).

Old Warden Aerodrome, near Biggleswade, Beds SG18 9ER. Telephone: 0767 627288

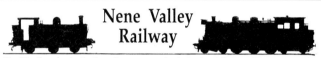

Nene Valley Railway

The 7½ miles stretch of railway line accompanies the banks of the River Nene, as it gently meanders westwards from Yarwell Mill towards Peterborough.

The headquarters of the NENE VALLEY RAILWAY are at WANSFORD (next to A1). Home to steam & diesel locomotives and rolling stock of British and European origin. Engine sheds are open all year for viewing with buffet, bar, museum, souvenir shop on operating days.

Orton Mere station has a buffet and souvenir shop, while Peterborough and Ferry Meadows (station for the Country Park), have toilet facilities and a selection of souvenirs.

Services operate in 1993 at weekends from the end of February to December. Mid-week services operate on certain days from May to the end of August. "Thomas" events throughout the year with Santa Specials on Weds, Sats & Suns in December.

Nene Valley Railway, Wansford Station, Stibbington, PETERBOROUGH PE8 6LR
Talking Timetable and Fax No: 0780 782921 Enquiries: 0780 782854

Steam back in time

You can travel from either Aylsham or Wroxham and experience the era of steam. Journey through 9 miles of beautiful Norfolk countryside between the historic market town of Aylsham and Wroxham – the bustling heart of the Norfolk Broads.

Open Spring to Autumn
Telephone 0263/733858 for a copy of the timetable

Steam engines subject to availability.

Please mention East Anglia Guide when replying to advertisements

East Anglian Railway Museum, Chappel

to Weybourne and Holt every Sun from March to October with a daily service in July and August. Museum exhibits, historic rolling stock, station buffet, souvenir shop at Sheringham. Nature trail from Weybourne Station. Also special Pullman dining trains and restaurant. *Easter-end Oct daily. For details of train times. Tel: (0263) 822045. Sample fares: Sheringham to Holt return £4.90/£2.50/£4.30. Station only 50p/25p.*

Station 146, Seething Airfield Control Tower, Seething Airfield, Brooke, Norwich (off the B1332 or A146): Renovated original USAAF wartime control tower holding 448th Bomb Group honour roll and several exhibits from World War II plus 448th Bomb Group collection of pictures, diaries and stories from veterans of 1943-45. *2 May, 6 Jun, 4 Jul, 1 Aug, 5 Sept, 3 Oct, 10-5. Also by appt Tel: (0508) 50787. Free.*

Strumpshaw Hall Steam Museum, Strumpshaw (2m off A47 Norwich-Yarmouth road): Collection of steam vehicles including beam engine, showman's road engine, portable and stationary Steam Engines. Steam Wagon and fairground organ. Railway running every day from 3pm. *14 May-2 Oct, daily (ex Sat), 2-5. £2/£1/£1.50.*

The Thursford Collection (6m NE Fakenham off A148): Collection of mechanical organs and Wurlitzer organ. Collection of steam road locomotives and various steam engines. *1 Apr-31 Oct, daily 1-5 (Jun-Aug 11-5). £4.20/£1.80/£3.80 (92).*

Wells & Walsingham Light Railway, Wells-next-the-Sea: The longest 10 inch gauge railway in Britain. 8-mile return journey along the old Great Eastern track, noted for its wonderful display of wild flowers and butterflies. New Garratt locomotive "Norfolk Hero" now in service. *9 Apr-end Sept, daily, first train from Wells 10am. Return £3.50/£2.*

Yarmouth Stadium, Yarmouth Road, Caister-on-Sea: Stock car, banger and hot rod racing presented by Spedeworth International. Enjoy an evening of thrills and spills with the family. Coach and car parking, covered stands, catering, licensed bar. *Mar-Dec, race days: Sun 7pm, Tue and Thu (high season) 8pm. Tel: (0945) 584736. Race days (0493) 720343. £5.50/£3/£3.*

SUFFOLK

East Anglia Transport Museum, Carlton Colville (3m SW Lowestoft, on B1384): The museum is under continual development and the visitor can see transport equipment, working trams, trolley-buses, commercial vehicles, narrow gauge railway, steam rollers. Cafeteria, picnic area, book/souvenir shop. *11-12 Apr; 3 May-26 Sept, Sun & Bank Hol; 5 Jun-25 Sept also Sat; 19 Jul-3 Sept, daily. 2-4, Sun & Bank Hol 11-5. £2.50/£1.20/£1.20 (92).*

Ipswich Stadium, Foxhall Heath, Ipswich: One of the fastest Oval raceways in the country in attractive heathland surroundings, the site of many major championship events. Stock car, banger and hot rod racing. National Hot Rod Championship of the World in July, the premier event in the Spedeworth motor racing calendar. *Coach and car parking, catering, licensed bars. Mar-Nov, Suns and Bank Hols 2.30. Also some special race dates Tel: (0473) 254697. £5/£2.50/£2.50. Special prices for premier events.*

Ipswich Transport Museum, Old Trolleybus Depot, Cobham Road: A collection of over 70 historic commercial vehicles, dating from 1850 to 1983. *11 & 12 Apr, 9 May, 13 Jun, 18 Jul, 4,11,18,22 & 25 Aug, 19 Sept & 10 Oct. 11-4.30. £1.40/70p/70p.*

Long Shop Museum, Main Street, Leiston: The award winning Museum consisting of three Exhibition Halls and a Gallery, The largest Industrial Museum in East Anglia, features the Long Shop built in 1853 one of the earliest examples of "Assembly Line" production. On display are steam engines, steam rollers and portables, agricultural machinery. Also the history of the town, the USAAF Air Base etc. *1 Apr-31 Oct, Mon-Sat 10-5, Sundays 11-5. £1.20/60p/60p.*

Mid Suffolk Light Railway, Brockford Station, Brockford: Working museum dedicated to the Mid Suffolk Light Railway. Restoration of station and trackwork. Preservation of artefacts and memorabilia. *1 Apr-31 Oct, Sun 10-5. £1/free.*

Norfolk and Suffolk Aviation Museum, Flixton Buck (3m SW Bungay on B1062): 16 historic aircraft on display, collection of models, paintings, flying relics. Royal Observer Corps museum and 446th Bomb Group museum. *Apr-Oct, Sun and Bank Hols, 10-5; Jul & Aug, Wed 7-9pm, Thu 11-5 and 7-9pm. Nov-Mar by appt. Donations welcome.*

Pleasurewood Hills American Theme Park Miniature Railway, Corton Road, Lowestoft: 1 mile long miniature steam railway. Over 50 other rides, shows and attractions on a "pay one price" system except for coin operated machines. *9-18, 24-25 Apr; 1-3, 8-9 May; daily from 15 May-19 Sept; 25-26 Sept; 2-3 Oct. 10-5 or 6 depending on season. £8.50/children under 4 free.*

Enjoy a ride at Thursford

Prices are in the order Adults/Children/Senior Citizens. Where prices are not available at the time of going to press, the 1992 (92) price is given. See Touring Maps on pages 104-108 for locations of places to visit.

MILLS

BEDFORDSHIRE

Bromham Mill, (off A428 Bedford-Northampton Rd, next to Old Bromham Bridge): Restored historic watermill and machinery. Milling demonstration on some Suns throughout the year. Interpretive exhibitions, arts and crafts gallery. *Apr-Oct, Wed-Fri 10.30-4.30; Sat, Sun & Bank Hols 11.30-6. 60p/30p/30p.*

Stevington Windmill, (6m W Bedford, just outside Stevington, off Bromham-Stevington road): Beautifully restored 18c post mill. *Keys available on deposit of 50p from Royal George Inn, Silver Street, Stevington (Tel: Oakley 2184). All year, 10-7 (dusk in winter). Free.*

CAMBRIDGESHIRE

Bourn Windmill, Caxton Road, Bourn: Bourn Windmill is an open trestle type mill, of a design hardly changed since the 13c. Records indicate that Bourn mill existed in 1636 and it is thought to be the oldest example of its type in the country. *12 Apr, 9 & 31 May, 27 Jun, 25 Jul, 30 Aug & 26 Sept. 2-5. £1/25p. Groups at other times by appt Tel: (0223) 243830.*

Downfield Windmill, Fordham Rd, Soham (5m SE Ely on A142): Brick tower mill dating from 1726 now in full working order. Full milling process can be seen if wind strong enough. Wholemeal flour ground in mill for sale. *Every Sun (ex 26 Dec & 3 Jan) and Bank Hol Mons, 11-5. 70p/35p.*

Hinxton Watermill, Mill Lane, Hinxton: 17c watermill restored to working order with working machinery. Flour ground and for sale. *9 May, 6 Jun, 11 Jul, 8 Aug, 5 Sept, 2.30-5.30. £1/25p.*

Houghton Mill (NT), on River Ouse, (2m downstream from Huntingdon): Mid 17c mill containing much of the machinery that was used until 1930 when the mill stopped working. *27 Mar-23 May, Sat, Sun & Bank Hol Mon; 24 May-11 Sept, Sat-Wed; 12 Sept-10 Oct, Sat & Sun. 2-5.30. £1.80/90p. Suns, £2.20/£1.*

Lode Watermill (NT), Lode (6m NE Cambridge off B1102): Watermill. *27 Mar-17 Oct, Wed, Thu, Fri, Sat, Sun & Bank Hol Mon, 1.30-5.15. Also corn grinding on Bank Hol Mons and first Sun in month. Included in Anglesey Abbey admission price (see Historic Houses section).*

Sacrewell Farm & Country Centre, Sacrewell, Thornhaugh (8m W Peterborough, off A47): Working watermill, 530 acres showing farming, conservation and history. Farm, nature and general interest trails. Gardens and a large collection of rural, domestic agricultural and craft bygones. Children's play area with maze. Light refreshments, gift shop. Simple catering for groups by appt. School visits a speciality. *All year, daily 9-9. £1.50/50p/£1. Family max £5. Group visits £3/£2.50/£2.*

The Windmill, Swaffham Prior (9m from Cambridge on B1102): Tarred brick and clunch four storied tower built c1860 and worked commercially until 1946. Restored by present owner and producing traditional stoneground wholemeal flour with French burr stones powered by four double-shuttered patent sails. *Apr-Oct, 1st & 3rd Sun in the month. Also 11 & 12 Apr; 3, 30 & 31 May; 29 & 30 Aug; 2-5. £1/50p/50p*

ESSEX

Aythorpe Roding Post Mill, Aythorpe Roding, Great Dunmow: 18c post mill that has been restored. *Apr-Sept, last Sun in month, 2-5. Free, donations invited. Groups by appt, Tel: (0245) 492211 ext 51663 or (0787) 269724.*

Bourne Mill (NT), Colchester: 16c fishing lodge converted into a mill. Machinery now in working order. *All Bank Hol Sun & Mon; Jul-Aug, Sun & Tue. 2-5.30. £1.30/65p.*

John Webb's Windmill, Thaxted: Display of rural and agricultural bygones on ground floor, also a restored 1835 fire engine. Shop. *1 May-30 Sept, Sats, Suns & Bank Hols. 2-6. 50p/25p.*

Mountnessing Windmill (on B1002 off A12 between Brentwood and Chelmsford): 19c post mill now restored to working order. *Apr-Sept, 3rd Sun in month, 2-5. Free, donations invited. Groups by appt, Tel: (0245) 492211 ext 51663 or (0787) 269724.*

Stansted Mountfitchet Windmill, Stansted (10m S Saffron Walden, on B1383): Best preserved tower mill in Essex, built 1787. Most of original machinery remains including rare bolter and curved ladder to fit cap. *Apr-Oct, first Sunday in every month, also Bank Hol Sun and Mon, every Sun in Aug, 2-6. Groups by appt, Tel: (0279) 813160, 50p/25p.*

HERTFORDSHIRE

Kingsbury Watermill Museum, St Michaels Street, St Albans: Elizabethan watermill museum on the River Ver with working waterwheel and mill machinery. New restaurant specialises in freshly baked waffles with savoury and sweet toppings. Gift and pottery shops. *All year, Tue-Sat 11-6, Sun 12-6. Closed Mon ex Bank Hols. Winter closes 5. 85p/45p/55p.*

NORFOLK

NWT: Norfolk Windmills Trust, c/o County Hall, Norwich. Tel: (0603) 222709.

Berney Arms Mill (English Heritage), nr Reedham (6m S Acle, off B1140): Most splendid and highest remaining Norfolk marsh mill in full working order. 7 floors and 70 ft high. Built late 19c by Yarmouth millwrights, Stolworthy. Landmark for miles. Situated on lonely part of Halvergate marshes. Accessible by boat and by train to Berney Arms Station (1/4 mile walk). Contains exhibition on windmills. *1 Apr-30 Sept, daily, 9-1 2-5. 75p/40p/55p.*

Billingford Windmill (NWT) (1m E Scole, on A143): A very attractive, fully restored cornmill with five-storey red-brick tower, white boat-shaped cap, sails and fantail. *All year. Keys available at Horseshoes Public House 11am-3pm & 6pm-11pm. 70p/30p.*

Bircham Mill, Great Bircham (8m SE Hunstanton, on B1153): Norfolk's finest remaining corn mill, with much working machinery. Sails turning on windy days. Tea rooms, shop. Guided tours for groups by arrangement. *8-18 Apr; 19 Apr-20 May, Sun, Wed & Bank Hol Mons; 20 May-30 Sept, daily (ex Sat); 10-6. £2/£1.25/£1.75.*

Clayrack Windpump, How Hill Nature Reserve

Boardman's Mill (NWT), How Hill, nr Ludham: Interesting open-framed timber trestle windpump with turbine in working order. *All year, daily. Donations welcome.*

Clayrack Windpump (NWT), How Hill, Ludham: Remains of Ranworth Hollow Post taken to How Hill and rebuilt. *All year, daily. Free.*

Cley Windmill, Cley-next-the-Sea (4m NW Holt, off A149): 166-year-old tower mill converted to Guest House, still with sails and brake wheel. Five floors, magnificent views of village, harbour and marshes. *Easter-30 Sept, daily, 2-5. £1/50p/50p.*

Dereham Windmill, Cherry Lane, Norwich Road, Dereham: A brick tower mill built in 1836 and restored between 1984-87. The mill is complete with cap, fantail and sails. Some machinery intact. Exhibition on Norfolk and Suffolk windmills. *1 Apr-26 Sept, Thu, Fri & Sat 12-3; Sun 2.30-4.30. Free.*

Gunton Park Sawmill (NWT), Gunton Park, Hanworth: Water powered sawmill, timber framed and weatherboarded. Saw frame inside fully restored. *Apr-Sept, 4th Sun in the month, 2-5. £1/free.*

Horsey Windpump (NT), Horsey (alongside B1159 at Horsey Staithe, 3m NW Winterton): This windpump is 4 storeys high and the gallery affords splendid views across the marshes. *27 Mar-31 Aug, daily 11-5 (Jul & Aug until 6). £1.20/60p. Car Park £1.*

Letheringsett Watermill, Letheringsett (1m W. Holt off A148): Restored working watermill demonstrating the craft of grinding wheat into flour by stones. Tues-Thur (Suns in summer) 2-5. Vintage Ruston Hornsby oil engine on view. Open for sale of flour and animal feedstuffs. *All year, Tue-Fri, 9-1, 2-5; Sat 9-1; Whitsun to mid Sept, also Sun 2-4.30. Tue, Thu, Sun & Bank Hols demonstrations 2-4.30. Closed Good Fri. Open Easter Sun & Mon. £2/£1.25/£1.50 (when demonstrating) £1/75p at other times.*

Little Cressingham Mill and Pumphouse (NWT), Fairstead Lane, Little Cressingham: Combined wind and water mill being restored. Pumphouse with water powered cylinder pump built by Joseph Bramah; hydraulic rams. *9 May, 13 June, 11 July, 8 Aug, 12 Sept. £1/25p.*

St Olaves Windpump, (NWT). Near St Olaves Bridge, Fritton, Great Yarmouth. Tiny timber trestle windpump in working order. *Open daily, all year. Key held by Mr Miller, Bridge Stores, St Olaves. Donations Welcome.*

Snettisham Watermill, with its original 18c machinery restored to working order. See the miller grind corn and explain the history of the mill. Walk by the river and mill pool in beautiful gardens with a waterfall and ducks. Mill shop for flour, preserves and souvenirs. "Lego" mill museum. *15 Jul-9 Sept, Thu; Aug Bank Hol Sun & Mon. 10-5.30. £1.50/75p/£1.*

Starston Windpump, Starston (1m NW Harleston, off B1134): Restored windpump. *Daily, free.*

Stow Mill, Paston, nr Mundesley (1m S Mundesley): Tower mill, built in 1827 with working fantail and sails. Restoration to full working order in progress. *All year, daily 10-dusk or by appt, Tel: (0263) 720298. 50p/30p.*

Stracey Arms Windpump, nr Acle (NWT) (between River Bure and A47 Acle New Rd): Exhibition and history of windpumps in Broadland. Restored drainage pump. Access by ladders to cap showing brakewheel and gears. *Easter-30 Sept, daily. 70p/30p.*

Stracey Arms houses an exhibition of Broadland windpumps

Sutton Windmill, Sutton (1m SE Stalham, off A149): Tallest mill in the country, milling machinery complete, new 73ft sails now being made. 9 floors open to visitors. *1 Apr-30 Sept, daily, 10-5.30. £2/£1.*

Thurne Dyke Windpump (NWT): Restored windpump with display boards. *1 May-30 Sept, Sun & Bank Hol Mon, 2-5. Free, donations welcome. By appt for school groups, contact NWT.*

SUFFOLK

Buttrums Mill, Burkitt Rd, Woodbridge: Fine 6-storey tower mill built in 1835. Now restored with four fully shuttered patent sails, fantail and intact machinery. Display on history and workings of mill. *1 May-26 Sept, Sun & Bank Hol Mon 2-6. At other times by appt only. Contact Suffolk County Council Tel: (0473) 265162. 50p/20p.*

Herringfleet Marsh Mill, Herringfleet nr Lowestoft: Last surviving smock drainage mill in the Broads area. Last full size working windmill in the country with four common sails and a tailpole. *Interior only open on special open days, advertised locally. Exterior open all year and reached via public footpath. Free.*

Holton St Peter Post Mill, Halesworth (1m E Halesworth on B1123, reached via footpath from gateway of mill house): Restored post mill dating from mid 18c on a 2 storey roundhouse. 4 sails and working fantail. *Exterior accessible via footpath at all reasonable times. Interior open spring & Aug Bank Hols, 10-6. Free.*

Pakenham Watermill, nr Ixworth (5m NE Bury St Edmunds): Fine 18c working watermill on Domesday site, complete with oil engine and other subsidiary machinery. Recently restored by Suffolk Preservation Society to win a Europa Nostra Conservation award. Overlooking Mill Pool, and along river bank it is ideal for picnics, sketching and painting. Stone ground flour, light refreshments, souvenirs and merchandise for sale. *9 Apr-30 Sept, Wed, Sat, Sun & Bank Hol Mons. Open Good Fri. Other times by appt, Honorary Curator Tel: (0359) 70570 or (0787) 247179. £1.25/60p/£1.*

Saxtead Green Windmill, Saxtead Green, nr Framlingham (English Heritage): 18c post mill with 3-storey roundhouse. Four patent sails, two pairs of stones and a fantail. *1 Apr-30 Sept, Mon-Sat, 10-1 2-6. £1.10/85p/55p.*

Thelnetham Windmill, Mill Rd, Thelnetham, nr Diss. Early 19c four floor towermill with conical cap, powered by four large 'patent' sails which drive two pairs of French millstones. The mill is working whenever possible (wind permitting) on open days. Visitors may purchase stone-ground flour & other grain products. *Easter, May Day and Spring Bank Hols, Sun & Mon. 4 Jul-26 Sept, Sun & Bank Hol Mon. 11-7. Also by appt, Tel: (0473) 742388. 60p/20p.*

Thorpeness Windmill, Thorpeness (2m N Aldeburgh): Working windmill housing displays on the Suffolk Heritage Coast and Thorpeness village as well as mill information. *Easter, May, June & Sept, Sat, Sun & Bank Hol Mons; July & Aug, daily, 2-5. Free.*

Woodbridge Tide Mill, Woodbridge: A carefully restored tide mill. *1 May-30 Sept, daily; also Easter and weekends in Oct. 11-5. Groups at any time by appt, Tel: (0473) 626618. Mill operates at varying times depending on tide, for details see Mill notice board. 80p/40p.*

Prices are in the order Adults/Children/Senior Citizens. Where prices are not available at the time of going to press, thhe 1992 (92) price is given.
See Touring Maps on pages 104-108 for locations of places to visit.

33

ENJOY THE PAST TODAY

By June Shepherd

Deep in the dungeon, a voice said: "This is what it was like down here for medieval prisoners", before our party plunged into total darkness. We all joked, but for that minute before the lights were switched on again, we were realistically whizzed back centuries during our tour of the dungeons of Norwich Castle, the home of a wide-ranging museum.

This guided Battlements and Dungeons tour (the charge is extra to the museum admission price), lasts nearly an hour, so leave yourself enough time to see everything else in the Castle museum - paintings, porcelain, silver, archaeology and

welcome chat, children, questions and laughter. Take the Museum of East Anglian Life in the centre of Stowmarket, for instance. This spacious outdoor museum presents a unique record of the region's rural life, yet it is also a fun place to visit for all ages. Families can happily spend all day here (there are exhibits under cover if the weather is wet). Many families do as we did, take a picnic to eat on the banks of the Rattlesden River, before strolling round to admire Remus, the museum's working Suffolk Punch. Many other attractions include the world's only remaining Burrell steam ploughing engines, different local breeds of farm animals, and authentic buildings re-erected on this peaceful site, like the old Smithy, moved here - amazingly - from the village of Grundisburgh.

The earliest European collections were privately financed, by wealthy families or the Church. From these gradually developed the great cathedral treasuries, vast Renaissance picture collections, and specialist collections eventually leading to museums such as the Ashmolean in Oxford, opened to the public in 1663. Then gradually from the 19th century onward evolved the museum accepted as a housed collection open to the public, developing the role we all recognise today: institutions which conserve, study and exhibit, but also educate and - yes - ENTERTAIN the public.

This region offers a staggeringly wide choice of museums, from those housing important collections such as The Fitzwilliam in Cambridge - one of Britain's oldest public museums - and the vast, breathtaking Imperial War Museum at Duxford, to far smaller private ones that have grown around the collection of one person, like the tiny Cottage Museum at Great Bardfield.

Charlie the Clockwork Bartender and his companions live at Cockthorpe Hall Toy Museum, only a couple of miles away from the Norfolk Coast, near Holt. Here, David and Christine Kidd have filled seven rooms with the magical toys they have collected over 20 years. Toy trains made by famous makers, plus a host of Teddy bears, dolls houses, lead soldiers, games and puzzles, all in sound condition, make this an Aladdin's cave of childhood. Because it wouldn't be practical to have the tinplate clockwork and battery toys in motion all the time, a continuous video-film of how they work is shown - a good idea, although a few chairs for viewers in this room would be welcome. The tea-room and adjoining gift shop are small, but the tea is good and the shop thought fully stocked. David Kidd provides lecture-demonstrations for school-children and party visits - by arrangement.

Some collections are housed in or around buildings which are themselves "museum pieces", like True's Yard, where you can see the last couple of fishermen's cottages remaining in the once-thriving fishing quarter of King's Lynn; and Moyse's Hall, Bury St Edmunds, one of our finest national examples of Norman domestic architecture. This 12th century flint and stone building houses clearly presented displays on archaeology and local history, including gruesome relics of the notorious murder of Maria Marten and her Polstead murderer, William Corder, who was hanged outside Bury St Edmunds gaol before a crowd of thousands.

Another unique place is Kettle's Yard in Cambridge, formerly the home of the late Jim and Helen Ede, who converted three condemned cottages, and later invited Cambridge undergraduates in to enjoy their private collection of 20th century art. Pebbles, feathers and simple everyday objects complement important works by such artists as Ben Nicholson and the primitive Cornish artist Alfred Wallis. On leaving Cambridge in the mid nineteen-seventies, the Edes gave house and contents to the University of Cambridge because they couldn't bear to separate their collection from its home. The original cottage area today retains the restful atmosphere

Toys at Cockthorpe Hall Toy Museum

natural history displays and a fantastic teapot collection - if you are visiting in the afternoon, say, and want to try one of these tours, which are informative as well as great fun. A young mum in our party happily volunteered to sit in the museum's replica "ducking stool", much to her family's amusement. "Hands-on" experience of this kind helps to make today's museums attractive, lively places to visit.

Gone are the days when museums were a last resort for rainy afternoons. The dry, almost intimidating atmosphere often met with in earlier years has generally given way now to bright interiors, stimulating presentation of exhibits, and helpful, relaxed staff who actually seem to

Perhaps we enjoy museums simply because we are all collectors at heart, and museums grew, after all, from man's passion for collecting. Human beings have always hoarded unusual, beautiful or valuable objects, then sought to find out more about them. We know that the Babylonian kings were as keen on collecting antiquities as some of us are today on collecting thimbles or corn dollies. Incidentally, in its early Greek form the word MUSEUM meant "seat of the Muses", indicating a place of contemplation, its later Latin form describing more a place of philosophical discussion. Only much later was the term used in Europe to describe a collection of curiosities.

of a private house full of much loved treasures. Indeed, to be admitted, you ring the bell and wait, as any visitor to a private house.

Don't leave Cambridge without visiting The Fitzwilliam, but first make sure which galleries you want to visit plus their opening times. These dazzling collections- antiquities, ceramics, paintings, prints, sculptures and much more - contain fascinating treasures. To pinpoint only one - a rare goblet attributed to the Venetian glassmaker Giacomo Verzelini, who brought his skills to England in the 16th century - this was discovered as a museum treasure only this century when it was spotted in use as a vase for flowers on a farmhouse table, the owners unaware of its true value. Admire the delicate diamond-point engraving and ponder on its history.

Particularly enjoyable are museums which illustrate this region's unique life and work, like the Broads Museum at Sutton near Stalham, built around one family's collection; the Broadland Conservation Centre at Ranworth, with its practical birdwatching gallery; the compelling Lifeboat Museum at Cromer, and the excellent Farmland Museum at Haddenham, which grew from a small boy's hoard of treasures. Prizewinning Gressenhall Norfolk Rural Life Museum near East Dereham is housed in and around a former workhouse - interesting and thought-provoking in itself - on an attractive secluded site complete with its own farm. Here you can see how Norfolk folk have lived and worked over the last two centuries, through stimulating displays of rural bygones, many imaginatively designed for children, who love this place. There is a Mother and Baby Room (with a practical high loo!) here, and a tea room offering tasty home-cooked snacks.

Silk weaving on hand loom at the Working Silk Museum

exhibition areas, and back to the shop stocked with handmade silken items. Everything is on one level here with no steps, making it a particularly good venue for disabled visitors.

What are "spangles" and why do English lace bobbins have beads? If you want the answer to these questions, make for the small but comprehensive Lace Museum at Alby Crafts in Norfolk,

greatly to our visit. A fine collection of well preserved machinery and equipment enhanced by skilled woodcuts and old books tells the fascinating story of printing from early hand setting methods to modern computerised technology.

At the National Horseracing Museum at Newmarket - what more appropriate setting? - you can absorb the atmosphere of the Sport of Kings and enjoy a delicious lunch. Or why not gain a glimpse of how the hardworking marsh people of the Broads lived a century ago by travelling to How Hill, Ludham, and seeking out tiny Toad Hole Cottage, an eel catcher's dwelling hidden in quiet woodland by the river Ant? By the way, if you spot a mouse in a corner of one of the bedrooms here, don't panic - it's stuffed!

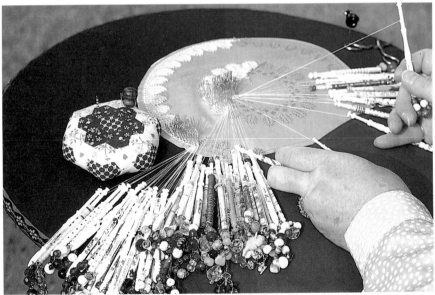
Lace being worked by hand at the Alby Lace Museum

I watched pure silk damask being woven for the Royal Palace at Hampton Court at the Working Silk Museum at Braintree, where old hand looms, rescued from oblivion and restored by Richard Humphries, are operated by skilled craftsmen. Their flying shuttles produce brilliantly coloured silk panels patterned with exquisite traditional designs, all woven to order. This unique working museum is housed in old buildings quaintly known as "New Mills". Clear directions guide visitors around the working and

where curator and instructor Lesley Thomas, who displays her selections from one of the best collections of lace outside London, will be happy to tell you about this ancient craft. Look our for Venetian, Flemish and French work as well as Lesley's own creations - she has even modelled a telephone in lace! Over the border in Suffolk, the guide who showed us round the William Clowes Printing Museum at Beccles was a retired employee of this printing and bookbinding firm. His knowledge and enthusiasm added

Visiting children at Gressenhall Rural Life Museum

MUSEUMS

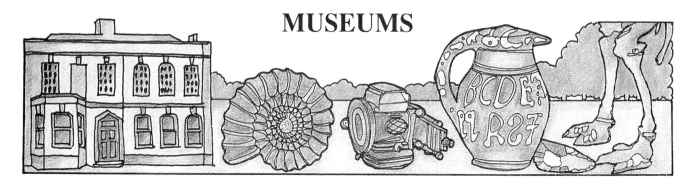

BEDFORDSHIRE

BEDFORD Bedford Museum, Castle Lane: Illustrates the region's history the from earliest times with displays from Bedford and the surrounding area. Programme of temporary exhibitions, childrens activities and other events. *All year, Tue-Sat 11-5, Sun & Bank Hol 2-5. Free.*

Bunyan Meeting Museum & Free Church, Mill Street: Bunyan memorabilia including his anvil and violin. Pilgrim's Progress in 169 languages and dialects, stained glass window depicting scenes. *1 Apr-30 Oct, Tue-Sat 2-4. 50p/30p/30p.*

Cecil Higgins Art Gallery & Museum, Castle Close: Award winning Victorian mansion. Internationally important collections of watercolours, drawings and prints. Permanent display of ceramics, glass and Bedfordshire lace. Facilities for the disabled. Set in pleasant gardens off the embankment. Groups by arrangement. *All year, Tue-Fri 12.30-5; Sat 11-5; Sun 2-5; closed Mon ex Bank Hols, Good Fri, 25 & 26 Dec. Free.*

ELSTOW Moot Hall, Elstow Green, Church End: Restored medieval market hall, now a museum housing a collection depicting 17c life. *Apr-Oct, Tue-Sat & Bank Hol 2-5, Sun 2-5.30. 60p/30p/30p.*

LUTON Museum & Art Gallery, Wardown Park, Old Bedford Road: Galleries feature lacemaking, archaeology and natural history. Changing programme of exhibitions in the art gallery. *2 Jan-24 Dec, Mon-Sat 10-5, Sun 1-5. Free.*

Mossman Collection, Stockwood Country Park, Farley Hill: Over 50 original vehicles and replicas providing a comprehensive history of horse drawn transport from Roman times to World War II. *2 Jan-24 Dec; Apr-Oct, Wed-Sun 10-5; Nov-Mar, Fri-Sun 10-4. Tel for adm charge (0582) 38714.*

Painting by J van der Hoecke, Fitzwilliam Museum

Stockwood Craft Museum, Stockwood Country Park, Farley Hill: A nostalgic look back at the rural trades and crafts that existed in years gone by. Live demonstrations of crafts most weekends. *2 Jan-24 Dec; Apr-Oct, Wed-Sun 10-5; Nov-Mar, Fri-Sun 10-4. Free.*

WOBURN Heritage Centre, Old St Mary's Church, Bedford Street, Woburn: The centre combines a museum of the history of Woburn with Tourist Information. *Apr-Oct, daily 2-4.30, free.*

CAMBRIDGESHIRE

CAMBRIDGE Cambridge and County Folk Museum, Castle St: Housed in an early timber-framed building, formerly the White Horse Inn, the museum has displays that show everyday life of the people of the city and county from 1650 to present day. *31 Apr-30 Sept, Mon-Sat 10.30-5, Sun 2-5. 1 Oct-31 Mar, Tue-Sat 10.30-5, Sun 2-5. Closed 25 Dec-1 Jan & Good Fri. £1/50p/50p. Students and UB40 holders 50p.*

Fitzwilliam Museum, Trumpington St: Lower Galleries: Antiquities, including Egyptian collection, ceramics and glass, coins and medals, manuscripts and miniatures, and other applied arts. Upper Galleries: Outstanding collection of paintings, drawings and prints, sculpture, furniture, clocks and majolica. Temporary exhibitions through the year. Coffee bar. Shop. *Tue-Sat (Lower Galleries) 10-2, (Upper Galleries) 2-5; Sun (All Galleries) 2.15-5. Closed Mons ex Easter Mon, Spring & Summer Bank Hols. Closed Good Fri, 24 Dec-1 Jan incl. Free. Guided tours 2.30 Sat & Sun, also by arrangement, charge.*

Kettle's Yard: Outstanding permanent collection of 20c paintings and sculpture, also an exhibition gallery presenting a continuous programme of modern art exhibitions with lectures, films, videos, performances, and other associated events. *House: Tue-Sun, 2-4 (parties of 10 or more not admitted without appt); Exhibition Gallery: Tue-Sat, 12.30-5.30; Sun, 2-5.30 during exhibitions. Closed Bank Hols and Christmas to New Year incl. Free.*

Museum of Technology, Riverside (off Newmarket Road): Preserved Victorian pumping station containing gas and steam engines, working printshop and other items from the industrial past. *All year, first Sun in every month, 2-5. Static 80p/40p/40p; Steam weekends £2/£1/£1. Tel: (0223) 68650 for details of steaming days.*

University Museum of Zoology, Downing St: Zoological specimens used in teaching and research. *All year, Mon-Fri 2.15-4.45; closed Easter, 24 Dec-3 Jan. Free.*

Whipple Museum of the History of Science: Collection of historic scientific instruments. Special exhibitions. *Mon-Fri 2-4 (except Bank Hols and possibly University vacations). Free.*

BURWELL Burwell Museum, Mill Close, Burwell: Rural museum housed in rebuilt 18c timber framed barn. *31 Mar-30 Sept, Sun 2-5. Open Good Fri & Easter Mon. Free.*

The Nursery, Cecil Higgins Art Gallery

Kettle's Yard, Cambridge

Stained Glass Museum, Ely Cathedral

ELY Ely Museum, High St: Local history, military collection. Recently completely re-furbished. Entirely new displays including audio visuals. *All year. Jan-Mar & Nov-Dec, Tue-Sat 11-4, Sun 1-4; Apr-Oct, Tue-Sat & Bank Hol Mons 10.30-1, 2.15-5, Sun 2.15-5. Closed mid Dec-1 Jan. £1/50p/50p. Parties by appt.*

Oliver Cromwell's House, 29 St Mary's Street: The family home of Oliver Cromwell, audio-visual presentation on his life, recreations of c17 kitchen and parlour scenes. TIC, souvenir and craft shop. *2 Jan-30 Apr & 1 Oct-31 Dec, Mon-Sat 10-5, open Easter Sun. 1 May-30 Sept, daily, 10-6; £1.50/£1/£1.*

Stained Glass Museum, Ely Cathedral: Examples of stained glass windows from the 13c to the present day in specially lighted display boxes. Models of workshop and history of craft and styles. *All year, Sat & Sun. 1 Mar-31 Oct, daily. Mon-Fri 10.30-4, Sat 10.30-4.30, Sun 12-3. Open school hols. Closed Good Fri, 25 Dec. £1.50/70p/70p.*

HUNTINGDON Cromwell Museum: Portraits and items relating to Oliver Cromwell and his family and the Parliament/Commonwealth side of the Great Rebellion or Puritan revolution 1640-1660. The collection is housed in the building where Oliver Cromwell and also Samuel Pepys went to school. *1 Apr-31 Oct, Tue-Fri 11-1, 2-5; Sat & Sun 11-1, 2-4; 1 Nov-31 Mar, Tue-Fri 1-4; Sat 11-1, 2-4; Sun 2-4. Closed Bank Hols ex Good Fri. Free.*

MARCH March and District Museum, High St: Primarily a 'folk' museum with a range of rural and domestic exhibits reflecting life in March and the area. Also photographs and local records. Outbuildings contain restored blacksmith's forge and Fen cottage. *All year, Wed 10-12; Sat 10-12, 2-4.30. Free, donations welcome. Parties by appt, Tel: (Secretary) (0354) 54783.*

PETERBOROUGH City Museum and Art Gallery, Priestgate: Local history, archaeology, geology, natural history, folk life, industry, militaria, costume, period shop and art gallery with many temporary exhibitions throughout year. *All year, Tue-Sat 10-5 subject to some Sat closure. Closed 25 & 26 Dec, 1 Jan and Good Fri. Free.*

RAMSEY Rural Museum (10m SE Peterborough, on B1069): Bygones of local and agricultural interest. *1 Apr-30 Sept, Thu & Sun 2-5. At other times by appt. Tel: (0487) 813223. Free.*

ST IVES Norris Library and Museum: Local collections from prehistory to bygones, including local literature. *1 May-30 Sept, Mon-Fri 10-1, 2-5; Sat 10-12, 2-5; Sun 2-5. 1 Oct-30 Apr, Mon-Fri 10-1, 2-4; Sat 10-12. Closed Good Fri. Free.*

SACREWELL Farm and Country Centre, Sacrewell, Thornhaugh (8m W Peterborough, off A47): Working watermill, 530 acres showing farming, conservation and history. Farm, nature and general interest trails. Gardens and a large collection of rural, domestic, agricultural and craft bygones. Children's play area with maze. Light refreshments, gift shop. Simple catering for groups by appt. School visits a speciality. *All year, daily 9-9. £1.50/50p/£1. Family max £5.*

THORNEY Heritage Centre, (7m NE Peterborough): Attached to Bedford Hall, Station Road, the Centre shows development of village from early Monastery, the changes made by the Dukes of Bedford in housing and fen drainage, Huguenot links, village social history. *1 Apr-31 Oct, Sat & Sun, 2-5; 1 Jun-30 Sept, also Wed 2-5. Free. Village Tours, Heritage Centre open any time by arr. Tel: (0733) 270368.*

WHITTLESEY Whittlesea Museum, Town Hall, Market St (5m E Peterborough, on A605): Archaeology, agriculture, hand tools, brickmaking, collection of local photographs. Sir Harry Smith exhibition. Brickyard worker's living room display. Costumes, temporary displays. Walled garden. *All year, Fri and Sun 2.30-4.30. Sat, 10-12. 50p/20p.*

WISBECH Wisbech and Fenland Museum, Museum Square: Decorative arts, archaeology, geology, local and natural history. Temporary exhibitions. *All year (closed over Christmas), Tue-Sat, 10-4 (1 Apr-30 Sept closes 5). Free.*

ESSEX

BASILDON National Motorboat Museum, Wat Tyler Country Park, Pitsea: Illustrates the history of the motor boat over the last century. *All year (ex 24 Dec-1 Jan), Thu-Mon, 10-4. Free.*

BILLERICAY Barleylands Farm Museum, Barleylands Road: Collection of vintage farm machinery illustrating rural life of the past, housed on a working farm. *All year, Wed-Sun 11-5. Open Bank Hols except 25 & 26 Dec. £2/£1/£1.*

BRAINTREE Town Hall Centre, Market Square. The Heritage Centre shows the town's development from the Stone Age to the present and describes Braintree's international importance in wool, silk, engineering and early American history. The gallery houses changing exhibitions. Study room with local interest books and photographic collection. TIC on ground floor. *All year, Mon-Fri 9-5, Sat 10-4. Closed Bank Hols. Study room open by appt only. Free admission except to special events.*

Oliver Cromwell's House, Ely

Colchester Castle set in an attractive park

The Working Silk Museum New Mills, South Street, Braintree: England's last hand loom silk weaving mill. Working looms from early 19c. Ancient textile machines restored and working. Show of silk textiles and mill shop. *All year, Mon-Sat, 10-12.30, 1.30-5; Sat, shop only ex tours at 2, 3 and 4. Evening tours at 7.30 by appt, Tel: (0376) 553393. Closed Bank Hols. £2.50/£1.25/£1.25.*

BURNHAM-ON-CROUCH Museum (9m SE Maldon): Local history; maritime and agricultural features of Dengie Hundred. *Mid Mar-mid Dec, Wed & Sat 11-4; Sun & Bank Hols 2-4.30. Burnham Week (last week Aug), daily, 2-4.30, 20p/5p.*

CANVEY ISLAND Dutch Cottage Museum: Early 17c cottage of one of Vermuyden's Dutch workmen (Vermuyden was the Dutch engineer who was principally responsible for the great drainage schemes undertaken through much of East Anglia in the early 17c) *24 May-29 Sept, Wed, Sun 2.30-5; Bank Hols 10.30-1, 2.30-5. Parties by appt, Tel: (0268) 794005. Free.*

CHELMSFORD Chelmsford and Essex Museum, Oaklands Park, Moulsham St: Permanent collections of geology, archaeology, bygones, glass, ceramics and natural history. Display of The Story of Chelmsford, Ice Age to AD1600. Also Essex Regiment Museum. *All year, Mon-Sat 10-5, Sun 2-5. Closed Good Fri, 25 & 26 Dec. Free.*

COLCHESTER Colchester Castle, is unique. It is the largest Norman castle keep in Europe, built over the remains of the magnificent Roman Temple of Claudius which was destroyed by Boudica in AD60. Colchester was the first capital of Norman Britain and the archaeological collections on display are among the finest in the country. Spectacular new displays and reconstructions. *All year, Mon-Sat, 10-5; 1 Mar-30 Nov also Sun 2-5. Closed 24-27 Dec. £1.50/75p/75p; Oct-May £1/50p/50p. Groups by appt, Tel: (0206) 712931/2.*

The Hollytrees, High St: Two centuries of fascinating toys, costume, decorative arts and curios displayed in an attractive Georgian Town House of 1718. *All year, Mon-Sat 10-5. Closed Good Fri, 24 Dec-27 Dec. Free.*

Natural History Museum, All Saints Church, High Street: Recently completely displayed museum of the natural history of North East Essex.

Hands on exhibits. *All year, Mon-Sat 10-5. Closed Good Fri, 24-27 Dec. Free.*

Social History Museum, Holy Trinity Church, Trinity St: Town and country life in the Colchester area over the last two hundred years displayed in this former church with its Saxon Tower. All year, *Mon-Sat 10-5. Closed Good Fri, 24 Dec-27 Dec. Free.*

EAST TILBURY Coalhouse Fort, Victorian Thames defence fortress with Thameside Aviation museum, military vehicles and artillery display. *All year, last Sun in the month plus most Bank Hols, 1-4.30. Other times by appt. Tel: (0375) 390000 ext 2414. £1.50/50p. Special events £2/£1.*

FINCHINGFIELD Guildhall and Museum (8m NW Braintree, on B1053): Art exhibitions in the Guildhall from Apr-Oct. Free. Museum of Local Antiques. *11 Apr-30 Sept, Sun 2-5.30, open Easter Mon. Donations welcome.*

GRAYS Thurrock Local History Museum (in Thameside Complex): Over 50 cases detail Thurrock's local history from prehistoric times to the modern day. *All year, Mon-Sat 9-8. Closed Sun & Bank Hols. Free.*

GREAT BARDFIELD Cottage Museum, Dunmow Road (7m NE Gt Dunmow, on B1057): 16c charity cottage. Collection of mainly 19 and 20c domestic and agricultural artefacts. Some rural crafts, mainly strawplaiting and corndollies. *Easter-end Sept, Sat, Sun & Bank Hols. 2-6. Free.*

Great Bardfield Cage, Bridge Street: 19c village lock up. *Easter-end Sept, Sat, Sun & Bank Hols. 2-6. Free.*

Bardfield Centre, Braintree Road: Art gallery in redeveloped medieval barn complex. Permanent display of the work by Edward Bawden and the Bardfield artists. Paintings for sale. *Easter-end Sept, Sat, Sun & Bank Hols. 2-5.30. Free.*

HARLOW Museum, Third Avenue: Local history (important Roman and post-medieval collection), natural history, geology and folk life.

Prittlewell Priory Museum, Southend-on-Sea

Tymperleys Clock Museum, Trinity Street: A fine collection of Colchester made clocks displayed in Tymperleys, a restored late c15 house. *1 Apr-31 Oct, Mon-Sat 10-5. Closed Good Fri. Free.*

DEDHAM The Sir Alfred Munnings Art Museum, Castle House (3/4m from village centre): Castle House contains many paintings, drawings, sketches and other works by the late Sir Alfred Munnings, KCVO, President of the Royal Academy 1944-1949. *2 May-3 Oct, Sun, Wed, Bank Hol Mon, also Thu & Sat in Aug, 2-5. £2/25p/£1. Groups of 20 or more by appt, Tel: (0206) 322127.*

Housed in Georgian manor house, set in park with pond and butterfly garden. *All year (ex 25 & 26 Dec), Sun, Mon, Tue, Wed & Thu 10-5 (Tue closes 9). Closed 12.30-1.30 Sun. Free.*

Harlow Study and Visitors Centre, Netteswell Bury Farm: Study centre is a 13c church. Visitors centre is a medieval tithe barn, containing an exhibition telling Harlow's new town story. *All year (ex 21 Dec-1 Jan & Bank Hols), Sun-Thu 9.30-4.30. Free.*

HARWICH Maritime Museum, Low Lighthouse. The Green: Special displays related to lifeboats, Royal Navy and commercial shipping. Fine views over unending shipping movements in harbour. *Easter-Oct, Sun, 10-12, 2-5. 50p/free/50p.*

Central Museum, Southend-on-Sea

KELVEDON Feering and Kelvedon Local History Museum, Branch Library (4m NE Witham, off A12): Manorial history, artefacts from Roman settlement of Canonium. Agricultural tools and bygones. *1 Mar-31 Oct, Mon 2-5, Sat 9.30-12.30. 1 Nov-28 Feb, Sat 10-12.30. Closed Bank Hols. Also open by appt Tel: (0376) 570307. Free.*

Harwich Maritime Museum

MALDON Agricultural and Domestic Museum, Church St, Goldhanger. Items of rural interest dating back to 18c including vintage tractors, agricultural machinery and domestic items. *Easter-28 Nov, Wed 2-6, Sun 10-6 and by appt, Tel: (0621) 88647/853856.*

SAFFRON WALDEN Museum, Museum St: Collections of local history, archaeology inc Ancient Egyptian room, ceramics, glass, furniture, costume, toys, ethnography. Also special exhibitions. Natural history and geology displays in preparation. Castle ruins in grounds. Museum's 19th century farm tools and vehicles collection displayed in stable block at Audley End House. *All year, 1 Apr-31 Oct, Mon-Sat 10-5, Sun & Bank Hol 2.30-5; 1 Nov-31 Mar, Tue-Sat 11-4, Sun & Bank Hol 2.30-4.30. Closed 24 & 25 Dec. £1/free/50p*

SOUTHEND-ON-SEA Central Museum and Planetarium, Victoria Ave: Room settings, archaeology, the history of S.E. Essex, natural history and social history displays. Only planetarium in South East outside London. *All year. Museum: Mon 1-5, Tue-Sat 10-5; Planetarium: Wed-Sat, 10-4. Closed Easter and Bank Hols. Museum free, charges for Planetarium only, £1.80/£1/£1, family £4.90. Parties by appt.*

Prittlewell Priory Museum: Local history, natural history and an important collection of radios and communications equipment in old building which is remains of a 12c Cluniac Monastery. *All year, closed Easter & Bank Hols, Tue-Sat 10-1, 2-5. Groups welcome by appt. Free.*

Southchurch Hall: Early 14c timber-framed moated manor house with Tudor addition. *All year, Tue-Sat 10-1, 2-5. Closed Easter & Bank Hols. Groups welcome by appt. Free.*

SOUTHMINSTER Ewenny Farm Alternative Environment Centre, Southminster Road: Traditional windpump, wind generator, solar electric displays, solar heating, organic garden, wildlife garden, tree nursery, herbs. Video display in visitors centre. *All year (ex Christmas hols), daily, 10-6 or dusk if earlier. £2/£1.*

STANFORD-LE-HOPE, Walton Hall Farm Museum, Walton Hall Road, Linford: Main collection housed in 17c barn and farm building. Farming bygones; rare breed and other animals; representations of Victorian and Edwardian

childs nursery and old time dairy. *1 Apr-end Sept, Thu-Sun & Bank Hol Mons, 10-5; 1 Oct-end Mar, Sat & Sun 10-4. £2/£1/£1.*

STANSTED House on the Hill Toy Museum, adjacent to Mountfitchet Castle: Exciting, animated toy museum covering 7,000 sq ft, featuring a huge collection of toys from Victorian times to the 1970's offering a nostalgic trip back to childhood. Many animated displays. Collectors' shop. *Mid Mar-mid Nov, Tue-Sun. Open Mons for Bank and school hols. Winter open Sat & Sun, also daily during school hols. 10-4. Closed 24-26 Dec. £2.80/£1.80/£2.50.*

WALTHAM ABBEY Epping Forest District Museum, Sun St: Early timber-framed building with fine Tudor oak panelling, herb garden, agricultural and allied crafts, temporary exhibitions, local and social history of Epping Forest District. Shop. Light refreshments. *All year, Fri, Sat, Sun, Mon, 2-5; Tue, 12-5 (closed 25-26 Dec & 1 Jan). Free.*

WALTON Heritage Centre: Interpretive museum of local history, rural & maritime, in former lifeboat house. *22 Jul-29 Sept, daily, 2-5; 50p/free.*

WEST MERSEA Mersea Island Museum, High Street, West Mersea. Local history, natural history display of methods and tools used in marine and wildlife. Art exhibitions, social history, fossils and minerals. *1 May-26 Sept, daily ex Mon (open Bank Hol), 2-5. Parties by appt 10-12.30. Tel: (0206) 383301. 50p/20p/25p.*

HERTFORDSHIRE

ASHWELL Village Museum, Swan Street (off A505 between Royston and Baldock): A small village museum containing interesting items from an agricultural community. *All year, Sun & Bank Hol Mon 2.30-5. 40p/10p.*

HATFIELD Mill Green Museum & Mill, Mill Green: Fully restored water powered corn mill and local history museum. Visitors can see corn ground in the traditional way and buy flour. Programme of temporary exhibitions. Craft demonstrations held on summer weekends. *All year (ex Christmas), Tue-Fri 10-5, Sat, Sun & Bank Hols 2-5. Adm charge.*

Hitchin Museum

The Sir Walter Rothschild Zoological Museum

HERTFORD Hertford Museum, 18 Bull Plain: Fine collections from the county and beyond. Archaeology, social history, natural history, geology, fine art and photographs. Changing exhibitions and events programme. Shop and Jacobean garden. Disabled access to ground floor and garden. *All year, Tue-Sat 10-5. Free.*

HITCHIN Museum & Art Gallery, Paynes Park: Displays of local, domestic and working life. The costume gallery covers two centuries of fashion and the regimental collection of the Herts Yeomanry is housed here. Reconstructed Victorian chemist shop, complemented by a physic garden. Art exhibitions change monthly. *All year, ex Bank Hols, Mon-Sat 10-5, Sun 2-4.30. Free.*

HODDESDON Lowewood Museum, High Street: Exhibitions and displays explaining the history of the towns and villages that form the Borough of Broxbourne. Activities, talks, demonstrations and other events. *All year, Tue-Sat 10-1, 2-4. Free.*

Rye House Gatehouse Exhibition, Rye Road: Intriguing 15c moated building built by Sir Andrew Ogard, a fine example of early English brickwork. Rye House created a national scandal with the discovery in 1683 of the 'Rye House Plot' to assassinate King Charles II. *Apr-Sept, Sat 1-5, Sun & Bank Hol 11-5. Adm charge.*

LETCHWORTH First Garden City Heritage Museum, 296 Norton Way South: Exhibition of items relating to the Garden City Movement and the development and social history of Letchworth Garden City. Displayed in the former office and home of the architect Barry Parker. *All year (ex 25 & 26 Dec), Mon-Fri 2-4.30, Sat 10-1 2-4. Free.*

Letchworth Museum, Broadway: Local museum with displays of archaeology and natural history from North Hertfordshire. Programme of changing exhibitions of art, crafts and various topics of local interest. *All year, Mon-Sat 10-5. Free.*

RICKMANSWORTH Batchworth Lock Canal Centre, 99 Church Street: The canalside museum centre has a fine display of Paget Tomlinson pictures tracing the development of the narowboat. Rickmansworth Waterways Trust is hosting the Rickmansworth Canal Festival 21-23 May and runs a varied programme of lock events in the summer. *All year, daily, Tue-Sun 12-5. Free.*

ST ALBANS Grebe House, Herts & Middlesex Wildlife Trust, off St Michael's Street in Verulamium Park: The Centre has displays illustrating local wildlife and conservation activities. Wildlife garden and shop. *All year (ex Christmas-New Year), Mon-Fri 10-4, Sat & Sun 12-4. Free.*

Museum of St Albans, Hatfield Road: Discover the story of the cathedral city of St Albans, told through a lively series of displays using the museum's historical and ecological collections.

Broadland Conservation Centre, Ranworth

Home of the Salaman collection of trade and craft tools. Wildlife garden. *All year, Mon-Sat 10-5, Sun 2-5. Adm charge.*

Verulamium Museum, St Michael's: On the site of one of the major cities of Roman Britain. Recreated Roman rooms, hands-on discovery areas, excavation videos, access to reserve collections and gallery tours. *All year, Mon-Sat 10-5.30 (Nov-Feb closes 4), Sun 2-5.30 (Nov-Feb closes 4). Adm charge.*

Organ Museum, 320 Camp Road: Permanent playing exhibition of mechanical musical instruments. Light refreshments and shop. *All year, Sun 2-4.30. £1.50/60p/£1.*

STEVENAGE Stevenage Museum, St Georges Way: Tells the story of the town from the stone age to the present, through objects including a Roman silver coin hoard and a

1950's sitting room. Exhibition showing the history of sport until 1 May. Monthly programme of Saturday events. Full access to disabled. *All year, Mon-Sat 10-5. Closed Bank Hols. Free.*

TRING The Walter Rothschild Zoological Museum, Akeman Street: Founded by 2nd Baron Rothschild in 1892, the museum contains the finest collection of mammals, birds, reptiles and insects in the country, including the famous dressed fleas. Extinct, rare, beautiful and bizarre exhibits in a unique Victorian atmosphere. *All year (ex 1 Jan, Good Fri & 24-26 Dec). Mon-Sat 10-5, Sun 2-5. £1.50/75p/£1.*

WATFORD Central Library & Art Gallery, Hempstead Road: The Watford exhibition gallery mounts temporary exhibitions throughout the year. These cover the work of local artists, art societies and photographic clubs. The central library provides a full information service on activities, events and services in Watford and the surrounding area. *All year (ex 10 Apr & Bank Hols), Mon-Sat 9.30-8 (Wed closes 1, Sat closes 4). Free.*

Watford Museum, 194 High Street: Local history with special emphasis on printing, brewing, wartime and the Victorian period. Displays on Watford Football Club. Art gallery and temporary exhibition gallery with displays changing monthly. *All year (closed 25 & 26 Dec), Mon-Sat inc Bank Hols 10-5. Free.*

WELWYN Roman Baths, The Bypass: 3rd century bath house, the one visible feature of a villa complex, preserved in a specially constructed vault. *All year ex Christmas, Thu, Fri, Sat, Sun & Bank Hols 2-5 (dusk if earlier). Adm charge.*

NORFOLK

ALBY Bottle Museum, Alby Craft Centre (5m S Cromer, on A140): The only bottle museum in the UK, the George Dennis collection of Norfolk bottles of all descriptions. Around 3000 are constantly on view. *24 Mar-13 Dec, Tue-Sun, 10-5. 30p/10p.*

ALBY Lace Museum, Alby Craft Centre: Large workshop with working lacemaker, part of Alby Craft Centre (see craft section). *21 Mar-14 Dec, Tue-Fri & Sun, 10-1, 1.30-5. Free.*

BURSTON Strike School (3m NE Diss): Building erected to house scholars of strike school. Interpretative exhibition of artefacts, documents and photographs of the longest strike in British history – 25 years. *All year, daily 7-dusk (closed 1 Jan, Good Fri, 25 & 26 Dec). Free.*

Victorian Fisherman's cottage, Cromer Museum

COCKLEY CLEY Iceni Village and Museums (3m SW Swaffham): Iceni encampment reconstruction, believed on original site. Saxon church c 630 A.D. Folk and East Anglian Museum in historic cottage. Agricultural implement, vintage engine and carriage museums. Nature Trail. Gift shop and light refreshments. Picnic area. *1 Apr-31 Oct, daily, 12-5.30. 1 Jul-30 Sept opens 11. Group bookings Tel: (0760) 721339. £2.50/£1/£1.50/students £1.50 (92).*

COCKTHORPE Cockthorpe Hall Toy Museum: Unique collection of antique and vintage toys, 1860 to 1970's. Over 3000 toys on display in west wing of c16 Cockthorpe Hall. Tea/coffee shop, homemade cakes, toy and souvenir shop. *1 Mar-30 Mar & 1 Nov-31 Dec, daily 11-4. 31 Mar-31 Oct, daily, 10-5. Closed 24-26 Dec. £2/£1/£1.75.*

CROMER Cromer Museum, East Cottages, Tucker St: Late Victorian fisherman's cottages displaying history, geology, archaeology and natural history of the Cromer area. *All year (closed Good Fri, 24-26 Dec, 1 Jan). Mon-Sat, 10-5 (closed Mon 1-2), Sun 2-5. 80p/40p/50p.*

Lifeboat Museum: Models, pictures, photographs. Lifeboat, "Ruby & Arthur Read II" new Tyne Class Lifeboat, can be viewed at the Lifeboat House on the pier, same times as museum. Oakley lifeboat "H F Bailey" on display which served at Cromer from 1935 to 1947 and saved 818 lives. History of Cromer Lifeboats displayed in pictures, Bloggs medals displayed. School parties and organised visits welcomed. Talks and film shows can be arranged. *1 May-30 Sept, daily 10-5 (ex in very bad weather). Free.*

Lifeboat House, end of the pier open mornings throughout year. Tyne class lifeboat.

DISS Diss Museum, Market Place: 19c photographs, clothes and tools. Local history and prehistory. *12 Apr-30 Sept, Wed & Sun 2-4.30, Fri, Sat & Bank Hol Mons 10-4.30. Oct-Dec, Wed 2-4.30, Fri 10-4.30.*

DOWNHAM MARKET Bridge Farm - A Country Christmas, (1/2m from the railway station on the banks of the River Ouse): A working arable farm with over a mile frontage to the River Ouse. The site of a medieval hermitage. The chapel of the nativity is unique. Journey through 'The Mists of Time' back to a Dickens Christmas with Victorian Street scenes. Car and cart museum. *Oct-Dec, tours Wed 3pm, Tel: (0366) 383185 to check time. Groups 15+ at any time by appt. £3.50/£2/£3.*

EAST DEREHAM Bishop Bonner's Cottage: Local domestic and agricultural exhibits in early 16c cottage. *1 May-30 Sept, Tue-Sat, 2.30-5. Donations welcome.*

FAKENHAM Museum of Gas and Local History: The town gasworks in use from 1846-1965 is now a scheduled ancient monument. On show are the complete works (with working exhausters and gas holder); displays of working gas meters and calorimeter equipment; a model of a North Sea Gas Rig; local history material. *9-15 Apr; 2-6 May; 30 May-3 Jun; 25 Jul-5 Sept. During these periods Tue, Thu & Bank Hols, 10-4; Sun, 2-5. £1.50/25p/£1. Other times by appt, Tel: (0328) 851696.*

GREAT YARMOUTH Old Merchant's House (EH), Row 111, South Quay: Domestic ironwork of 17 and 19c in 17c houses. Two rooms have been restored to their original condition with ornate plaster ceilings. *1 Apr-30 Sept, daily, 10-1, 2-6. Admission by tour only. £1.10/55p/85p (92).*

Gt Yarmouth Museums' Exhibition Galleries, Central Library: Local and loan exhibitions of paintings and other arts and crafts, plus displays from Gt Yarmouth Museums' art collections. When exhibition is showing (Tel: (0493) 858900 to check). *Mon-Fri 9-5.30 (sometimes closed 1-2). Sat 9-12.30, 1.30-5. Closed Bank Hols. Free.*

Maritime Museum for East Anglia: Maritime history of East Anglia, including herring fishery, lifesaving, shipbuilding and inland waterways. *Summer, daily ex Sat, 10-5. For winter opening details Tel:(0493) 855746. Adm charge.*

Elizabethan House Museum: House built 1596, containing panelled 16c rooms. Exhibits illustrate domestic life in the 19c. Victorian toys and Lowestoft porcelain. *Summer, daily ex Sat, 10-1, 2-5. For winter opening details Tel: (0493) 855746. Adm charge.*

The Tolhouse Museum, Tolhouse St: Medieval building with local history exhibits. Once the town's courthouse and gaol. Dungeons. Brass rubbing centre. *Summer, daily ex Sat, 10-1 2-5. For winter opening Tel: (0493) 855746. Free.*

Lydia Eva Steam Drifter, Town Quay: The last survivor of over 3000 drifters which came every autumn to Yarmouth and Lowestoft to fish for herring. Displays the hardships of life aboard and ashore in an industry which dominated two towns for a century. Lydia Eva was built in 1930 in King's Lynn and her engines and boiler were fitted in Great Yarmouth. She was one of the last steam drifters to be built and destined to be the very last survivor. *Jul-Oct, daily, 10-4.30. Also at Lowestoft Harbour Easter-Jun. Free.*

GRESSENHALL Norfolk Rural Life Museum and Union Farm, (2m NW East Dereham, on B1110): Former workhouse illustrating the history of Norfolk over the last 200 years; agriculture, rural crafts etc. Union farm is a working 1920's farm with traditional breeds of livestock, heavy horses and nature trail. Very extensive site with special exhibitions and events throughout the season. Picnic area, cafeteria, giftshop. *4 Apr-31 Oct, Tue-Sat 10-5, Sun 12-5.30, closed Good Fri. £3/80p/£1.80.*

HOLKHAM "Bygones at Holkham", Holkham Park, Wells-next-the-Sea: Housed in the beautiful 19c buildings adjacent to Holkham Hall, this unique collection of over 4,000 items includes displays of motor cars, fire engines, tractors, traction engines, farming and gardening implements. Victorian domestic items, a smithy, a laundry, a dairy, original 1900 harness room, shoe shop, and brewing section, etc. Cafeteria, souvenir shop, ample parking. *30 May-30 Sept, daily (ex Fri & Sat), 1.30-5. Also Easter, May, Spring and Summer Bank Hol Sun & Mons, 11.30-5. Bygones & Park £2.70/£1.20; Hall, Park & Bygones £4.70/£2.*

KING'S LYNN Arts Centre and Guildhall of St George (NT): Largest surviving 15c medieval guildhall in England. Part of the King's Lynn Art Centre promoting regular concerts, theatre, films and exhibitions. Annual arts festival July. *All year, Mon-Fri 10-5; Sat 10-4. Closed Good Fri. Free.*

Lynn Museum: Natural history, archaeology, local history; also temporary exhibitions. *All year, Mon-Sat, 10-5. Closed Bank Hols. 60p/30p/40p.*

King's Lynn Arts Centre & Guildhall of St George

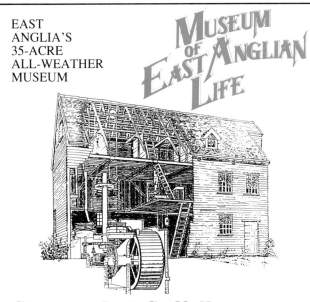

Please mention East Anglia Guide when replying to advertisements

Old Gaol House Museum and Regalia Rooms: Opening in April 1993, a new attraction set in the original cells of the old town gaol, telling the stories of some of Lynn's most infamous criminals. Walkman audio tour, sound and light effects. Also features the town's magnificent civic treasures, including the oldest medieval loving cup and royal charters dating from King John. *Spring Bank hol-end Oct, daily 10-5. Nov-Spring Bank hol, Fri-Tue 10-5 (ex Christmas, New Year). £2/£1.50.*

Town House Museum of Lynn Life, 46 Queen Street: Discover the merchants, tradesmen and families who for 900 years have made Lynn such a prosperous place. Historic room displays including costume, toys, a working Victorian kitchen and a 1950's living room. *All year, Tue-Sat 10-5; 30 May-26 Sept also Sun 2-5. £1/50p/60p*

True's Yard, North Street: The last two remaining fishermen's cottages of King's Lynn's fishing quarter, the North End fully restored, with a museum, gift shop and tea room. Research facilities available for those wishing to trace their ancestry in King's Lynn, or for students researching the area. *All year (ex 25 Dec), daily 9.30-4.30. Nov-Feb closed Fri. £2/£1.50/£1.*

LITTLE DUNHAM Dunham Museum: Station Road, Little Dunham, King's Lynn. (5m NE Swaffham). Exhibition buildings showing collection of old working tools and machinery. Dairy, Leathersmith, Shoemakers. Stationary engines and bygones. *1 Apr-30 Sept, 10-5.30; By appt 1 Oct-31 March, 11-3. Closed 25 & 26 Dec. £1/25p.*

LUDHAM Toad Hole Cottage Museum: How Hill, Ludham. Cottage museum demonstrating the home and work life of a family on the marshes, about 100 years ago. *1 Apr-31 May & 1-31 Oct, Sat, Sun, Bank Hols & Half Term week, 11-5. 1 Jun-30 Sept, daily, 10-6. Free.*

NORTH CREAKE The Forge Museum: nr Fakenham. Working forge situated on the B1355, 3m from Burnham Market and Burnham Thorpe, Nelson's birthplace. At one of the oldest real forges in left in England, you can watch the blacksmith working iron by hand. View the double forge fired by bellows and witness the delights of an age gone by. In a small room alongside the forge are bygones on display. Here you can browse and learn of the many facets of past life in a small East Anglian village. Tea rooms and working forge. *9 Apr-30 Sept, daily 10-5. £1/50p/50p.*

True's Yard, King's Lynn

NORWICH Castle Museum: HQ of Norfolk Museums Service. Norman castle keep built 12c and museum housing displays of art, archaeology, natural history, Lowestoft porcelain, Norwich silver, a large collection of paintings and famous collection of British ceramic teapots. Changing programme of temporary exhibitions, guided tours of dungeons and battlements. Cafeteria. *All year, Mon-Sat 10-5, Sun 2-5. Closed Good Fri, 23-26 Dec & 1 Jan. £1.60/60p/£1.20.*

Strangers' Hall Museum of Domestic Life: Late medieval town house, with furnished rooms illustrating the tastes and fashions of various periods between 16c and 19c. Fine costumes and textile collection. *All year (ex Good Fri, 23-26 Dec & 1 Jan), Mon-Sat 10-5. 80p/50p/40p.*

The Bridewell Museum, Bridewell Alley: Displays illustrate the history of trades and industries in Norwich from the 17th century. *All year,*

(ex Good Fri, 24-26 Dec & 1 Jan). Mon-Sat 10-5. 80p/40p/50p.

St Peter Hungate Church Museum and Brass Rubbing Centre, Princes St: One of the 36 medieval churches within the old city walls, used to display church art and furnishings including an important selection of medieval English alabaster carvings. Brass rubbing facilities. *All year (ex Good Fri, 24-26 Dec, 1 Jan). Mon-Sat 10-5. Free. Charge of £1-£10 for brass rubbing.*

Royal Norfolk Regimental Museum, Shirehall: Enter the museum from the Market Avenue or from the Castle Museum via the eerie prisoners tunnel and walk-through model of a first world war communication trench. Displays tell the story of the county regiment from 1685 to the present day. *All year (ex Good Fri, 23-26 Dec & 1 Jan). Mon-Sat 10-5, Sun 2-5. 80p/50p/40p; Castle & Regimental museum £1.60/£1.20/60p.*

Sainsbury Centre for Visual Arts, University of East Anglia: The Robert and Lisa Sainsbury Collection is wide-ranging and of international importance. With the recent addition of Sir Norman Foster and Partners superb Crescent Wing, 700 paintings, sculptures and ceramics are on permanent display with Picasso, Moore, Bacon and Giacometti shown alongside art from Africa, the Pacific and the Americas. The Centre also houses the Anderson collection of Art Nouveau. Three special exhibitions a year. The Centre has a restaurant, buffet and coffee bar. Accessible to disabled. *Galleries open all year (closed 24 Dec-2 Jan) Tue-Sun, 12-5. £1/50p/50p.*

Norwich Gallery, Norfolk Institute of Art & Design, St George Street: Temporary exhibitions of contemporary art. *Open Mon-Fri 10-6, Sat 10-4. For details of exhibitions Tel: (0603) 610561.*

RANWORTH Broadland Conservation Centre: Exhibition about conservation in Norfolk Broads, and wildlife. Birdwatching gallery with binoculars and telescope. *1 Apr-31 Oct, Sun-Thur 10.30-5.30; Sat 2-5.30. Groups by appt Tel: (060549) 479. Adm charge.*

Castle Museum, Norwich

Lowestoft and East Suffolk Maritime Museum

SHERINGHAM Museum, Station Road: Museum of local interest. Shop adjacent selling souvenirs. *1 Apr-31 Oct, Tue-Sat 10-4, Sun 2-4.30. Free.*

SUTTON Broads Museum (1m SE Stalham, off A149, follow signs to Sutton Mill): Museum with one of the most comprehensive collections of domestic, farm and trade tools, bank notes, local bygones under one roof in East Anglia. The collection of hundreds of interesting items has grown up from the private collection of the Nunn family which was established over a period of 30 years. *1 Apr-30 Sept, daily 10-5.30. £2/£1.*

SWAFFHAM Swaffham Museum: London Street. 18c building, formerly brewer's main house. Local history, china, armour and weapons. Display on local man Howard Carter and the discovery Tutankhamum's tomb. *27 Mar-30 Oct, Tue, Thu & Sat. 26 Jun-4 Sept also Wed & Fri. 10-4. Adm charge, free to children and school groups.*

THETFORD Ancient House Museum, White Hart St: 15c timber framed house with fine carved ceiling. Displays on local history and Breckland natural history. Especially: Saxon Thetford; Grimes Graves flint mines and local flint-knapping. Occasional temporary exhibitions. *All year (ex 1 Jan, Good Fri, 24, 25 & 27 Dec). Mon-Sat, 10-5 (closed Mon 1-2); 30 May-26 Sept also Sun 2-5. Free all year ex Aug, 60p/30p/40p.*

THORPE ABBOTTS 100th Bomb Group Memorial Museum, Old Airfield (1m Dickleburgh, off A140 or A143, at Billingford): 8th Air Force and 100th Bomb Group exhibits. Housed in original 8th Air Force control tower, now fully restored. Guided tours. *All year (ex 25 Dec), Sat, Sun & Bank Hols. 5 May-29 Sept, also Wed. 10-5. Free.*

THURSFORD The Thursford Collection, Thursford (6m NE Fakenham, off A148): The world's greatest collection of steam road locomotives, showman's traction, ploughing and barn engines. Nine mechanical organs. Wurlitzer cinema organ, various steam engines. Organs play every day. Live concerts on the Wurlitzer every Tue evening at 8pm from end June-end Sept. Refreshment and souvenir shops. Picnic and children's play area. *1 Apr-31 Oct, times vary, to check Tel: (0328) 878477. £4.20/£1.80/£3.80 (92).*

WALSINGHAM Shirehall Museum: Almost perfect Georgian courtroom with original fittings. Also many items illustrating history of Walsingham, with a display on pilgrimage. *9 Apr-30 Sept, daily, Mon 10-1, 2-5; Tue-Sat 10-5; Sun 2-5. Oct, Sat 10-5, Sun 2-5. 60p/30p/40p.*

WELLS Maritime Museum, Old Lifeboat Museum, The Quay: Museum housing the maritime history of Wells including fishing, the port, wildfowling, coastguard, lifeboat and bait digging. *9 Apr-mid Oct, daily ex Mon 2-5, Sat & Sun also 10-1. 50p/25p (92).*

WESTON LONGVILLE The Dinosaur Natural History Park, (9m NW Norwich, off A1067): Life size dinosaurs in natural woodland setting. Adventure rides. Play area. Wooded maze. Bygone museum. Information centre. Refreshment area. Picnic area. Gift shop. *8 Apr-31 Oct, daily 10-6, £3/£2/£2.*

WEYBOURNE The Muckleburgh Collection, Weybourne Military Camp (026- 370-210) (on A149 between Sheringham and Blakeney): The UK's largest private military collection open to the public. Tanks, armoured cars, artillery and missiles. Guns from the Falklands and the Gulf War. The Suffolk and Norfolk Yeomanry museum and an extensive range of military models and War Department photographs, all under cover. A new maritime display which includes the Royal Navy, Merchant Navy and the RNLI. Licensed restaurant and souvenir shop. *29 Mar-31 Oct, daily 10-5. £2.60/£1.60/£2 & HMF (92).*

WOLFERTON Wolferton Station Museum, (6m NE King's Lynn, off A149): Former Royal Station retiring rooms, built for Edward VII and Queen Alexandra. Furniture and items from Royal trains including Queen Victoria's travelling bed. *1 Apr-30 Sept, Mon-Fri 11-5.30, Sat (craft shop & grounds only) 10.30-4.30, Sun 1-5. £1.85/80p/£1.40/disabled £1.10.*

WYMONDHAM Heritage Museum, Middleton St: Displays of local and historical interest. *10 Apr-29 May, Thu & Fri 2-4, Sat 10-4, 1 Jun-25 Sept, Mon-Fri 2-4, Sat 10-4. Closed Bank Hol Mons. 50p/10p/25p.*

SUFFOLK

ALDEBURGH Moot Hall: 16c listed ancient building with museum of items of local interest. *9-12 Apr. 1-31 May, Suns 2.30-6. 1-30 Jun & 1-30 Sept, daily 2.30-5. 1 July-31 Aug, daily 10.30-12.30, 2.30-5. 35p/free.*

BECCLES William Clowes Printing Museum: Extensive range of preserved machinery and equipment. Numerous wood cuts, books all dating from the early 1800's. Factory tours by arrangement. *7 Jun-27 Aug, Mon-Fri 2-4. Free.*

BRANDON Heritage Centre, George Street: Offers the opportunity to go back in time to the Stone Age. Visit a flint knappers workshop and relive the town's history from neolithic times to the present day. *1 Apr-30 Sept, Thu & Sat 10.30-5 (1 Oct-19 Dec closes 4), Sun 2-5. Also Bank Hol Mons. 50p/40p/40p.*

BUNGAY Museum: Waveney District Council Offices, Broad Street: Local history, including coins, pictures and photographs. *All year, Mon-Fri, 9-1, 2-4. Closed Bank Hols. 30p/free/20p.*

BURY ST EDMUNDS Art Gallery: Market Cross. Robert Adam's only public building in the east of England, originally designed as a playhouse, now using the upper floor for changing exhibitions of painting and allied arts. *All year, Tue-Sat, 10.30-4.30. Closed Good Fri. 50p/free/30p.*

Manor House Museum, Honey Hill: A new museum of Art and Horology opening 29 Jan. After 2 years of careful restoration and refurbishment, this fine Georgian mansion has been transformed in to a magnificent centre where you can discover clocks, watches, paintings, furniture, costume, ceramics aand objets d'art from 17c-20c. There will be special exhibitions and events, workshops and activities. Cafeteria and shop. *All year, daily (ex Good Fri, 25 & 26 Dec), Mon-Sat 10-5, Sun 2-5. £2/£1/£1.*

Moyse's Hall Museum: 12c Norman domestic building now housing local history, archaeological exhibits, including the Maria Marten Red Barn murder relics. *All year, Mon-Sat 10-5, Sun 2-5. Closed 25-26 Dec & Good Fri. Free.*

Suffolk Regiment Museum, Gibraltar Barracks, Out Risbygate St: Military historical exhibits of the Suffolk & Cambridgeshire regiments, including weapons, uniforms, medals and drums. *All year, Mon-Fri, closed Bank Hols, 10-12, 2-4. Free.*

CAVENDISH Sue Ryder Foundation Museum (8m NW Sudbury, off A1092): Displays showing the reason for establishing the Foundation and its work past, present and future. Refreshments including lunches. *All year, daily, 10-5.30. Closed 25 Dec. 80p/40p/40p.*

Moot Hall, Aldeburgh

CLARE Ancient House Museum (7m NW Sudbury, on A1092): 15c Priest's House now contains local bygones. *10-12 Apr; 31 May-2 Oct, Wed, Fri, Sat, Sun & Bank Hol 2.30-4.30, Sun also 11-12.30. 60p/30p/50p.*

COTTON Mechanical Music Museum Trust (5m N Stowmarket): The extensive collection includes various types of organ, street pianos, polyphones, gramophones, music boxes, musical dolls, fruit bowls, even a musical chair and the Wurlitzer pipe organ. *6 Jun-26 Sept, Sun, 2.30-5.30. £2/50p.*

Royal Naval Patrol Service Memorial, Lowestoft

DUNWICH Museum (4m SW Southwold): History of town of Dunwich from Roman times, chronicling its disappearance into the sea over the centuries. Local wildlife. *Easter-31 Oct, daily 11.30-4.30; Free (groups £10 per party).*

EASTON FARM PARK (turn off A12 Wickham Market bypass onto B1116. Follow directions to Easton). Victorian farm setting for many species of farm animals including rare breeds. Modern milking unit with viewing area. Unique Victorian dairy. Suffolk Punch Horses. Large collection of vintage farm machinery, country bygones and old laundry. Green trail, pets paddock, adventure playground, gift shop. Food and farming exhibition. Licensed tea room. *21 Mar-30 Sept, daily, 10.30-6 (last adm 4). £3.70/£2/£3.*

Laxfield Museum

FELIXSTOWE, Landguard Fort and Museum View Point Road: Items relevant to the history of the fort, an early 18th century monument. In Museum: HMS Beehive Room (Nautical) RAF, Local History rooms and WWII exhibition. The museum now houses a large part of the St. Audry's Hospital, Melton, collection which dates from 18c to the present day. *31 May-4 Oct, Sun, Wed & Thu, 2.30-5. Museum 20p/free. Guided tour of fort £1/60p.*

FLATFORD Bridge Cottage, (NT). Flatford, East Bergholt: 16c building beside the mill(not open) made famous by Constable's paintings. Teas, Shop. *27 Mar-31 Oct, Wed-Sun & Bank Hol Mon, 11-5.30; June-Sept, daily, 10-5.30. Closed Good Fri. Free. Car Park charge (not NT).*

FRAMLINGHAM Lanman Museum, in the castle: Rural exhibits relating to everyday life in Framlingham and the surrounding area, including paintings and photographs. *9 Apr-30 Sept, daily (ex Sun & Mon mornings - open Bank Hol Mon mornings), 10-1, 2-4.30. 30p/10p/10p.*

HALESWORTH Halesworth & District Museum, The Almshouses, Steeple End: Local history & archaeology exhibitions in almshouses below art gallery. *1 May-30 Sept, Sun, Tue & Bank Hols 2-5, Wed 10-1. Donations welcome.*

IPSWICH Christchurch Mansion: Extensive Tudor town house in park, central Ipswich, furnished period rooms 16th to 19th century. Outstanding decorative art collections of china and glass. Suffolk Artists' Gallery and Victorian displays. Wolsey Art Gallery with lively temporary exhibition programme. *All year, Tue-Sat 10-5 (dusk in winter), Sun 2.30-4.30 (dusk in winter). Open Bank Hol Mons. (Closed 1 Jan, Good Fri & 24-27 Dec). Free.*

Ipswich Museum: Romans in Suffolk exhibition; Mankind galleries featuring objects from Africa, Asia, the Pacific, Australia and the Americas; Suffolk geology; Victorian natural history gallery with superb collection of British birds; temporary exhibition programme. New Victorian Natural History Gallery. *All year, Tue-Sat, 10-5. (closed 1 Jan, Good Fri & 24-27 Dec). Free.*

Tolly Cobbold Brewery, Cliff Road: Victorian brewery built in 1896, with working equipment from original brewery of 1723. Still producing beers. Contains exhibits, memorabilia, steam engine, videos. Brewery Tap. *All year, daily (ex 25 Dec), tours at 11.30 & 2.30. Brewery tour £2.75.*

LAVENHAM Taxidermy Studios & Wildlife Park, Thatched House, Brent Eleigh: Large studio showing taxidermy. Bird of prey centre and deer park. *Opens spring 1993 subject to planning permission. Daily ex 25 Dec, 9-dusk. £3.25/£1.75/£1.75.*

LAXFIELD & District Museum (6m N Framlingham): Guildhall containing farm tools, geological and natural history. Cottage kitchen and village shop display. Observation bee-hive. Costume room. *31 May-end Sept, Sat & Sun 2-5. Free.*

LOWESTOFT Lowestoft & East Suffolk Maritime Museum, Whapload Rd: Models of fishing and commercial boats, old and new. Also paintings, shipwrights' tools and fishing gear. *1 May-30 Sept, daily, 10-5. 50p/25p/25p.*

Royal Naval Museum, Sparrow's Nest: Ship models, naval documents, uniforms, photographs and certificates. *16 May-17 Oct, daily (ex Sat) 10-12, 2-4.30. Free.*

Archaeology & Local History Society's Museum, Broad House, Nicholas Everitt Park, Oulton Broad: Local history, Lowestoft china, fossils, flints and medieval artefacts from field searches. *3-17 Apr, Mon-Sat 10.30-1, 2-5, Sun 2-5; 24 Apr-16 May, Sat & Sun 2-5; 22 May-3*

Felixstowe Museum, Landguard Fort

Christchurch Mansion, Ipswich

Oct, Mon-Sat 10.30-1, 2-5, Sun 2-5. 9-31 Oct, Sat & Sun, 2-4. 55p/30p/30p (92).

Lydia Eva Steam Drifter, The Yacht Basin, Lowestoft Harbour: The last survivor of over 3000 drifters which came every autumn to Yarmouth and Lowestoft to fish for herring. Displays the hardships of life aboard and ashore in an industry which dominated two towns for a century. Lydia Eva was built in 1930 in King's Lynn and her engines and boiler were fitted in Great Yarmouth. She was one of the last steam drifters to be built and destined to be the very last survivor. *Easter-Jun, daily, 10-4.30. Also at Great Yarmouth Town Quay Jul-Oct. Free.*

MILDENHALL & District Museum, King Street: Local history, particularly of RAF Mildenhall and the Mildenhall Treasure. Archaeology, natural history and local bygones. Displays

Gainsborough's House, Sudbury

showing contrast of Fenland and Breckland. *All year, Wed-Sun. 2.30-4.30, Fri 11-4. Free.*

NEWMARKET National Horse Racing Museum, High Street: Housed in Regency subscription rooms opened by the Queen in 1983. In 5 permanent galleries the great story of the development of horse racing is told. Everything from the skeleton of "Eclipse" to the finest sporting art. Equine Tours offer the Museum visitor a unique chance to see history come alive. Tour the town to see the famous training establishments, the horses working on the ancient Heath and the stallions at The National Stud (tour booking essential). Licensed wine bar/tea room, walled garden, gift shop. Vestey Gallery of British sporting art. *30 Mar-5 Dec, Tue-Sat & Bank Hol 10-5, Sun 2-5; Jul & Aug, Mon-Sat 10-5, Sun 12-5. Other times by appt. Tel: (0638) 667333. £2.50/75p/£1.50.*

ORFORD Dunwich Underwater Exploration Exhibition, The Craft Shop, Front Street: Exhibits showing the progress of the underwater exploration of Dunwich, once the capital of East Anglia, now reduced to a tiny village through coastal erosion. Details of underwater studies, mainly associated with marine archaeology. *All year, daily, 11-5 (closed 25 & 26 Dec). 40p.*

OULTON BROAD Boat World: Working exhibition of boatbuilding craft skills. Visitors can look inside a variety of interesting and historic craft. Maritime book shop and tea rooms. *1 May-30 Sept, Mon-Fri 10-4. £1.95/£1.60/£1.60.*

SIZEWELL Visitor Centre, Sizewell B Site, nr Leiston: Visitor centre giving details about all aspects of electricity supply industry. Site minibus tours (subject to availability). View the site from the viewing platform. *1 Apr-30 Sept, daily 10-4. 1 Oct-31 Mar, Mon-Sat 10-4. Free. Closed Christmas.*

SOUTHWOLD Lifeboat Museum: RNLI models, photographs of lifeboat, relics from old boats. *1 Jun-30 Sept, daily 2.30-4.30. Free.*

Southwold Museum: Local history and bygones, archaeology, natural history. Collection of exhibits connected with old Southwold Railway and Battle of Sole Bay (1672) *9-18 Apr, 1 May-30 Sept, daily, 2.30-4.30. Free. Donations welcome.*

Southwold Sailors' Reading Room: Maritime books, photographs and models. *All year, daily, 9-9 (when in use by members). Closed 25 Dec. Free.*

STOWMARKET Museum of East Anglian Life (12m NW Ipswich, on A1308 off A45). Attractive 30-acre riverside site in centre of Stowmarket. Working exhibits bring the past alive. Watermill, craft workshops, agricultural displays and representation of domestic life all demonstrate East Anglia's heritage. The museum houses the only Burrell steam ploughing engines in the world. There are craft demonstrations and special events at weekends. Extensive new museum shop. Refreshments room. *10 Apr-end Oct, daily 10-5. £3.25/£1.60/£2 (92).*

SUDBURY Gainsborough's House: Elegant Georgian town house with attractive garden; birthplace of Thomas Gainsborough. Paintings by Gainsborough and contemporary furniture. Also changing exhibitions of contemporary and historic art and designer craft work. Print Workshop. *2 Jan-8 Apr, Tue-Sat 10-4, Sun 2-4; 10 Apr-31 Oct, Tue-Sat 10-5, Sun and Bank Hol Mons 2-5; 1 Nov-Dec, Tue-Sat 10-4, Sun 2-4. Closed Good Fri, Christmas-New Year. £2/£1/£1.50.*

Thorpeness Windmill Museum

THORPENESS Windmill Museum, Thorpeness (2m N Aldeburgh): Working windmill housing displays on the Suffolk coast and Thorpeness village as well as mill information. *Easter, May, Jun & Sept, Sat, Sun and Bank Hol; Jul & Aug, daily. 2-5. Free.*

WOODBRIDGE Museum, Market Hill: Museum illustrating the history of Woodbridge and its people. Also exhibits of Anglo Saxon remains at Sutton Hoo and Burrow Hill. *27 Mar-31 Oct, Thur, Fri, Sat and Bank Hols 10-4, Sun 2.30-4.30. (Daily in Aug ex Wed). Groups welcome by appt (not restricted to above times). Tel: (0394) 383509. 50p/15p.*

WOOLPIT Bygones Museum, The Institute: Museum depicting the life of a Suffolk village. Brickmaking display, photographs. Displays changed annually. *10 Apr-26 Sept, Sat, Sun & Bank Hols, 2.30-5. Free.*

Prices are in the order Adults/Children/Senior Citizens. Where prices are not available at the time of going to press the 1992 (92) price is given. See Touring Maps on pages 104-108 for locations of places to visit.

COUNTRYSIDE

LONG WALKS AND DISTANCE PATHS

BEDFORDSHIRE

Greensand Ridge Walk, 40 mile footpath from Leighton Buzzard to Gamlingay. Well signposted and waymarked. *Details from Bedfordshire County Council.*

Upper Lea Valley Walk, Follows the valley of the River Lea from Leagrave Common, via Luton town centre to East Hyde. *Details from Bedfordshire County Council.*

CAMBRIDGESHIRE

Bishops Way: 7-9 miles circular route on ancient tracks north of Ely. *Details available from Cambridgeshire County Council, leaflet 40p.*

Clopton Way: 10 mile linear walk from Wimpole to Gamlingay via the prehistoric trackway and deserted medieval village of Clopton. Links in with the Wimpole Way and Greensand Ridge Walk. *Details from Cambridgeshire County Council, leaflet 40p.*

Devil's Dyke: 7 1/2 mile long defensive fortification ditch dating from 500 AD, running from open chalklands and undrained fenland north of Reach to thick woodland south of Stechworth. *Leaflet available from Bedfordshire & Cambridgeshire Wildlife Trust, 5 Fulbourn Manor, Fulbourn, Cambridge, Tel: (0223) 880778.*

Grafham Water

Grafham Water Circular Ride: A circular ride of 13 miles around the reservoir. The route includes ancient woodlands, medieval granges and excellent views across the water. *Details from Cambridgeshire County Council, leaflet 30p.*

Nene Way: 10 miles, from Peterborough to Wansford along the valley of the River Nene. *Details from Ferry Meadows Country Park, Ham Lane, Peterborough. Tel: (0733) 234443.*

River Ouse: Waymarked riverside walk from Eaton Socon to Earith. Total length 26 miles. 7 *leaflets available at 15p each or £1 per set from Huntingdon Tourist Information Centre, Tel: (0480) 425831.*

Three Shires Way: A long distance ride of 45 miles from Grafham Water into Bedfordshire and Buckinghamshire to link with the Swan's Way. *Details from Cambridgeshire County Council, leaflet 40p.*

Wimpole Way: 13 miles through woodlands and fields from Cambridge to Wimpole Hall.

Details from Cambridgeshire County Council, leaflet 40p.

ESSEX

Epping Forest Centenary Walk: 15 miles through Epping Forest from Manor Park to Epping (links Essex Way to outskirts of London). *Booklet 74p (incl postage) from The Superintendent, Epping Forest, The Warren, Loughton.*

Essex Way: 81 mile walk from Epping to Harwich. *Booklet £1.74 (incl postage) from West Essex Ramblers Association, "Glenview", London Road, Abridge, Essex, Tel: (0992) 813330.*

Harcamlow Way: 140 miles in the form of a "figure-of-eight" footpath walk from Harlow to Cambridge and back. *Booklet £2.50 (incl postage) from West Essex Ramblers Association (address above).*

St Peters Way: 45-mile walk from Chipping Ongar to ancient chapel of St Peter-on-the-Wall at Bradwell-on-Sea. *Booklet £1.44 (incl postage) from West Essex Ramblers Association (address above).*

Three Forests Way: 60 miles circular walk linking the forests of Epping, Hatfield and Hainault. *Booklet £1.24 from West Essex Ramblers Association (address above).*

HERTFORDSHIRE

Chess Valley Walk, 10 mile walk from Chesham to the Grand Union Canal in Rickmansworth. *Details from the Countryside Management Service, County Hall, Hertford.*

Cole Green Way, follows the course of a disused railway between Welwyn Garden City and Hertford. *Details from the Countryside Management Service, County Hall, Hertford.*

Ver Colne Valley Walk, 15 mile path linking Redbourn, St Albans and Watford running alongside the Rivers Ver and Colne. *Details from the Countryside Management Service, County Hall, Hertford.*

NORFOLK

Angles Way: A 70 mile walk along the Waveney and Little Ouse valleys. *Free leaflet from Norfolk County Council (SAE please).*

Around Norfolk Walk: A 220 mile walk following the Peddars Way, Coast Path, Weavers Way and Angles Way, taking in most of Norfolk's varied scenery. *Free leaflet from Norfolk County Council (SAE please).*

Great Eastern Pingo Trail: 8 mile walk, partly along disused railway line, taking in Breckland scenery. *Leaflet 58p (inc p&p) from Norfolk County Council.*

Marriott's Way: 20 mile footpath and bridleway between Norwich and Aylsham along former railway line. *Free leaflet from Norfolk County Council (SAE please).*

Peddars Way and Norfolk Coast Path with Weavers Way: Official long distance footpath of 93 miles, between Knettishall Heath and Holme, then along the coast to Cromer. Through heath and Breckland woods and varied coastal scenery. Plus Norfolk County Council Recreational Path from Cromer to Great Yarmouth of 56 miles. *(Guide which includes accommodation*

list, £1.65 plus 28p p&p) from East Anglia Tourist Board or Peddars Way Association, 150 Armes Street, Norwich NR2 4EG. Official guide available from HMSO £8.99 plus postage.

Wash Coast Path: A 10 mile route between Sutton Bridge Lighthouse and West Lynn giving spectacular views of the saltmarshes and the Wash. *Free leaflet from Norfolk County Council (SAE please).*

Weavers Way: 57 mile walk from Cromer to Great Yarmouth via Blickling and Stalham. *Free leaflet from Norfolk County Council, (SAE please).*

SUFFOLK

Constable Trail: A 9 mile walk through the landscape and villages associated with the artist's childhood and life. Four shorter walks available. *Booklet £1.25 inc postage from Peddar Publications, Croft End, Bures, Suffolk CO8 5JN. Tel: (0787) 227823.*

Gipping Valley River Path: Located along the 17 mile long former tow path between Ipswich and Stowmarket alongside the River Gipping. *Laminated walkcards from Suffolk County Council. £1.50.*

Icknield Way, A long distance path following mainly broad green lanes and easy tracks in seven counties, linking the Peddars Way to the Ridgeway. *Free leaflets from Suffolk County Council (SAE please).*

Painters Way: 28 mile walk along the valley of River Stour, from Sudbury to Manningtree through countryside which inspired Gainsborough, Constable and Munnings. *Booklet £1.25 inc postage from Peddar Publications, Croft End, Bures, Suffolk, CO8 5JN. Tel: (0787) 227823.*

Suffolk Coast Path: 45 mile path along coast from Bawdsey to Kessingland. *Free leaflet from Suffolk County Council (SAE please).*

COUNTRY AND LEISURE PARKS

BEDFORDSHIRE

Dunstable Downs, Beds County Council: Highest point in the county with superb views over the county and the Vale of Aylesbury. Watch the gliders and walk among the chalk downland flora. Visitors Centre.

Harrold Odell Country Park, Beds County Council: Landscaped lakes attract many wildfowl varieties. Extensive reedbeds, river meadows and riverbanks. Visitors Centre.

Priory Country Park, Barkers Lane, Bedford: 228 acres of open country, 80 acres of which are water. Wildlife conservation areas, angling, sailing and Visitor Centres.

Stewartby Lake Country Park, Beds County Council: Disused clay pit, now the largest expanse of water in the county. Attracts many birds in autumn and winter. Water sports.

Stockgrove Country Park, Beds County Council: Parkland, oak woodland, coniferous plantations, lake and diverse wildlife. Visitors Centre.

COUNTRY AND LEISURE PARKS

Sundon Hills Country Park, (Upper Sundon, Luton) Beds County Council: 250 acres of rolling chalk downland with excellent views of surrounding area.

CAMBRIDGESHIRE

Ferry Meadows Country Park, Nene Park, nr Peterborough (off A605 2m W of city centre): Sailing, windsurfing, hire craft available at Watersports Centre. Fishing, miniature steam railway, boating, picnicking, walking, nature reserve, visitor centre, conservation garden.

Grafham Water (5m SW Huntingdon off B661): This 2 1/2 sq mile man-made reservoir has fishing and sailing facilities and many water

birds. 3 Nature Trails, 2 bird hides (one with facilities for disabled), pleasure boat trips. Picnic sites, restaurant, cafe, free parking, public footpaths, toilets (disabled facilities), cycle hire and visitor/exhibition centre.

Hinchingbrooke Country Park: 156 acres of woods, lakes and meadows. Watersports, activities, walks and displays at the visitor centre. Facilities for the disabled. Ranger Service.

Wandlebury (3m SE Cambridge off A1307): Parkland with Iron Age hill fort, picnics, woodland walks and nature trail. Dogs on leads.

Wimpole, nr New Wimpole: Walks in park landscaped by Bridgeman, Brown and Repton, surrounding Wimpole Hall. NT.

ESSEX

Belhus Woods (1m N Aveley), Essex County Council: 158 acres. Woodlands, lakes and open areas for walking and picnicking. Fishing from 8 to dusk and proposed horse-ride. Visitor Centre. Ranger Service.

Chalkney Wood, Earls Colne, Essex County Council: Ancient woodland site of 63 acres.

Cudmore Grove, East Mersea, Essex County Council: Access to a pleasant beach and grassland for picnics. 35 acres. Information Room. Ranger Service.

Danbury (5m E Chelmsford), Essex County Council: 41 acres. Danbury Country Park is set

Please mention East Anglia Guide when replying to advertisements

in the former pleasure gardens of the mansion and provides for quiet enjoyment of the lakes and exotic trees and shrubs. Ranger Service.

Epping Forest: 6,000+ acres, mostly within Essex, owned by the Corporation of the City of London. Much of it is SSSI and includes ancient woodlands of beech, oak and hornbeam, grasslands and attractive water areas. Two Iron Age earthworks visible. Epping Forest Centre at High Beach.

Garnetts Wood, Barnston, nr Dunmow, Essex County Council: Ancient woodland of 62 acres.

Grove Woods, Rochford District Council: 40 acres of recent woodland between Eastwood and Rayleigh. Walks among old orchards and overgrown ruins of small holdings. Waymarked circular route, surface suitable for wheelchairs.

Hadleigh Castle Country Park, Essex County Council, Southend and Castle Point Borough Councils. 450 acres of downland, woodland and marshes. Wildlife area. Ranger Service.

Hainault Forest Country Park, London Borough of Redbridge: 902 acres of open space, playing fields, lakes, golf course and ancient woodland. Foxburrows Farm contains rare breeds of farm animals. *All year, free. Park 7-dusk, farm 9-4.*

Harlow Town Park: Fully landscaped 164 acre park with scenic walks and views. Pets corner, pitch n putt, adventure playground, paddling pool. Cafes and riverside complex.

Hatfield Forest (4m E Bishop's Stortford): 1,000 acres of wooded medieval landscape and nature reserve with lake. Miles of peaceful woodland walks including 1 1/4 mile waymarked nature trail. *Vehicle access, Good Fri-31 Oct, daily 10-5, exit gate closes 8. (Ground conditions permitting). £2.20 per car.*

High Woods Country Park, Colchester Borough Council: 330 acres of attractive woodland, grassland, farmland and wetland. Numerous footpaths. Visitors Centre, bookshop and toilets.

Hockley Woods, Rochford District Council: 260 acres of ancient coppice woodland, the largest in Essex. Pleasant walks and a horse trail. Picnic and play area. 2 waymarked routes.

Langdon Hills (1m SW Basildon), Essex County Council: Divided into two parks, Westley Heights and One Tree Hill, the Country Park overlooks the Thames estuary and has a range of scenery including open grassland, deciduous woodlands, and sandy heaths. Horse ride through park. Information at One Tree Hill plus AA viewpoint. Ranger Service.

Lee Valley Regional Park: Stretches 23 miles along the Lee Valley from London's East End, through Essex and to Ware in Hertfordshire. Parkland, picnic sites, angling, camping, sports centres, marinas, bird watching and a farm. *Countryside Centre at Abbey Farmhouse, Crooked Mile, Waltham Abbey. For further information, Lee Valley Information Line, Tel: (0992) 700766.*

Maldon Promenade: 100 acres of formal and informal parkland adjoining River Blackwater. Riverside walks, picnics, children's play areas.

Marsh Farm Country Park, South Woodham Ferrers, Essex County Council: 320 acres of country park operating as a modern livestock farm. Country walks round the sea wall, farm tracks and nature reserve. Visitor Centre. Picnic areas. *See also Animal Collections.*

Thorndon (2m S Brentwood), Essex County Council: 540 acres. Thorndon North is almost totally woodland with pleasant walks and a horse ride. Thorndon South has woodland walks, fishing and some extensive views of the Thames estuary. Ranger Service. Countryside Centre.

Aldenham Country Park

Wat Tyler Country Park, Pitsea: Country park with an emphasis on conservation and natural history. Attractions include a marina, craft workshops, National Motorboat museum and relocated historic buildings.

Weald (1m NW Brentwood), Essex County Council: 428 acres of woodland, lakes and open parkland open to the public for informal recreation. Fishing and horse riding (by permit). Visitor Centre, Ranger Service.

Programme of Ranger Guided Activities: Talks can be arranged. Further details from the Ranger Service, Weald Country Park, South Weald, Brentwood. Tel: (0277) 261343.

HERTFORDSHIRE

Aldenham Country Park, Aldenham Road, Elstree: Recreational parkland with a lake. Home of the Aldenham herd of Longhorn cattle. A recognised rare breed survival trust. Visitor centre. *Daily ex 25 Dec.*

Ashridge Estate, (NT): Covers 6 sq miles in Hertfordshire and Buckinghamshire, running along the main ridge of the Chiltern Hills from Ivinghoe Beacon to Berkhamsted. The Ivinghoe Hills offer excellent views. The rest of Ashridge is almost level, with fine walks through woods and open commons. Monument to the 3rd Duke of Bridgewater. *Estate all year. Monument & Information Centre 1 Apr-end Oct, Mon-Thu & Good Fri 2-5, Sat, Sun & Bank Hol Mon 2-5.30. Monument £1, parking £1 summer weekends.*

Cassiobury Park, Watford: Once part of the Earl of Essex's estate. 96 acres of parkland providing facilities for organised sports, entertainment and recreation. Scenic walks along the River Gade and Grand Union Canal.

Fairlands Valley Park, Six Hills Way, Stevenage: 120 acre park with 11 acre lake. Sailing centre and small boating lake. Variety of wildfowl and the main lake is stocked with fish for anglers.

Stanborough Park, Stanborough Road, Welwyn Garden City: Beautiful countryside recreation park offering a wide range of leisure facilities including sailing, windsurfing, canoeing, fishing and rowing. Childrens play area, picnic areas and a nature trail. *Car park charge weekends and school hols.*

NORFOLK

Fritton Lake (6m SW Gt Yarmouth on A143): Wood, grassland and formal gardens. Lake, rowing and fishing. 9 hole golf, 18 hole putting. Adventure playground. Cafe, shop and craft workshops. 250 acres.

Holt Lowes and Country Park (1m S Holt on B1149): Conifer wood and heathland with walks, nature trail. Car parking, picnic areas and toilets. 98 acres woodland and 113 acres heathland.

Mannington Countryside nr Saxthorpe (18m N Norwich, off B1149): 20 miles of waymarked walks and trails through woodlands, meadows and farmland. Car park, coffee and snacks at Information Centre. *Walks from 9 daily. Infor-*

mation Centre when Gardens are open (see Gardens entry), also Wed, Thu & Fri in winter. Car Park £1.

Sandringham (7m NE King's Lynn on A149): Wood and heathland. Nature trail. 650 acres.

Sheringham Park (NT), Sheringham (car access off A148 Cromer to Holt road): Rhododendrons, woodland, spectacular views of park and coastlines. *Open all year, sunrise to sunset daily for pedestrians. Access charge and car park £2.10.*

Thetford Forest Park: 50,000 acres of pine forest straddling Norfolk and Suffolk. Waymarked walks and trails lead from the car parks into the forest. Forest Office, Santon Downham, Tel: (0842) 810271.

Wolterton Park: 340 acres of historic parkland with marked trails. Orienteering, adventure playground, Hawk and Owl Trust exhibition. Special events programme. Toilets. *Park open daily, 9-5. Car Park £2.*

SUFFOLK

Alton Water, Holbrook Road, Stutton, nr Ipswich: Water park with walks, nature reserves and picnic areas. Cycle tracks and cycle hire. Watersports centre offering sailing and windsurfing. Coarse angling, day tickets available. Visitor centre serving snacks.

Brandon (1/2m S Brandon): Lake, lawns, tree trail, orienteering course, Victorian walled garden, Visitor Centre, toilets, woodland picnic areas and forest walks. 32 acres. *Park open daily until sunset.*

Clare Castle, Clare, nr Sudbury: Ruins of Clare Castle and baileys. A former railway station with visitor centre, water-fowl, nature trail, history trail, walks, picnic areas, toilets. 25 acres. *Open daily. Free.*

Ickworth Park, Horringer (3m SW Bury St Edmunds, on A143): Park of NT house. Walks through woodland and by canal. Leaflet available from machine at car park 50p. *£1/50p payable on entrance to park.*

Knettishall Heath (5m E Thetford): Attractive Breck landscape, heather, grass heath and mixed woods, Peddars Way long distance footpath starts at W end. Angles Way, the Broads to the Breks path finishes at E end. Toilets and extensive picnic area. 400 acres. *All year (ex 24-26 Dec), daily, 9-dusk. Free.*

West Stow Country Park (6m NW Bury St Edmunds, off A1101): Grassland, heathland, lake and river with many pleasant walks. Also reconstructed Anglo-Saxon village (see Ancient Monuments section for full details). 125 acres. Children's play area. Visitor centre, car parking, picnicking and toilet facilities. *Open daily, 10-5*

USEFUL ADDRESSES

Leisure Services, Bedfordshire County Council, County Hall, Bedford. Tel: (0234) 228330.

Rural Group, Department of Property, Cambridgeshire County Council, Shire Hall, Castle Hill, Cambridge. Tel: (0223) 317445.

Planning Department, Essex County Council, County Hall, Chelmsford. Tel: (0245) 492211.

Countryside Management Service, Planning and Estates Department, County Hall, Hertford. Tel: (0992) 555255.

Department Planning and Property, Norfolk County Council, County Hall, Martineau Lane, Norwich. Tel: (0603) 222776.

Planning Department, Suffolk County Council, County Hall, Ipswich. Tel: (0473) 265131.

BROADLAND

There is nowhere quite like the Broads anywhere else in Britain. Not only is the landscape unique, the Broads are also renowned for their richness and diversity of wildlife and rarities such as the stunning Swallowtail, Britain's largest butterfly.

Contrary to what one might expect, this landscape is not entirely natural and in fact has been heavily influenced by mans activities. These vast, shallow inland waterways are actually the result of peat diggings which began around the ninth century when local people would carve turves to use for fuel. At this time and until the fourteenth century, the rivers were rather drier than they are today, although soon the diggings became increasingly subject to flooding, and eventually work ceased.

In some areas where the water was much shallower, the plants wasted no time and these areas were quickly overgrown by reed-mace, bulrush and other peat forming plants. Mans interference in the development of the Broads was not limited to this one material. Reed and sedge were also harvested and indeed still are, for use in the local thatching industry. At Hickling Broad National Nature Reserve (managed as a Nature Reserve by the Norfolk Naturalists Trust), the income from the sale of reed and sedge makes a valuable contribution to the upkeep of the Reserve.

dominated by a number of factors. The once gin clear water of the Broads now more closely resembles pea soup thanks to pollution largely form agricultural land and sewerage treatment works. This soupy appearance is actually algae, which thrive on the phosphates and nitrates that over-enrich these waters. Algae are also thought to be responsible for the loss of aquatic vegetation and increased sedimentation rates, choking up the channels. The resultant loss of vegetation has made the banks susceptible to erosion, and 'wash' caused by motor powered boats has exaggerated this problem. However, the story is not all doom and gloom; Broadland still retains its national and international importance for wildlife and large scale efforts are being made to clean up the water of the Broads and restore the once abundant plant and animal life.

To the naturalist, the bit attraction of the Broads, is the sheer diversity. The conditions are right for a remarkable number of birds, insects and animals. The Norfolk Naturalists Trust owns or manages Nature Reserves throughout the Norfolk Broads (as do the Suffolk Wildlife Trust over the border in neighbouring Suffolk) where you can get close to wildlife in a protected environment where, in many cases, it would otherwise be virtually impossible.

Ranworth Broad

all the way to the Norfolk coast). Alternatively, a trip to Ranworth Broad can be combined with a visit to the church of St. Helen in Ranworth village. The tower of the church is open to visitors and from here you will have one of the finest views over Broadland

If your sea-legs are not up to much, sticking to dry land can also reveal an abundance of nature's delights. The Broadland Conservation Centre is a floating, thatched visitor centre, from which you can take advantage of the panoramic views over the open water of Ranworth Broad. It can be reached by taking the boardwalk from the car park adjacent to the staithe which is specially adapted for disabled access. You will notice several large oak trees at the start of this walkway, although as you progress, the habitat becomes increasingly swampy and you will pass through areas of old coppiced alder woodland, willow, honeysuckle, ferns and sedges until you eventually come to the open water of the Broad. A series of information boards explain this progression and what you are likely to see there. The whole route is only about 1/3rd of a mile so you can see a great variety in a short time.

For those of you with more time and energy, Hickling Broad will fulfil the wilder side of Broadland. The new visitor centre and car park form the focus of this 1360 acre site which in 1976 was designated as being a wetland of international importance for birds. A trail guide leaflet will help you devise your own route around the Reserve.

Whenever you visit the Broads, you will notice the abundance of wildlife, with flocking wildfowl the dominant feature of the open water during the winter months where sporting pursuits of windsurfing and sailing take over during the warmer weather. Much effort goes into maintaining the conditions that keep Broadland at the top of the wildlife popularity polls. We hope that your visit will outweigh all your expectations of Britain's newest National Park.

Peaceful Cockshoot Broad

As well as this, harvesting these crops maintains a variety of habitats for wildlife and helps to keep these traditions alive.

Since the late 1940's, there has been talk about protecting the Broads as a National Park. This status was eventually granted and this is now Britain's newest National Park.

Wildlife conservation in Broadland has a long history. However, since the Second World War, the ecology of the area has been increasingly

One of the best ways to see wetland is, naturally by boat! Guided tours around Nature Reserves are run throughout the summer months at Hickling Broad and Ranworth Broad (which is otherwise closed to traffic). They are popular so booking is essential. As an added bonus, the Hickling Wildlife Safari stops at the 60 ft tree tower and from here you may get a 'birds eye view' of the spectacular Marsh Harriers patrolling their territory or at least a spectacular view over the Broads (on a clear day this view extends

If you would like to know more, a new booklet has recently been published on Nature Conservation in Broadland by English Nature (£1) Tel. 0603 620558, or for more information on the Norfolk Naturalists Trust Nature Reserves, telephone 0603 625540.

NATURE RESERVES

Ordnance Survey grid references have been provided for some of the reserves which are less easy to locate. For further details please contact the Naturalists' Organisations, addresses and telephone numbers on p53.

BEDFORDSHIRE

Felmersham Gravel Pits, nr Felmersham [SP 991584] (BCWT): Disused gravel workings composed of open water, marsh, grassland, hedges and developing woodland with rich plant life. Excellent site for damselflies and dragonflies.

Flitwick Moor, off Flitwick-Maulden road, turn off by Folly Farm [TL 046354] (BCWT): Once valley fen and heath; now contains a variety of habitats including damp birch woodland, open water, unimproved grassland and sphagnum moss.

King's Wood Heath and Reach, [SP 928298] (BCWT): Access only to plots owned by Trust - details from the Conservation Officer. Ancient woodland. Largest and most important deciduous wood in Bedfordshire. Spring flowers include wood anemone, primrose and bugle.

The Lodge, RSPB Headquarters (1m E Sandy off B1042): Mature woodland, pine plantations, birch and bracken slopes with a remnant of heath and an artificial lake. 4 nature trails. Formal gardens. Many breeding birds, muntjac deer are often seen. *Reserve and gardens, daily 9-9 or sunset when earlier. £1.50 (free RSPB members.*

Old Warden Tunnel, [TL 114446] (BCWT): Cutting and tunnel baulk of disused railway. Slopes of cutting rich in plants such as cowslip and hairy violet.

Sewell Cutting, runs between Sewell Lane and French's Avenue, Dunstable [TL 004227] (BCWT): An old railway cutting, first class site for flowering plants, mosses and butterflies.

Sharnbrook Summit, nr Souldrop [SP 963626] (BCWT): Lime-rich soil excavated from the railway cutting supports an excellent range of plants including zig-zag clover, wild liquorice and hairy violet.

Totternhoe Knolls, nr Dunstable [SP 986216] (BCWT): A long, partly wooded chalk ridge, subject to quarrying since Saxon times. Plants include kidney and horseshoe vetch, clustered bellflower and wild thyme.

CAMBRIDGESHIRE

Coe Fen and Paradise Nature Trails, Cambridge (BCWT): Nature trails on common land next to River Cam. *Guide books from Beds & Cambs Wildlife Trust.*

Fowlmere, E of A10 Cambridge to Royston road, nr Shepreth (RSPB): Reedbeds, pools, watercress beds. Kingfishers, turtle doves, water rails. *Access free at all times from reserve car park. Warden: Mike Pollard, 19 Whitecroft Road, Meldreth, Royston, Cambridgeshire.*

Nene Washes, nr Whittlesey, 5 miles E Peterborough (RSPB): Wet meadows and marshland with breeding waders and wintering ducks and swans. *Entry by permit from warden: C Kitchen, 21a East Delph, Whittlesey, nr Peterborough.*

Wicken Fen

Ouse Washes, nr Manea reached from A141 Chatteris-March road (RSPB/BCWT): Extensive wet meadows. Breeding black-tailed godwits. The most important inland site in Britain for wintering ducks and swans. Observation hides, information centre and toilets. *Access free at all times from reserve car park. Warden: C Carson, Limosa, Welches Dam, Manea, March.*

Roswell Pits, Ely (BCWT): Nature trail around flooded claypits close to city. Rich vegetation and bird life. Access from Springhead Lane, off B1382. *Leaflet available from Beds and Cambs Wildlife Trust.*

Welney Wildfowl & Wetlands Refuge, nr March. The Wildfowl Trust has numerous hides and a large observatory overlooking some 900 acres of the Ouse Washes. Almost 3,500 wild swans and many thousands of wildfowl in winter, in summer notable for wide variety of breeding birds and wild flowers. *Unescorted visits daily 10-5 (except Xmas). Nov-Feb, winter evening party visits to watch swans under floodlights, pre-booking essential Tel: (0353) 860711. £2.85/£1.40/£2.10 (family £7.10).*

Wicken Fen (NT): Practically the last remaining undrained fen with general access; especially interesting for plant and insect life, waterfowl in winter and breeding marsh birds in summer. Display. *Open daily, except 25 Dec, dawn-dusk. Parties must book in advance, Tel: (0353) 720274. £2.50/£1.25.*

ESSEX

Abberton Reservoir, nr Colchester (EBWS): Special protected area for wild duck, swans and other water birds. Visitor centre with panoramic views. 2 nature trails and 5 bird hides. Access to perimeter road restricted to EBWS permit holders, although visible from roads. *Daily, 9-5, ex Mon, 25 & 26 Dec (open Bank Hol Mon).*

Colne Estuary, (EN) East Mersea; foreshore, beach and marshes. *All year.*

Fingringhoe Wick Nature Reserve 3m SE Colchester (EWT). The centre has displays and a shop. Observation tower, toilets, car parks, 2 nature trails, 8 bird hides. Good views over the salt marsh. Some facilities for disabled visitors. *Closed Monday.*

John Weston Reserve, Walton-on-the-Naze (EWT): 70-ft high cliffs rich in fossils and providing an estuarine grassland with thickets and ponds. Nearby is an important landfall for migrating birds. Essex Skipper butterfly and Emperor moth may be seen. *Clifftop walks open all year to general public. Nature trail below cliffs.*

Langdon Nature Reserve, SW Basildon and reaches to within 1 mile of town centre (EWT): Ancient woodland, meadows and former plotland area. Original plotland building now converted to museum. Good network of footpaths and impressive range of birds and mammals. Very good for insects, particularly butterflies. *Open all year. Car park.*

Leigh: (EN/EWT) Mudflats, saltmarsh and part island. Access to footpaths and nature trail. *All year.*

Roding Valley Meadows (EWT): Flower rich hay meadows bounded by thick hedgerows, and marshes are the the the main features of this large and outstanding reserve on both sides of the river Roding between Loughton nd Chigwell. Car park. Nature trails. *Open all year.*

Stour Wood and Copperas Bay, off B1352 road from Manningtree to Ramsey (RSPB): Mixed woodland and mudflats on Stour estuary. Ducks, geese and waders numerous in autumn and winter. Nightingales and woodpeckers can also be seen. Access at all times to hides overlooking estuary from reserve car park. Donations welcome. *Warden: R Leavett, 24 Orchard Close, Great Oakley, Harwich.*

HERTFORDSHIRE

Duchie's Piece, nr Tring [SP 952129] (HMWT): A fine example of chalk grassland, renowned for its butterflies. At the top of the reserve the grassland grades into beech woodland. *Open at all times.*

Hertford Heath, [TL 350106 & TL 354111] (HMWT): Damp heathland with several ponds. The other section of the reserve is mature hornbeam coppice and more recent oak and birch woodland. *Open at all times.*

Hunsdon Mead, 1m NE Roydon [TL 350106] (HMWT): A large wet meadow which has been managed in the same way for at least 600 years. It is enclosed by the River Stort and the Stort Navigation and is rich in wild flowers. Please keep to the towpath or permissive path by the River Stort until the hay is cut. *Open at all times.*

Rye House Marsh Reserve, Rye House, Rye Road, Hoddesdon (RSPB): A variety of wetland habitats. 5 hides (2 accessible to wheelchairs), reached by good pathways, from where you can watch the varied wildlife. *Daily 9-dusk. £1.50/50p/£1.50 (RSPB members free).*

Telegraph Hill, on the minor road between Lilley and Hexton [TL 117288] (HMWT): The Icknield Way, an ancient trackway passes through the reserve, which is a matrix of chalk grassland and shrub, fringed by old beech trees. *Open at all times.*

Tewin Orchard and Hopkyns Wood, [TL 268155] (HMWT): These two reserves are set next to each other near Tewin. The orchard, with apple and pear trees attracts many forms of wildlife. Hopkyns Wood is a shady oak and hornbeam wood. *Open at all times.*

Therfield Heath, [TL 335400] (HMWT): One of the few remaining areas of unimproved chalk grassland in East Anglia. Renowned for its large colony of pasque flowers which bloom in early spring on Church Hill. *Open at all times.*

NORFOLK

The Norfolk Coast

Norfolk has an extensive coastline with some of the finest sand dunes and saltmarshes in Britain.
Blakeney Point (NT): Shingle spit, sand dunes, seals, shop and display in Lifeboat House. Access for disabled. Hides. Access by boat from Morston or Blakeney. *All year. Morston and Blakeney car park charge.*

Cley Marshes (NNT): Fresh water and salt marshes: large number of rare migrants which appear each year. *Apr-Oct, 10-5. Closed Mons, open Bank Hols. Access by permit, available from Visitor Centre 10-5.*

Cley Visitor Centre (NNT): Built on high ground overlooking the Cley Marshes Reserve, the Centre affords magnificent views; displays on conservation and history of the Cley area. Gift shop. *Admission free. Permits for Reserve obtainable from the Centre. Apr-Oct, Tue-Sun, 10-5. Closed Mons, open Bank Hols.*

Holkham (EN): Sand and mud flats, salt marsh, sand dunes with Corsican pines. *All year.*

Birdwatching at Holkham

Holkham Hall Lake: Freshwater 1 mile in length on which moorhen & coot, grebes, cormorants, swans, geese and ducks can be seen. *Admission free. Advance notice to Estate Office for large groups please, Tel: (0328) 710227.*

Holme Bird Observatory Reserve (NOA): 6 acres. Permanent warden. 300 species. Hides. Nature trail. *Visitors welcome all year, permits available on the spot.*

Scolt Head Island (EN): Island reserve with extensive salt marshes and sand dunes. Nature Trail. *Access by ferry from Brancaster Staithe and Overy Staithe, Apr-Sept.*

Snettisham, signposted from A149 road from King's Lynn to Hunstanton (RSPB): Gravel pits on the Wash. Spectacular flocks of waders at high tides, breeding terns, ducks. Observation hides. Information centre. *Free access at all times from public car park at beach. Warden: P Fisher, 13 Beach Road, Snettisham, King's Lynn, Norfolk.*

Titchwell, off A149, W of Brancaster (RSPB): Reedbeds, lagoons, saltmarsh and sandy beach. Nesting avocets, marsh harriers and bitterns. Good variety of birds throughout the year. Access at all times along the west bank. Observation hides, visitor centre, shop, toilets. *£2 car park charge for non members. Warden: N Sills, Three Horseshoes Cottage, Titchwell, King's Lynn, PE31 8BB.*

Winterton Dunes (EN): Large sand dune area with coastal plants and birds. *All year.*

Broadland

Berney Marshes and Breydon Water, nr Great Yarmouth (RSPB): Flooded grazing marsh and estuary mudflats. Waders and wildfowl present throughout the year. No road access. Norwich-Great Yarmouth train stops at Berney Arms halt. Also reached by foot along Weaver's Way or by boat from Breydon Marine, bookable in advance with the warden: *C Self, RSPB, Ashtree Farm, Breydon Marina, Butt Lane, Burgh Castle, Great Yarmouth.*

Broadland Conservation Centre, Ranworth (NNT): A floating gallery for bird watching moored on Ranworth Inner Broad; displays on conservation and the history of the Broads approached by 1/4 mile nature trail through woodland. *1 Apr-28 Oct, Sun-Thur 10.30-5.30; Sat 2-5.30. Adm charge.*

Bure Marshes (EN): Extensive fen, broads, fen woodland and Hoveton Great Broad; nature trail can only be reached by boat, upstream from Salhouse Broad. *Early May-mid Sept (ex weekends).*

Cockshoot Broad (NNT): Boarded walkway (3/4 mile) along River Bure and Cockshoot dyke leading to bird hide overlooking the Broad. Abundance of wildlife. *All year. Free.*

Hickling Broad (EN, NNT): Large Broad, open reed and sedge beds, oak woodland. Passage waders in large numbers in spring and autumn; bittern, heron and bearded tit in summer. Stronghold of swallowtail butterfly. Boats may pass along the public channels. Visitor Centre: Stubb Rd, Hickling, open 10-5 on weekdays (except Tues). Tel: (069261) 276. Water trail 2 1/2 hr trip in boat. *May & Sept Tue, Wed & Thur. June, July & Aug Mon-Fri. Depart 10am and 2pm from Pleasure Boat Inn. Advance booking essential.*

Horsey Mere (NT): Winter wildfowl, with occasional swans; extensive reed beds and proximity to sea give it a special attraction to birds of passage. *Restricted access by boat.*

How Hill, Wildlife Water Trail, Broads Authority: Water trail by small electric launch. Trail covers river and dykes through marshes and fens of the How Hill Nature Reserve. Guide describes area, walk to bird hide. *1 Apr-31 May & 1-31 Oct, Sat, Sun, Bank Hols & Half Term week, 11-3. 1 June-30 Sept, daily, 10-5. £2.50/£1.50.*

Strumpshaw Fen, signposted from Brundall off A47 Norwich to Great Yarmouth road (RSPB): Broads, reedbeds and woodland with many birds including marsh harriers and kingfishers. Wild flower meadows, dragonflies and butterflies also notable. Information centre, observation hides and toilets. *All year 9-9 or sunset when earlier. Non members £2.50/£1.50. Warden: M Blackburn, Staithe Cottage, Low Road, Strumpshaw, Norwich, NR13 4HS.*

Surlingham Church Marsh, north of A146 Norwich-Lowestoft road (RSPB): Former grazing marsh with dykes and pools. Nesting little ringed plovers and common terns. Circular walk of 1 1/2 miles starting by Surlingham church. Observation hides. Wellingtons or boots advisable. *Free access at all times. Warden: M Blackburn (see Strumpshaw Fen).*

Inland Norfolk

East Wretham Heath (NNT): Grassland heath with some woodland. Typical Breckland country, which in other areas has been much altered by recent afforestation. Sandy soil supports many continental plants unusual in England. *All year (ex Tues, Christmas and New Year) 10-5 (dusk in winter). Free.*

East Winch Common, off the A47 at East Winch (NNT): One of the few large remnants of heathland in the county. Plants include heather, purple moor grass, sundew and beautiful marsh gentian. Dragonflies, damselflies and a variety of birds. Nature trail. *Daily, dawn-dusk.*

Foxley Wood, 6m NE East Dereham (NNT): Largest ancient woodland in the county. Wide rides benefit butterflies and the site is rich in wildflowers in the spring and summer.

Honeypot Wood, from the A47 W East Dereham take the road to Wendling (NNT): Honeypot wood is a remnant of the ancient woodland that once covered Norfolk, there are rare plants and wild flowers in abundance. Concrete rides enable wheelchairs to get about the wood with comparative ease. *Daily, dawn-dusk.*

Lolly Moor, Westfield village, 3m S East Dereham (NNT): A small site with damp grassland, fen and wet woodland, actively managed for the Trust by local conservationists. The public are welcome to enter the reserve and there is a short nature trail. Please keep to paths.

Narborough Railway Line, 1m S Narborough village (NNT): A disused railway embankment composed of chalk ballast and supporting one of the best examples of chalk grassland in the county. The site is being managed jointly with Norfolk Branch of the British Butterfly Society. *Access at all times.*

Thompson Common, 4m S Watton via B111 (NNT): A mosaic of grasslands, pingos (shallow ponds formed during the ice age), scrub and woodland. Shetland ponies and roe deer graze the common. *Public nature trail open at all times. Vistors are requested to keep to the clearly marked trail.*

Wayland Wood, 1m SE Watton, access from A1075 (NNT): An ancient and historic wood, still managed in the traditional way as coppice with oak standards. Wayland is mentioned in the Domesday book. Its name is derived from the Viking name of the wood "Wanelund", meaning sacred grove. *Open at all times.*

Weeting Heath (NNT and NCC): Area of heathland supporting rich flora and fauna. Bird hides only (Apr-Aug). Payment to visit hides to be made to Warden on site.

SUFFOLK

Bonny Wood, [TM 076520] Barking Tye, nr Stowmarket (SWT): Ancient woodland with marvellous spring flowers. *Leaflet available. Open at all times.*

Bradfield Woods [TL 935581] nr Bury St Edmunds (SWT): Outstanding ancient woodland coppiced since medieval times. *Open throughout the year. Visitor Centre. Leaflet available. Guided walks for groups by arrangement with the warden Tel: Rattlesden 7996.*

Bromeswell Green, [TM 296504] nr Melton (SWT): Variety of woodland, estuary and meadow habitats. *Nature trail and leaflet. Open at all times.*

Carlton Marshes [TM 508918] nr Lowestoft (SWT): Grazing Marsh and Fen; Wetland Birds. *Access by public footpath at all times. Visitor Centre. Leaflet available. Guided walks for groups by arrangement with the warden. Suffolk Broads Wildlife Centre on site. Tel: (0502) 564250.*

Cavenham Heath (EN): Area of heathland supporting wide range of birds. Access to area south of Tuddenham-Icklingham track only. Parking at Temple Bridge. *All year, free.*

Cornard Mere, [TL 887388] nr Sudbury (SWT): Wetland important for birds and flowers. *Leaflet available. Open at all times.*

Large tree hide at Minsmere Bird Sanctuary

Wolves Wood, near Hadleigh

Darsham Marshes [TM 420691] (SWT): Marsh, fen and woodland. Excellent birdlife and flora. Leaflet available. *Open at all times.*

Dunwich Heath (NT): One mile of sandy beach and gravel cliff with 214 acres of heathland. Exhibition, tea room, shop and holiday flats. *All year. Car park £1 (£1.50 Jul & Aug).*

Framlingham Mere [TM 284638] (SWT): Wet meadows and large shallow mere. Near castle. Circular walk. Good water birds. *Open at all times.*

Groton Wood, [TL 976428] nr Sudbury (SWT): Superb broadleaved wood, with large ancient small leaved lime grove. Bluebells and orchids. *Leaflet available. Open at all times.*

Havergate Island, Orford (RSPB): Britain's largest colony of avocets also breeding terns. Many wading birds in spring and autumn. Short boat crossing by permit in advance from *The the warden J Partridge, 30 Munday's Lane, Orford, IP12 2LX (please enclose SAE). Members £2.50, non-members £5 payable on arrival.*

Lackford [TL 803708] 6m NW Bury St Edmunds (SWT): Award winning large gravel pits restored for wildlife. Much to see in summer and winter. Hides. *Open at all times.*

Landguard, [TM 285315] nr Felixstowe (SWT): Wonderful coastal sand flora. Migrant and coastal birds. *Warden on site.*

Martins Meadows, [TM 227573] nr Monewden (SWT): One of the finest hay meadows in Britain. Keep to edges of meadows.

Minsmere, nr Westleton (RSPB): 2,000 acres of marsh, lagoon, reedbed, heath and woodland. Immense variety of birds including bitterns, marsh harriers and avocets. *Open daily (ex Tue) 9am-9pm or sunset when earlier. Closed 25 & 26 Dec. Non-members £3/£1.50/£2. Access at all times from Dunwich cliffs to free public hides on beach. Warden: G Welch, Minsmere Reserve, Westleton, Saxmundham, Suffolk.*

Newbourne Springs [TM 271433] (SWT): Woods, fen, heath and reedbed with abundant songbirds in spring, including nightingales. Reserve visitor centre, car park.

North Warren, off B1122 one mile N Aldeburgh (RSPB): Heathland, fen and grazing marshes. Breeding waders, heathland birds. *Access free at all times. Warden: R Macklin, Firethorn Cottage, Rectory Road, Middleton, Saxmundham.*

Redgrave & Lopham Fen [TM 046797] (SWT): Large sedge and reed bed at source of rivers Waveney and Little Ouse. Boardwalk accessible for the disabled. *Access from car park at all times. Reserve Office Tel: (037988) 618.*

Reydon Wood [TM 476790] (SWT): Ancient woodland and green lane. Nature trail provided. *Access from car park at all times.*

Walberswick and Westleton Heaths, nr Saxmundham (EN): Extensive area of heathland and coastal habitats supporting a varied flora and fauna. *Access by public footpaths only.*

Wolves Wood, beside A1071 2m E Hadleigh (RSPB): Mixed deciduous wood with nightingales, woodpeckers and hawfinches. Observation hide and information centre. Access at all times from car park. Donations welcome. *Warden: c/o Stour Wood Reserve, 24 Orchard Close, Great Oakley, Harwich.*

NATURALISTS' ORGANISATIONS

(with abbreviations as used in text).

Broads Authority, 18 Colegate, Norwich, Norfolk. Tel: (0603) 610734.

BCWT: Beds & Cambs Wildlife Trust, 5 Fulbourn Manor, Fulbourn, Cambridge. Tel: (0223) 880788.

EBWS: Essex Birdwatching Society, The Saltings, 53 Victoria Drive, Great Wakering, Southend-on-Sea, Essex.

EWT: Essex Wildlife Trust, Fingringhoe Wick Nature Reserve, nr Colchester, Tel: (0206) 729678.

HMWT: Herts & Middlesex Wildlife Trust, Grebe House, St Michael's Street, St Albans, Herts, Tel: (0727) 58901.

NT: The National Trust, Blickling, Norwich, Norfolk, Tel: (0263) 733471.

EN: English Nature (East Region), 60 Bracondale, Norwich, Tel: (0603) 620558.

NNT: The Norfolk Naturalists' Trust, 72 Cathedral Close, Norwich, Tel: (0603) 625540.

NOA: Norfolk Ornithologists' Association, Aslack Way, Holme-next-the- Sea, nr Hunstanton, Tel: (048525) 266.

RSPB: Royal Society for the Protection of Birds, Headquarters: The Lodge, Sandy, Beds, Tel: (0787) 680551. East Anglia Office, 97 Yarmouth Road, Thorpe St Andrew, Norwich, Tel: (0603) 700880.

SWT: Suffolk Wildlife Trust, Park Cottage, Saxmundham. Tel: (0728) 603765.

The Wildfowl and Wetlands Trust, Slimbridge, Gloucester, Tel: (0453) 890333.

CAMBRIDGE

When in Cambridge make the most of your visit.

Join a Walking Tour, accompanied by a Blue Badge Guide.

Tours leave the Tourist Information Centre daily throughout the year.

For further information or details regarding the special arrangements necessary for groups, please contact:

The Tourist Information Centre, Wheeler Street, Cambridge CB2 3QB

Tel: (0223) 322640/463290
Fax: (0223) 463385

MALDON DISTRICT
THE MARITIME EXPERIENCE!

With two attractive rivers, historic towns and villages, miles of unspoilt coastline and an extensive network of footpaths through the countryside, there is much on offer for the visitor to enjoy. For more information please contact the tourism promotion officer, Maldon District Council, Princes Rd., Maldon, Essex CM9 7DL. Tel: 0621 854477 ext. 315

Norwich Guided Tours
The Guildhall

Tourist *i*nformation Centre

Guildhall, Gaol Hill, Norwich, NR2 1NF.

- Guided Tours

- City Regalia

- Guided Coach Tours

Please Contact Tourist Information Centre for details. **Telephone (0603) 666071**

Norwich City Council

Please mention East Anglia Guide when replying to advertisements

54

HERITAGE TOWNS AND VILLAGES

ALDBURY

Just east of Tring, this picturesque village has been used for many television programmes and films. Its half timbered houses grouped around the village green and duck pond form an archetypal English village. An avenue of trees leads across Aldbury Common to the Bridgewater Monument, erected in 1832 to commemorate the pioneer of Britain's canal system, the 3rd Duke of Bridgewater.

AMPTHILL

Ampthill, one of Bedfordshire's finest historic towns lies 8 miles south of Bedford. Radiating out from its crossroads are picturesque narrow streets lined mainly with Georgian houses, many of which were restored in the early 1950's by the former president of the Royal Academy, the architect and writer, Sir Albert Richardson. There are also many interesting Tudor buildings, and a cross now marks the spot where the 15th century castle stood, where Catherine of Aragon was sent while Henry VIII arranged the annulment of their marriage. Market day Thursday. Early closing Tuesday. *Further information from TIC.*

BEDFORD

The River Great Ouse, one of England's most attractive rivers, flows through the County town of Bedford, before passing on to the Wash. The Borough Council has greatly enhanced this stretch of river, by creating miles of riverside walks and gardens, restoring locks and constructing a marina. The river attracts dedicated rowers to the town's regatta in July, and a colourful river festival is held in even numbered years. Bedford's most famous son was the separatist preacher John Bunyan, author of The Pilgrim's Progress, who was imprisoned for his beliefs for many years in Bedford County Gaol. His life story is portrayed and the Bunyan Museum, and the 16th century Moot Hall at Elstow. The town is dominated by fine buildings, and its prosperity dates from the late 17th century when the town became an important distribution point for goods up and down the river. Market days Wednesday and Saturday. Early closing Thursday. *Further information from TIC.*

BERKHAMSTED

Berkhamsted is today a lively market town on the Grand Union Canal. In 1066 William the Conqueror was offered the English Crown here. There are scanty remains of the Norman castle which was once a favourite royal residence. Two miles north of Berkhamsted lies the 4000 acre Ashridge Estate, which includes woodlands, commons and hills up to Ivinghoe Beacon. Market day Saturday. *Further information from TIC.*

BISHOP'S STORTFORD

The River Stort runs through the centre of this thriving market town which lies close to the border between Hertfordshire and Essex. There is a 15th century church in the town, and the old vicarage was the birthplace of Cecil Rhodes, which is now a museum depicting his life and the history of the commonwealth. Remains of the 11th century castle can still be seen, and there are several old inns of interest. Market days Thursday and Saturday. Early closing Wednesday. *Further information from TIC.*

BUNGAY

An unspoilt market town standing on Suffolk's border with Norfolk, on the banks of the River Waveney. The Domesday Book noted 5 churches in Bungay and of these 2 remain. Bungay Castle, rebuilt in about 1300, stands as a reminder of the town's turbulent past. Largely rebuilt after the Great Fire in 1688, the town has many fine Georgian buildings. The Market Place contains the Butter Cross, on top of which is the figure of Justice. There is wide variety of shops, all within easy walking distance of the Market Place. The town is encompassed by a well-signed footpath walk, the Bigod Way, providing a range of country walks 2 to 10 miles in length. *For free Tourist Guide, Tel: 0986 893243.*

BURNHAM-ON-CROUCH

The largest town in the area known as the Dengie Hundred, a peninsula abutting into the North Sea, bounded northward by the River Blackwater and southward by the River Crouch, dates back to prehistoric times. Throughout its history it has maintained a strong maritime flavour culminating today in its title "Pearl of the East Coast", evocative of the beautiful views across the River Crouch with its numerous yachts. As well as a picturesque setting, there are various attractions including a large yacht harbour, two museums, a sports centre, pleasant shopping area and a good selection of pubs and restaurants. Early closing Wednesday. *Information from the Tourist Information Officer, Maldon District Council, Princes Road, Maldon, Essex CM9 7DL. Tel: (0621) 854477.*

BURY ST EDMUNDS

An ancient market town, full of history and Suffolk charm, and ideally situated for touring East Anglia. Cambridge, Ely and the Suffolk coast are within easy reach, as are Ickworth House, Clare Priory and Euston Hall. The country park at West Stow features a unique reconstructed Anglo-Saxon village and there are country parks at Clare and Nowton on the outskirts of the town. Bury St Edmunds has a wealth of historic buildings. The boards are still trodden at the Theatre Royal, a Regency theatre designed by William Wilkins, and the Market Cross Art Gallery was designed by Robert Adam. Moyse's Hall Museum in the Market Place is a Norman building which houses local history collections and the Manor House, a brand new museum of fine arts and time keeping, is due to open in 1993. There is a leisure centre with indoor swimming pool, a cinema and open air markets on Wednesdays and Saturdays. The Bury festival takes place each May. Early closing Thursday. *Tourist Information Packs (£2 inc postage) from TIC.*

CAMBRIDGE

ESSEX

Heritage

Coast

Countryside

For further information, details of where to stay, places to visit and events, please contact the Essex Tourist Information Centre, County Hall, Chelmsford, Essex CM1 1GG, or phone (0245) 283400 (24 hrs.).

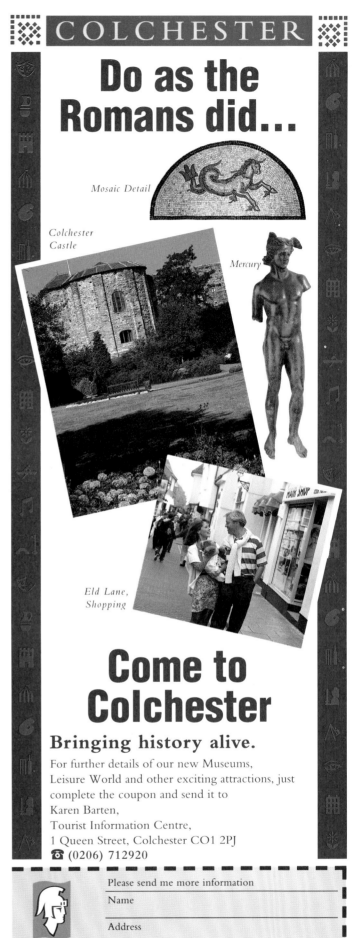

COLCHESTER

Do as the Romans did...

Mosaic Detail

Colchester Castle

Mercury

Eld Lane, Shopping

Come to Colchester

Bringing history alive.

For further details of our new Museums, Leisure World and other exciting attractions, just complete the coupon and send it to
Karen Barten,
Tourist Information Centre,
1 Queen Street, Colchester CO1 2PJ
☎ (0206) 712920

COLCHESTER

COLCHESTER BOROUGH COUNCIL

Please send me more information

Name

Address

EAG 92

The river, and the Roman road, made Cambridge an important settlement and market from early times. The Saxon tower of St Benet's Church, the mound built by William the Conqueror for his castle, and several medieval churches all survive. The Folk Museum (Castle Street) and the University Museum of Archaeology and Anthropology (Downing Street) have interesting items from the city's past. The University was established in the 13th century, and the first college, Peterhouse, was founded in 1284. The later medieval colleges, including King's and Trinity, were all built in or beside the existing town. The more modern colleges are scattered over west Cambridge, with the new faculty buildings. (Individual visitors may generally walk through the college grounds, but party organisers must contact the Tourist Office preferably well before their visit.) The Fitzwilliam Museum is one of the principal museums of fine and applied arts in Britain. Market days Mon-Sat. *Leaflet and Guide from TIC.*

COLCHESTER

Colchester is a marvellous mix of the old and new. Centuries old streets blend in with the country's most modern shopping centres. Large stores, small specialist shops we have them all. Away from the shops, Colchester's famed history is everywhere to be seen. Parts of the original Roman wall can still be seen and Balkerne Gate near the Mercury Theatre is one of the largest surviving monuments of Roman Britain. The Norman castle, built on Roman foundations has a brand new permanent exhibition. The Natural History museum just opposite has been re-displayed to reflect both current environmental concerns and an increased awareness of the wonders of the natural world. The new leisure centre has a two level pool with falling rapids, sauna world and 24 lane bowling alley. There is also a 1200 seater hall which hosts many famous names. Other attractions well worth a visit are St Boltolph's Priory and St John's Abbey gate house. Colchester is also home to the University of Essex which contributes considerably to the town. Among local personalities who have lived in Colchester are John Ball, one of the leaders of the peasants' revolt of 1381, and William Gilberd, physician to Queen Elizabeth I. Daily walking tours of the town in the summer months. Market day Saturday. Early closing Thursday. *Further information from TIC.*

DEDHAM

Dedham Vale is described as 'Constable Country', and it was this countryside which inspired John Constable's paintings. A footpath leads along the edge of the River Stour to Flatford Mill and Willy Lott's cottage, the scene of his famous 'Hay Wain'. The village has a charm fitting with the mellow countryside. The grammar school which the young painter attended still exists although it now stands as 2 private houses. St Mary's Church commands the central position in the village, the building of which was financed by the wool merchant Thomas Webbe. South of the village the road passes Castle House, the home of the painter Sir Alfred Munnings. Early closing Wednesday. *Further information from TIP, Duchy Barn.*

DISS

Diss is a thriving market town set in the Waveney valley. It still retains much of its picturesque old world charm despite seeing a certain amount of modern development. The older part of the town is found around its market place and the site of the six acre mere – a lake which is a haven for ducks. St Mary's church is a fine imposing building which dominates the market place and has watched history pass it by for seven centuries. The streets leading from the church, the market place and mere feature a wealth of interesting architecture, and a variety of specialist shops and restaurants. Market and auction day Friday. Early closing Tuesday. *Further details from TIC.*

DUNSTABLE

At the junction of the 4000 year old Icknield Way and Roman Watling Street lies Dunstable, created early in the 12th century by Henry I. An Augustinian priory was founded here in 1131, and was later chosen by Henry VIII for the trial of his first wife, Catherine of Aragon. Very fine Norman work remains from the priory, including the nave arcade and the west front. The town is on the edge of the highest point in Bedfordshire, the Dunstable Downs, which offer stunning views over the county and are rich in wildlife. Market days Wednesday, Friday and Saturday. Early closing Thursday. *Further information from TIC.*

ELY

Ely Cathedral is a superb architectural achievement of the Middle Ages and is a dominating feature of the Fenland skyline. The Octagon is an engineering masterpiece and the Lantern above it is one of the finest examples of 14th-century carpentry. The great Lady Chapel (1321) retains the beauty of its carvings and tracery. It has a fine long Nave and the choir has 14th century stalls. Stained glass museum in North Triprium. Nearby is Oliver Cromwell's House which houses a themed tourist information and visitor centre. The Ely museum occupies one of the many old monastic buildings which surround the Cathedral. Along and near the Riverside Walk are interesting old houses and the attractive Maltings public hall. Market day Thursday. Early closing Tuesday. *Mini-guide available from TIC.*

EPPING

Epping, now a busy little market town, dates from the 13th century and was once an important coaching centre. Some of the old coaching inns still survive along the attractive main street. Epping's long High Street follows the line of one of the 'purlieu banks' that marked the edge of the forest, which today, extends for some 270 acres north of the town. The Forest, almost 6,000 acres in total, is famous for its beautiful hornbeam trees. Market day Monday. Early closing Wednesday. *Book of maps of District (75p) and free guide from Council Information Desk, Civic Offices, High St. Tel: (0378) 560000.*

EYE

Retains the peaceful atmosphere and character of a small 18th century market town resting in the heart of the Suffolk countryside. The first definite evidence of a settlement dates from Roman times. The castle mound, which dates back to 1156, affords panoramic views of Eye and its surrounding countryside. The Church of St. Peter and St. Paul, founded in the 12th century with its magnificent tower and rood screen is particularly worth a visit. Town trail available. Early closing Tuesday. *Further information from Stowmarket TIC.*

FINCHINGFIELD

The village green and pond are at the heart of this delightful village. Clustered on the gently sloping hillside above are plastered cottages, half-timbered and Georgian houses. The church of St John the Baptist with its Norman tower and Georgian style bell-cote looks down over the village. The churchyard is entered through the arch of the 15th century Guildhall, where there is a small museum.

FRAMLINGHAM

A quiet market town with many attractive buildings. The striking 12th century castle, built by Roger Bigod, is mainly intact and marvellous views may be seen from its battlements. The Lanman Museum in the castle grounds provides a valuable insight to the lives of the town's people. The Church of St. Michael contains historic tombs and effigies. It has close links with the Mowbrays and Howards, two important medieval families. The town has an interesting shopping centre and good sports centre. Market day Saturday. Early closing Wednesday.

HADLEIGH

This busy market town in the valley of the River Brett is of special historical and architectural importance. At one time a Viking Royal Town, it later rose to become the 14th most prosperous town in the country through its wool trade during the 14th century and 15th century. The medieval heart of Hadleigh, St Mary's Church, the Deanery Tower and the Guildhall bears witness to its historical importance. Today the long High Street has a wide variety of shops offering personal and friendly service. Hadleigh offers free parking. Market days Friday and Saturday. Early closing Wednesday. *Leaflet and accommodation list from TIC.*

HARWICH AND DOVERCOURT

Harwich still has a strong flavour of the medieval sea-faring township it once was. Christopher Jones, master of the Mayflower was married here, and Charles II took the first pleasure cruise from Harwich. During the time Samuel Pepys was MP for the town. Harwich was the headquarters of the King's navy. Now, lightships, buoys and miles of strong chain are stored along the front and passengers arriving on the North Sea ferries at Parkeston Quay see the nine-sided High Lighthouse as the first landmark. Southwards along the coast is Dovercourt, with its new indoor swimming pool, the residential and holiday suburb of Harwich. Market day Friday. Early closing Wednesday. Holiday guide to the Essex Sunshine Coast from *Council Offices (EDU), Thorpe Road, Weeley, Clacton on Sea, Essex, CO16 9AJ. Information also from Harwich TIC. Tel: (0255) 256161.*

HATFIELD

The hillside village of old Hatfield is full of charming old buildings including a row of Georgian houses. The magnificent Hatfield House which dominates the village, has been the home of the Cecil family since 1611, when the first Earl of Salisbury, Robert Cecil had it built. Its great hall is endorsed with fine paintings, panelling and carving. In the gardens lies the surviving wing of the Old Palace, home of Elizabeth I for much of her childhood. The new town of Hatfield was built in 1946, and has attracted many large companies. It has recently seen the opening of Britain's first American style shopping and leisure complex, The Galleria. Market days Wednesday and Saturday. Early closing Monday and Thursday. *Further information from TIC.*

HEMINGFORD GREY

A mile south west of St. Ives lies this peaceful village by the edge of the River Great Ouse. A moated Norman manor house is set among the village's timber, brick and thatched cottages. St. James's church on the waterside bears an unusual stump on its tower, the original spire was blown into the river by a hurricane in 1741.

Hemingford Grey is linked with its neighbouring village Hemingford Abbots where some attractive houses are grouped around St. Margaret's church.

HERTFORD

This ancient county town is the meeting point of four rivers. The 28 mile Lee Navigation runs from here to the Thames in London. The town has many buildings of historical interest, most notably the castle, occupied for nearly 1000 years. In the grounds are remains of the 18th century round towers, and 12th century curtain wall. The 15th century gatehouse is now home to East Hertfordshire District Council. Other buildings of note include the Shire Hall, by James Adam (brother of Robert) completed in 1769, and the 17th century Hale's Grammar School. Market day Saturday. Early closing Thursday. *Further information from TIC.*

HOLT

A small, attractive country town just inland from the coast and nestling in undulating North Norfolk countryside. The main street is lined by Georgian buildings mainly built after the fire of 1708. The town has many picture galleries and bookshops. Holt is well known for the public school Greshams, founded in 1555. The North Norfolk Steam Railway has its terminus on the outskirts of the town, connecting Holt with the seaside resort of Sheringham. Market day Friday. Early closing Thursday. *For a free guide write to: Coast and Countryside, Dept EG93, Brochure Despatch Centre, Unit 28, Mackintosh Road, Rackheath Industrial Estate, Norwich, Norfolk NR13 6LH. Tel: 0603 721717 (24 hours).*

IPSWICH

Ipswich is England's oldest heritage town. As Suffolk's county town it is a major commercial and shopping centre. Ipswich has 12 medieval churches, 5 of which are floodlit in the winter months. The Tudor Christchurch Mansion (1548) furnished as a country house contains the finest collection of Constable and Gainsborough paintings outside London. It is set in beautiful parkland 5 minutes from the town centre and is open every day. The Wolsey Art Gallery has an extensive programme of temporary exhibitions; the Ancient House has the country's finest example of pargeting; Ipswich Museum contains replicas of the Sutton Hoo and Mildenhall Treasures, Roman Villa display, (taped commentary available) (Tue-Sat). Sport and leisure facilities are excellent including the award winning Crown Pools, most indoor and outdoor sports are available. Ipswich Town Football Club provides Premier Division professional football, with speedway and stock car racing making perfect outdoor excitement. First class live entertainment is provided by The Corn Exchange, the Wolsey Theatre and the Regent Theatre. There are 7 cinema screens, 2 nightclubs and a wide variety of restaurants. Market days Tuesday, Friday and Saturday. Early closing Wednesday. *Regular guided tours and a (signposted) Town Trail from TIC. A tourist and accommodation guide (free) is available.*

KERSEY

Kersey church on its hilltop site dominates the village which runs steeply down The Street to a water-splash where ducks rest peacefully. Some call it the "prettiest village in England" and it certainly lives up to this. Many fascinating historic buildings line the main street, large merchants houses, weavers cottages and two medieval pubs. Kersey's past prosperity as a settlement important for the manufacture of Kersey cloth, is reflected in the magnificence of the 14th century St Mary's Church.

KING'S LYNN

King's Lynn entertained King John before his last journey to Newark Castle, where he died. His baggage-train, following after him, badly miscalculated the tide and was lost crossing the Wash. People still look for the treasure and Lynn makes visitors believe in treasure trove. Medieval streets run down to the quays, merchant's houses with their private warehouses still present an aspect of considerable wealth and two guildhalls still function. One is the Town Hall, now housing a new crime and punishment attraction as well as the splendid civic treasures, including a magnificent set of Charters dating right back to the days of King John (access through TIC) and the other is the King's Lynn Arts Centre home of the King's Lynn Festival (held the last two weeks of July). There are three museums including the new Town House Museum of social history and True's Yard, a museum of King's Lynn's fishing quarter, two market places (with markets on Tuesday, Friday and Saturday), many fine buildings to visit, plus Lynnsport and Leisure Park, East Anglia's newest and largest sports and leisure complex, and a cinema. The surrounding countryside is attractive, and contains several historic houses open to the public, including Sandringham, as well as a variety of other attractions. Early closing Wednesday. *Brochure from TIC.*

LAVENHAM

A beautifully kept example of a Suffolk wool town with superb ancient buildings. The church of Peter and St Paul stands proud to the south of the village with its 141 ft tower. The manufacture of various kinds of cloth and the preparation of wool and yarn were the main source of Lavenham's wealth for at least 500 years. The 16th century Guildhall is one of the finest Tudor half-timbered buildings in the country. Overlooking the market place it now contains an exhibition of local history items and the woollen cloth industry. *Further information from TIC.*

LEIGHTON BUZZARD

Situated on the Grand Union Canal, Leighton Buzzard has in modern times become famous for sand. It is essentially a market town and has a wide Georgian High Street with mews shops, an ancient street market and a fine parish church, which dates from 1277. It has a 190 foot spire, medieval graffiti and 13th century ironwork. The 15th century pentagonal market-cross at the centre of the town, has played host to witch trials, horse auctions and the calling of marriage banns. The Leighton Buzzard Narrow Gauge Railway was built in 1919 to carry sand from the quarries, but now offers passenger trips around the town. Market days Tuesday and Saturday. Early closing Wednesday. *Further information from South Bedfordshire District Council, High Street North, Dunstable, Bedfordshire LU6 1LF. Tel: (0582) 474014.*

LITTLE WALSINGHAM

A busy pilgrimage centre since the middle ages. The high street opens out into a square in the centre of which is a 16th century octagonal pump-house. Many of the religious buildings can still be seen including the Abbey and hostels used by the pilgrims over the centuries. There is an Anglican shrine built in 1931 which may be visited and a few miles away at Houghton St Giles is the Slipper Chapel. *Further information available from TIC. For a free guide write to: Coast and Countryside, Dept EG93, Brochure Despatch Centre, Unit 28, Mackintosh Road, Rackheath Industrial Estate, Norwich, Norfolk NR13 6LH. Tel: 0603 721717 (24 hours).*

LUTON

The fortunes of Luton were largely founded on the straw hat industry, which grew in 17th century throughout the south of the county. Luton is proud of this tradition and tells the history of the industry in its museum. In recent years it has become a centre for modern industry, including car manufacturing. The Mossman Collection is a unique and nationally important collection of horse-drawn vehicles. The collection is located in Stockwood Park, together with the Stockwood Craft Museum and the Hamilton Finlay Sculpture Garden. Market days Monday to Saturday. Early closing Wednesday. *Further information from TIC.*

MALDON

The attractive little town of Maldon lies on the Rivers Chelmer and Blackwater and is an important yachting centre and home of Thames sailing barges which can be seen by the Hythe quay. The town, granted a Royal Charter in 1171, has many interesting old buildings, including the 15th century Moot Hall, 17th century Plume library, riverside and canal walks and between the main streets run the attractive lanes and "chases" which are such a feature of the town. Fishing and sailing facilities. Explore the town or the surrounding district by obtaining various free publications, including the ETB Mini-Guide, from the *Tourist Information Officer, Maldon Council, Council Offices, Princes Road, Maldon, Essex, CM9 7DL. Tel: 0621 854477 Extn.379.* Market days Thursday and Saturday. Early closing Wednesday.

MUCH HADHAM

A pretty, unspoilt village, which lies in the Ash Valley between Ware and Bishop's Stortford. Edmund Tudor, father of the Tudor monarchs was born here, and the Bishops of London had their summer palace here, parts of which still stand. The home of the acclaimed sculptor Henry Moore is at nearby Perry Green. *Further information from Hertford TIC.*

NEEDHAM MARKET

A small town in the Gipping Valley with many pleasant country and riverside walks. It boasts Mid Suffolk's most popular recreation site, Needham Lake, with its fishing and picnic facilities. There are many attractive buildings in the town and of particular interest is the church interior with its dramatic hammerbeam roof. Craft and antique shops add further interest. Early closing Tuesday. *Further information from Stowmarket TIC.*

NEWMARKET

James I was the first king to visit Newmarket, primarily because the hunting was so good, but it was his Scottish nobles who introduced racing to England and found the heath at Newmarket so ideal for the matches which were then run usually between two horses at a time. Charles II was single-minded in his devotion to racing from the first, and Newmarket became during the racing season, in fact if not in name, the alternative court to Whitehall. The Rowley Mile racecourse takes its name from his hack Old Rowley. Nell Gwynn's cottage can still be seen, having escaped the fire of 1683 which consumed most of old Newmarket. The town became firmly established as the centre of horse racing and breeding a position which it still maintains, embodied in the handsome buildings of the Jockey Club in the High Street. Market days Tuesday and Saturday. Early closing Wednesday. *Tourist information: Public Library, Rookery Precinct Tel: (0638) 661216. Also Forest Heath District Council Information Centre, Rookery Precinct Tel: (0638) 719000.*

NORWICH

It was George Borrow who wrote of Norwich "A fine old city, truly, view it from whatever side you will; but it shows best from the east." Indeed from St James' Hill on Mousehold Heath on a warm day in summer when the sky is blurred with heat, the view down on the city seems to come from an illustration to a medieval Book of

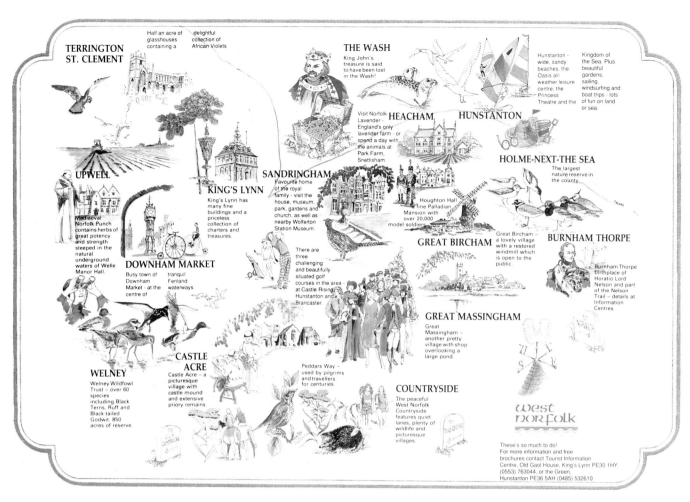

TERRINGTON ST. CLEMENT

Half an acre of glasshouses containing a delightful collection of African Violets

THE WASH
King John's treasure is said to have been lost in the Wash!

Hunstanton - wide, sandy beaches, the Oasis all-weather leisure centre, the Princess Theatre and the

Kingdom of the Sea. Plus beautiful gardens, sailing, windsurfing and boat trips - lots of fun on land or sea.

HEACHAM HUNSTANTON

Visit Norfolk Lavender - England's only lavender farm - or spend a day with the animals at Park Farm, Snettisham

HOLME-NEXT-THE-SEA
The largest nature reserve in the county

UPWELL

SANDRINGHAM
Favourite home of the royal family - visit the house, museum, park, gardens and church, as well as nearby Wolferton Station Museum.

KING'S LYNN
King's Lynn has many fine buildings and a priceless collection of charters and treasures.

Mediæval Norfolk Punch contains herbs of great potency and strength steeped in the natural underground waters of Welle Manor Hall.

Houghton Hall fine Palladian Mansion with over 20,000 model soldiers

Great Bircham - a lovely village with a restored windmill which is open to the public.

BURNHAM THORPE
Burnham Thorpe birthplace of Horatio Lord Nelson and part of the Nelson Trail - details at Information Centres.

DOWNHAM MARKET
Busy town of Downham Market - at the centre of   tranquil Fenland waterways

GREAT BIRCHAM

There are three challenging and beautifully situated golf courses in the area - at Castle Rising, Hunstanton and Brancaster.

GREAT MASSINGHAM
Great Massingham – another pretty village with shop overlooking a large pond.

WELNEY
Welney Wildfowl Trust – over 60 species including Black Terns, Ruff and Black-tailed Godwit. 850 acres of reserve.

CASTLE ACRE
Castle Acre – a picturesque village with castle mound and extensive priory remains.

Peddars Way – used by pilgrims and travellers for centuries.

COUNTRYSIDE
The peaceful West Norfolk Countryside features quiet lanes, plenty of wildlife and picturesque villages

west norfolk

There's so much to do!
For more information and free brochures contact Tourist Information Centre, Old Gaol House, King's Lynn PE30 1HY. (0553) 763044, or the Green, Hunstanton PE36 5AH (0485) 532610

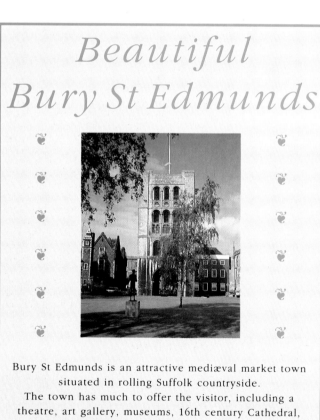

Please mention East Anglia Guide when replying to advertisements

Hours. The 33 medieval churches within the old walls, the course taken by the walls themselves, and the impregnable arm of the River Wensum describe the old city very much as it must have been. Descending into the town, the Norman Castle keep assumes a dominance it does not have viewed from above, and the delicate height of the Cathedral spire assumes its true proportions. The old Guildhall looks out on to the market place, a patchwork of stall awnings known locally as "tilts", which offers local produce in profusion. Narrow flint-cobbled streets, such as Elm Hill, lead past elegant town houses. Alleys and courtyards invite exploration. On the edge of the city the modern University includes the award winning Sainsbury Centre for Visual Arts. In addition to the Castle Museum, with its excellent Art Gallery, there are several other museums and galleries. Shopping facilities include many fascinating specialist shops. The ancient capital of East Anglia, Norwich is an ideal base from which to explore the region's wealth of market towns and villages, the many medieval churches, the unique Broads, and the coastline with its tranquil harbours, nature reserves, fishing villages and traditional seaside. Market days Mon-Sat. Early closing Thursday. *Norwich Guide (£2 + 50p p&p) and free leaflets from TIC.*

ORFORD

A thriving port when Henry II had a castle built there in 1165. At that time the shingle spit separating the river from the sea ended near the quay. Since then the spit has extended 5 miles to the south west resulting in the port's decline, but not affecting the village's beauty. The river crossing to Orford Ness is now a place for mooring pleasure boats. The 90ft keep, all that remains of the castle, provides excellent views of the brick and timber cottages below and across to the marshes beyond. Good restaurants and walks. Early closing Wednesday.

PETERBOROUGH

Peterborough is a remarkable city: combining the best elements of past and present. Peterborough offers a blend of thousands of years of history enhanced by many new facilities. A visit to Peterborough will introduce you to the complete remains of a 150 million year old plesiosaur in the City Museum; the preserved timbers and artefacts of 3000 year old Flag Fen Bronze Age Excavation; medieval wallpaintings in Longthorpe Tower; a magnificent Norman Cathedral; and the charm of Thomas the Tank Engine on the Nene Valley steam railway. Peterborough's present offers a wide range of facilities. Nene Park is a 500 acre expanse of lakes, woodlands and water meadows where visitors can camp, sail, row, canoe, fish, ride or walk. There are golf courses, an ice rink, a ten pin bowling alley and other sports facilities. A multi screen cinema, nightclubs, theatre and other live shows provide more relaxed entertainment. Market days are Tuesday, Wednesday, Friday and Saturday. Late night shopping Thursday. *Various guide and information booklets are available from TIC.*

ROYSTON

Royston lies at the crossing of the ancient Icknield Way and Ermine Street, and is said to have been named after the Lady Roysia who placed a cross set in stone to mark this crossing. The town has several interesting houses and inns, and an unusual bell shaped cave, thought to be pre Roman. There is a small local history museum. Market days Wednesday and Saturday. *Further information from Royston Town Hall, Royston, Hertfordshire SG8 7DA. Tel: (0763) 245484.*

SAFFRON WALDEN

The ancient town of Saffron Walden has revolved around its market for many generations. The medieval market rows are well preserved and timber-framed buildings abound, many decorated by pargeting. The church, reputed to be

the largest in Essex, dominates the town and nearby are the remains of the Norman Castle. On the Common is a rare earth maze, also a restored hedge maze at Bridge End Gardens. The Museum is known for its ethnographic department and also houses a large collection of local interest including many Saxon finds. The Saffron Crocus can be seen flowering outside the Museum in the autumn. It has never been proved that Cromwell's headquarters were in the Sun Inn but Henry Winstanley was certainly born in the town. Nearby is the Jacobean mansion of Audley End. Market days Tuesday and Saturday. Early closing Thursday. *Town Trail leaflet from TIC.*

STOWMARKET

Stowmarket is a busy market town and an important shopping centre for the surrounding countryside. During the 17th and 18th centuries, the town was a noted centre of the woollen trade and the River Gipping was canalised between Stowmarket and Ipswich to carry the town's trade. A walk can be taken along the former towpath through the woods and meadows by the river. Stowmarket's Museum of East Anglian Life is worth a visit. Market days Thursday and Saturday. Early closing Tuesday. *Further information available from TIC.*

SUDBURY

Sudbury is a thriving market town, very much the centre of the smaller villages and communities which surround it. Mentioned in the Domesday Survey of 1086, a settlement is known to have existed here in Saxon times, and today Sudbury still retains many ancient and interesting buildings. Much of the town's Georgian wealth stemmed from the prosperous wool trade. The weaving industry here dates back to the 13th century, and even today the finest silk, including that used in the Princess of Wales' wedding dress, is woven in Sudbury. You can still see rows of three-storey weavers cottages, the wide-floor window showing where the loom would have stood. Gainsborough's House, where the famous painter was born, is now preserved as a delightful little museum with an exhibition gallery. Market days Thursday and Saturday. Early closing Wednesday. *Leaflet and accommodation list from TIC.*

SWAFFHAM

NORMAN CASTLE

BUTTERCROSS

MEDIEVAL CHURCHES

MUSEUM

COUNTRY WALKS

BUNGAY

"A wonderful town"

A FINE ANCIENT AND UNSPOILT MARKET TOWN STANDING ON SUFFOLK'S BORDER WITH NORFOLK ON THE BANKS OF THE RIVER WAVENEY WITH EXCELLENT FACILITIES FOR ALL VISITORS.

FOR FREE TOURIST GUIDE
TELEPHONE: 0986 893243

FISHING

GOLF

INDOOR SWIMMING POOL

BOATING

CAMPING & CARAVANS

Medieval Banquets at the Three Tuns

A Compleat Evening's Entertainment & Feast

Step five hundred years into the past and feast upon four fine courses washed down with mead, wine & ale served by comely wenches whilst you are entertained by the famous Minstrels all in an ancient *Haunted Hostelry*

Telephone 0986 893243

OUTNEY MEADOW CARAVAN PARK

TOURING CARAVANS & CAMPING
MODERN LAUNDRY AND SHOWERS
ROWING BOATS & CANOES FOR HIRE
COARSE FISHING AVAILABLE

TELEPHONE (0986) 892338

The Bungay Tandoori

Indian Cuisine   Fully Licensed

Tel: 0986 894691 or 893881

BEAUTIFUL SOUTH SUFFOLK

Hadleigh Guildhall

Whatever your interests you will find much to your liking in the South Suffolk area. Wide skies, fine countryside, the lovely estuaries of the rivers Stour and Orwell, historic towns such as Sudbury, Hadleigh and Long Melford and charming villages including world famous Lavenham and Kersey.

Over the centuries these fine features have been the inspiration of painters such as Constable, Gainsborough and Munnings. Why not follow in the footsteps in this well established but unspoilt tourist area? You will be pleasantly surprised.

Free visitor information from:-
Tourist Information, Ref EAG
Babergh District Council,
Corks Lane, Hadleigh IP7 6SJ
Telephone 0473 825846

SOUTH SUFFOLK TOURISM

The Bell Inn

The Street, Kersey,
nr: Hadleigh,
Suffolk, IP7 6DY

Our glorious 700 year old building, situated in the middle of probably the most filmed village in Suffolk. Complete with ducks, ford, haunted buildings and the feeling of going back in time!

We boast no yellow lines to hinder parking plus we have our own car park for cars and (up to) 11m coaches.

Our opening hours are:

Morning Coffee from 10-30am
Bar Meals (and Restaurant menu) between 11-30am and 2-00pm
Cream and Afternoon TEA s from 2-30pm 'thru to 5-00pm
Evening Bar Meals (and Restaurant menu) from 6-45pm until 10pm
Traditional Roast Lunch every Sunday - 11-30am until 2-00pm

Roaring open fires in the winter months

We have a large rear flowering garden (for 50 persons) and a walled patio (for 36 persons) - subject to weather !!!
If you are in the area, we would love to see you. Coaches welcome, but by appointment please.

☎ **0473 823229**

Please mention East Anglia Guide when replying to advertisements

First-time visitors to Swaffham are usually impressed at the extent of the triangular-shaped market place which gives the town an air of expansive tranquility, transformed every Saturday by the famous open-air market and lively public auction. Around the market place are many fine Georgian buildings. Close by stands the majestic Church of St Peter and St Paul, one of the finest of the Medieval churches in East Anglia. It has a magnificent hammerbeam roof, with carved angels. Swaffham is an ideal touring centre for the many attractions of North West Norfolk. Market day Saturday. Early closing Thursday. *Further information and free brochure from Swaffham TIP.*

ST ALBANS

As Verulamium, St Albans was one of the leading cities of the Roman Empire. Its modern name comes from that of the first christian martyr in Britain, executed in about AD 209. The town grew up around the impressive cathedral and Abbey church of St Alban. The city displays a range of English architecture, covering many centuries. In particular George Street and Fishpool Street contain many excellently restored houses, some dating back to the 15th century. The two main museums in St Albans are Verulamium Museum and the Museum of St Albans. The Roman theatre, in the grounds of the Gorhambury Estate was discovered in 1847 and dates from around AD 150. It is the only completely exposed Roman theatre in Britain. The city has a vast selection of shops and eating houses, and a particular feature is the street market held every Wednesday and Saturday. *Further information from TIC.*

STEVENAGE

Stevenage new town was the first of the post war new towns, and is much larger than the old town which lies to the north. The old town has an attractive High Street, with numerous old coaching inns. To the southwest of Stevenage is the spectacular Knebworth House, with its Gothic exterior. It has been the family home of the Lyttons for over 500 years, and the Victorian novelist, Sir Edward Bulwer-Lyton was responsible for much of its splendid decoration. Stevenage also has a museum which concentrates on local and natural history. The museum holds an important collection of Roman coins discovered in the area. Market days Wednesday to Saturday. *Further information from TIC.*

THAXTED

Thaxted has been a community since Saxon times, with its greatest days in the 14th and 15th centuries when it prospered because of its cutlery industry. It was at this time that the Guildhall was built and that the present shape of the town grew up, with little houses, some white, some colourwashed or half timbered, winding down the hill past the church into Town Street. The tall spire of the church is one of the landmarks of Thaxted, soaring 181 feet above the town. The other well-known sight is the windmill built in 1804 by John Webb. From the top floor the view of the town and surrounding countryside is quite outstanding. Market day Friday. Early closing Wednesday. *Further information from Saffron Walden TIC.*

THETFORD

Thetford has been a thriving market town since before the Norman Conquest, and many traces of its fascinating past remain, from the IronAge ramparts surrounding the Norman castle mound, to the stately priory ruins and the fine buildings of the town centre's Conservation area. Archaeological digs have revealed important Roman, Saxon and Iron Age finds. 1000 years ago Thetford was one of the largest towns in the country, excavations in the town are of national importance. Thetford is a wonderful centre for river and forest walks. It has an excellent little museum in the picturesque 15th century Ancient House, just a few yards from the birthplace of Thomas Paine, "Father of the American Revolution". The Charles Burrell Museum draws together an impressive collection of exhibits, to tell the story of this once world famous manufacturer of steam traction engines. There is a good Sports Centre and a thriving Arts Centre, with year-round arts and crafts exhibitions and workings. Thetford offers the best of both worlds a lively town in lovely countryside. Market days Tuesday and Saturday. Early closing Wednesday. *Further information available from Ancient House Museum, White Hart Street, Thetford. Tel: (0842) 752599.*

WISBECH

The present day character of Wisbech is mainly that of a prosperous Georgian market town. Indeed, the North Brink, the Crescent and Museum Square must be among the finest examples of Georgian street architecture in the country. The town grew up around its port, trading from medieval times but flourishing commercially with the draining of the Fens in the 17th century. The years 1700-1850 witnessed tremendous growth, which established the fine buildings seen today. Whilst the port has declined in importance, Wisbech remains the market centre for a large agricultural and horticultural area. Of particular note in the town are buildings including Elgood's historic brewery, Peckover House, the Old Market, the Market Place and the Crescent area (including the Wisbech and Fenland Museum). Octavia Hill, one of the founders of the National Trust, lived at No: 8 South Brink. Two new

shopping centres complement the traditional retail areas and the market is still held on Thursdays and Saturdays. Auctions of plants, household effects and bygones are held each Wednesday and Saturday at 10am. Early closing Wednesday. *Free Town Trail, Accommodation Guide and Tourist Map from TIC.*

WOBURN

A small and beautifully preserved Georgian town, acknowledged as one of the most important historic towns in Britain. Woburn Abbey, home of the Dukes of Bedford for over 300 years is set in a magnificent 3000 acre deer park. The house was rebuilt in the mid 18th century and contains an extensive art collection. Britain's largest drive through safari park, Woburn Wild Animal Kingdom is home to a variety of species, including tigers, lions, rhinos, elephants and seals. The Heritage Centre is housed in old St Mary's church, combining a museum of Woburn's history with Tourist Information. *Further information from Woburn Heritage Centre or Ampthill TIC.*

WOODBRIDGE

Built on the banks of the Deben, it is not hard to believe this quiet, mainly Georgian town has a history of shipbuilding and sail-making. It's famous Elizabethan Statesman, Thomas Seckford has left his mark on the town. His endowment of almshouses in Woodbridge and investment in properties in London means the Seckford Foundation is still in being today. The Shire Hall on Market Hill was built by him, and the Seckford family home is now a hotel outside Woodbridge. The famous Tide Mill has been restored to full working order and is open to the public. From the quay enjoy a walk along the sea wall path. St Mary's church has a large 15th century West tower with strange buttresses that change shape as they ascend. *Tourist information from: Council Offices, Melton Hill (0394) 383789.*

CRAFTS SPECIALITIES
AND GALLERIES

CAMBRIDGESHIRE

Crafts at the Close

Set in a converted barn in two acres of idyllic gardens, and with an adventure playground to keep the children happy, this specialist needlework centre is well worth a visit. Crafts at the Close stocks a wide range of fabrics, kits, publications and accessories for embroidery, cross-stitch tapestry and quilting, including a full range of DMC threads, Appletons crewel and tapestry wools. An Aladdin's Cave of finds for the discerning needleperson. Evening group visits available from May to September. Open Tuesday to Saturday 10am-5pm, Wednesdays and Sundays 1.30pm-5pm, closed all day Monday. Free parking. Crafts at the Close, 129 Meldreth Road, Whaddon, Nr Royston. (1 ½ miles off A1198 or A10 between Royston and Cambridge). Telephone (0223) 208103

Sacrewell Farm & Country Centre is interesting and educational - superb for parties and school visits - but above all it is **friendly** and **fun**. Meet our farmyard animals or enjoy the many "hands on" bygones, quizzes and games. Play on trampolines, roundabouts, swings or get lost in the maze. Travel any of the numerous farm, nature and general interest trails, bury yourself in the history of the place and relish the immense power and ingenuity of our ancient watermill which re-opens Summer 1993 after renovation. We are open every day, 9am-9pm. The Visitors Centre, with numerous exhibits and children's toys, provides refreshments and a souvenir/gift shop and is open daily 11am-5.30pm. Admission £1.50/£1.00/50p with party rates and conducted tours available. Ample parking; caravans and campers welcome; provision for picnics, inside and out. Situated off the A47, 8miles west of Peterborough. Telephone David Powell on (0780) 782222.

Chilford Hundred Vineyard

Not just a vineyard, more a wealth of interest for all the family: art gallery with prints and sculpture; banqueting halls; farm and industrial artefacts; children's play area; picnic space and, of course, the county's largest vineyard and winery, all in fascinating buildings featuring ornamental stonework from historic structures. Vineyard shop. Tour the winery and taste the wine. Visitors welcome 11-5, from 1 May-to end Oct; also group visits arranged throughout the year. Take A11/A604 and follow Chilford Hall Vineyard signs from Linton to Chilford Hundred Vineyard, Balsham Road, Linton, Cambridge CB1 6LE. (0223) 892641

Steeplegate Ltd

Unusual gifts of good taste in craft gallery beside the cathedral. Tea room. We sell treen, woodwork, leatherware, ceramics, jewellery and toys. Open all year, daily except Sunday, 9-5.30. 16-18 High Street, Ely, Cambs. Tel Ely (0353) 664731.

ESSEX

Trinity Antiques Centre

7 Trinity Street, Colchester, Essex. Tel: Colchester 577775. The Centre is housed in a 15th century building adjoining Tymperleys Clock Museum. 8 dealers with a variety of silver, jewellery, china, furniture, oriental items, postcards, copper, brass, linen etc. Open Mon-Sat, 9.30-5.

Dedham Art & Craft Centre

This thriving centre, created from a former Congregational church in the heart of Constable country, is a large venture now set out on three floors. On the GROUND FLOOR there is a fully equipped pottery studio. The main hall houses an extensive gallery of local crafts and paintings. Amanda Clement-Robinson shows her unusual, fascinating work ranging from hand-painted silk banners to unique screens and night lights. Quality books at bargain prices. Melissa Collier displays innovative craft jewellery from all over Great Britain. The restaurant/coffee shop serves a delicious selection of wholefood vegetarian fayre all day (lunches 12-2). Also stocked are wholefood supplies, supplements, cookery books and natural cosmetics. *For address and opening times see entry below.*

Dedham Centre First and Second Floors

On the FIRST FLOOR is the small Toy Museum - packed with Joy Parkin's intriguing collection of toys, pictures and childhood mementos. The many other craft units offer: traditional wooden toys, brassware and decorative frames, designer knitwear, quilling and other craft supplies, colourful ladies clothes, soft toys, and antique maps, prints and books. Resident artist Brian Argent Smith displays landscapes in pastel and watercolour whilst Kenneth Smith works on intricate studies of birds and animals. Prints. Commissions. A further selection of other artists' work is exhibited on the SECOND FLOOR in the "Skylight Gallery". Sarah Cornwell's glass painting workshop. Paul Wells-modelmaker. Open Mon-Sun, 10-5, all year (but closed Mon during Jan-Mar). Admission 40p/20p (Family £1). **High St, Dedham, Nr Colchester , Essex. One mile off main A12 between Colchester and Ipswich.** Telephone (0206) 322666 for general enquiries & (0206) 322565 for upstairs crafts people. Restaurant (0206) 322677.

Please mention East Anglia Guide when replying to advertisements

NORFOLK

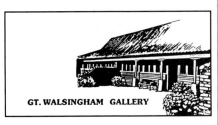

GT. WALSINGHAM GALLERY

Great Walsingham Gallery
This newly established Gallery is set in a beautiful courtyard of converted barns in the picturesque village of Great Walsingham. Exhibitions are held by contemporary and traditional artists together with displays of handmade furniture, quilts, baskets and pottery. On sale are framed and unframed fine art prints, photograph frames, mirrors and greetings cards. A picture framing service is offered as well as weeekend painting and craft courses. Member of the Fine Art Trade Guild. Open: Easter to end September, Monday to Friday 9.00-5.30, weekends 10.00-5.00; other times of the year, Monday to Friday 9.30-5.00, Saturday 10.00-12.30. Follow signs for the Textile Centre. Parking. Telephone (0328) 820900.

The Mustard Shop
Norwich is the home of Colmans, who have been milling mustard for over 160 years. Some varieties sold at this shop-cum-museum of mustard making are not generally available elsewhere. Reproductions of famous Colman posters, tea-towels, aprons, etc. 3 Bridewell Alley, Norwich. Tel. (0603) 627889

Hand Printed Textiles, Cards, Books and Gifts.

The Textile Centre
Now established in traditional Norfolk barns, the Textile Centre offers the opportunity to see the fascinating designs of Sheila Rowse being put to print. Sold countrywide for many years, her textile designs present a unique sense of personality rarely seen before. The screen printing process can be viewed during weekdays from the Craft Shop, where a variety of unusual gifts are on sale. Home made refreshments served, free car parking, facilities for the disabled. Open mid March to mid November, Monday-Friday, 9.30-5.30. Weekends & Bank Hols, 10-5. Educational and group visits welcomed by appointment. B1388 Hindringham Road , Great Walsingham, Norfolk. Tel (0328) 820009.

NORFOLK
CHILDREN'S BOOK CENTRE
SPECIALIST CHILDREN'S BOOKSHOP

Norfolk Children's Book Centre
Surrounded by fields, the Centre displays what we are told is the best collection of children's and teachers' books in East Anglia. Here you will find a warm welcome, expert advice and an abundance of the best, the latest and the classics in children's fiction and non-fiction. Open during school holidays Monday to Saturday 10-4, term time Wednesdays 10-12 and Saturdays 10- 4. Teachers please phone before calling. Find us between Aylsham and Cromer just of the A140. Look out for the signposted left turn 600 yards north of Alby Crafts. Telephone (0263) 761402

Taverham Craft Centre
Taverham Craft Centre is a purpose-built centre for the finest in traditional crafts, hand made on the premises by local craftspeople in a glorious countryside setting in the heart of the Wensum Valley to the west of Norwich. The workshops have been built to the highest standards in traditional style, and are grouped around a charming paved quadrangle. Inside you'll find many different crafts, from embroidery and lacemaking to wood-turning, painting and framing. Watch the craftspeople at work, talk to them about their skills, and come away with a pretty and practical keepsake. Plus garden centre, coffee bar, pet food and corn stores. Facilities for the disabled: coach parties welcome. Car parking for 1000 cars. Open daily, 10-5. Taverham Craft Centre, Fir Covert Road, Taverham, Norwich (situated 7 miles from Norwich on the A1067 Norwich/Fakenham road). Tel: (0603) 860522

Alby Crafts

Alby Crafts
The Gallery contains the skills of many British craftsmen, shown to perfection in this beautifully restored set of Norfolk farm buildings. Also Studio-workshops, Furniture Showroom, Lace Museum, Bottle Museum and Gift Shop. The Tea Room serves a varied menu of home made food. Extensive and interesting Gardens. Free car park. Coaches by appt. Open 14th March-19th December, 10-5, closed Mondays. On A140 between Cromer and Aylsham. Tel Cromer (0263) 761590

The Particular Pottery
A Particular Baptist Chapel (1807) in Kenninghall, Norfolk, has been sympathetically restored into a working pottery and showroom. The Particular Pottery provides a wide choice of pots and an opportunity to see the two resident potters at work on the wheel. Gillian Anderson supplies a range of functional domestic stoneware to various restaurants. She will accept dinner service orders. David Walters prefers to work in porcelain and concentrates on bowls (of all sizes) and one-off large platters, vases, urns etc, all with his distinctive stylish decoration. Find us on the B1113, between Diss & Thetford. We are open seven days a week and warmly welcome visitors. Tel: (095387) 8476.

The Picturecraft Art Gallery
North Norfolk's Art Centre
Discover one of the largest, privately owned art galleries in the country when visiting the historic Georgian town of Holt. Gold Award Winners of the coveted NatWest Business Award Scheme 1991. Difficult to find, so look for the brown & white "Art Gallery" Tourist Information signs in the town centre. No admission charges and large free car park. Extensive artists' material shop and specialist picture framing service. Video presentations on painting techniques. Demonstrations and one-man-shows (July-Oct). Easy access to all departments makes wheelchair visitors especially welcome. Members of the Fine Art Trade Guild and Guild of Master Craftsmen. Open Mon-Sat 9-5. Closed lunchtimes 1-2 and Thurs afternoons. Telephone Holt (0263) 713259 (3 lines). 23 Lees Courtyard, Off Bull Street, Holt. NR25 6HP

THE BLACK HORSE BOOKSHOP

Black Horse Bookshop
Latest books on a wide range of subjects, including almost everything in print about East Anglia. Other departments include maps, art books, architecture and reference books. Books posted to all parts of the world. Open 6 days a week. Official agent for HMSO. 8 & 10 Wensum St, Norwich. Tel (0603) 626871 and 613828

Please mention East Anglia Guide when replying to advertisements

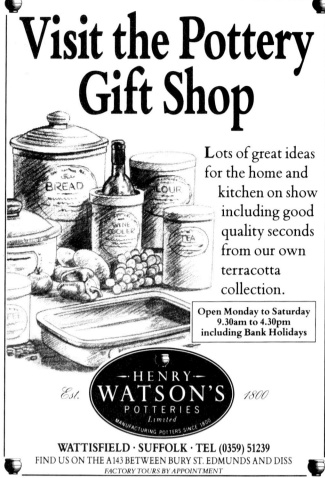

The Candlemaker and Model Centre

The Candlemaker and Model Centre at Stokesby, situated 9 miles from Great Yarmouth on the banks of the River Bure, boasts England's largest variety of handcrafted candles, with many that are unique. The Centre also has a good selection of local crafts and modeling kits. The candle shop and workshop is open daily (except Saturdays) from Easter to the end of October from 9am to 5.30 pm and during November and December from Thursday to Saturday 10am till 4pm with free admission. Free parking and river moorings in village. Telephone Great Yarmouth (0493) 750242.

Appleyard Craft Court

The old 1816 stockfeed and harness barn and surrounding farm buildings have been sympathetically renovated to provide a courtyard of crafts and shops to delight any visitor. Experience the aroma of freshly baked bread and pastries from the bakery or enjoy a relaxing lunch at Pantiles Bistro and sample one of the speciality teas or fresh filter coffee. Watch cider being made the Norfolk way and sample straight from the barrel or simply browse amongst the crafts and curios in the old Craft Barn. Why not finish your day with a trip to Banham Zoo - just opposite the courtyard. Coaches always welcome. Open 10-5 daily. Situated between Diss and Attleborough on the B1113. Tel: (095 387) 771.

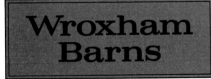

Wroxham Barns Ltd

This collection of beautifully restored 18th century barns, set in 10 acres of Norfolk parkland, provides the setting for one of the finest centres of rural crafts in East Anglia. Situated 1½ miles north of Wroxham you will find 13 craft workshops where resident craftsmen may be seen manufacturing a wide range of individual craftware. The Gallery Craft Shop offers an exciting selection of unusual gifts, crafts and knitwear, whilst the Old Barn Tea Room can provide delicious home made cakes, traditional cream teas and light lunches. As well as Williamson's traditional funfair, the parkland is home to Junior Farm- a farmyard full of friendly animals where children can help bottle feed the baby goats and piglets. Open daily 10am-6pm. Tel. Wroxham (0603) 783762.

Willow Farm Flowers

Willow Farm Flowers are situated at Neatishead in the heart of the Norfolk Broads. A small farm specialising in growing and supplying quality dried flowers direct to the public. The Shop and Flower Arranging workshop are open throughout the year with advice and help readily available. A huge selection of flowers by the bunch; baskets of all sizes, sundries and books. Dozens of Dried Flower Arrangements, large and small are always in stock or made to special order. Details of winter day classes available on request. A selection of flowers can be seen growing during the summer, Well signposted off the A1151 Wroxham to Stalham road. Open 7 days a week throughout the year (except closed Dec 24-31) Mon-Sat 10-4; Sun 2-4. Tel: Wroxham (0603) 783588.

Great Bircham Windmill

Norfolk's finest corn mill, set in unspoilt countryside on a site used for wind-milling since the 1700s. Climb the five floors to the top and view the milling machinery which is in working order. Tea Rooms, Bakery and Gift Shop. Open daily from 20 May-end Sept except Saturdays, and Suns and Weds from Easter, 10-6. Tel (048523) 393.

Norfolk Lavender

Caley Mill (on the A149) is the home of the National Collection of Lavenders. See many varieties of lavender and a large miscellany of herbs. Hear about the harvest, and the ancient process of lavender distillation. The Countryside Gift Shop stocks the full range of Norfolk Lavender's famous products, together with a wide choice of other gifts to suit all pockets. The Herb Shop has many varieties of lavender and herb plants together with gifts for gardeners. The Cottage Tea Room specialises in cream teas, homemade cakes and light lunches. Admission to Car Park and grounds free. Open daily 10-5, closed Christmas holiday. Tea Room opening – Please see Teas Section. Norfolk Lavender Ltd, Caley Mill, Heacham. Tel Heacham (0485) 70384

Embroidery and needlecraft specialists

The Handworkers' Market

Situated at the entrance to the main car park is this needlework and embroidery specialist shop. Well known for its marvellous stock of materials both here and abroad. We stock the full range of DMC threads. St Epin crewel wool in over 70 colours. Appleton's wool, both tapestry and crewel in over 390 colours. A vast selection of trammed and painted canvasses. Single and double thread canvas in French, German and English. Evenweave linens and cottons as well as many other fabrics. Over 80 different gold and silver threads. Real kid. Books on the many different aspects of needlework and design. We will gladly post whatever you want. Open all the year round 9.30-5. Closed lunchtime 1-2 and all day Thursday. The Handworkers' Market, 18 Chapel Yard, Holt. Telephone Holt 711251.

VISIT

A **BLACK SHEEP** SHOP

Black Sheep

Invite you to visit their Farm Store at Ingworth or Town Shop in Penfold Street, Aylsham both en route to Blickling. The Farm Store is open daily ex Mon, including Suns and Bank Hols. The Town Shop is open daily Monday-Saturday. In either you can be sure of a warm welcome. Knitting at Aylsham is often in progress and you will see the transformation of this superb wool into a collection of high quality country clothes, together with an exciting range of gifts. At Ingworth, from the Farm Store windows you just may catch a glimpse of a few members of the World renowned pedigree flock of Black Welsh Mountian Sheep! We've something for every member of the family – sweaters that are chunky, classic, patterned or plain; jackets, coats, skirts and hats; gloves, scarves, belts, mugs – even knitting wools and tweeds to make up to your own design. No tour of East Anglia is complete without visiting us, so don't conform – become a Black Sheep – come and pay us a visit! If you find it impossible to visit us then SEND FOR FREE COLOUR CATALOGUE to Black Sheep Ltd., Ingworth, Norwich, Norfolk NR11 6PJ, England. Aylsham (0263) 733142/732006.

Norfolk Children's Book Centre (see p 65)

SUFFOLK

Snape Maltings

This remarkable collection of old maltings buildings is set on the banks of the River Alde on the Suffolk Heritage Coast. Shops and galleries include House and Gardens (furniture, rugs, quilts, kitchenware and fine foods plus pots and plants in the garden); Snape Craft Shop; Gallery; Countryware; Children's Shop and a special Christmas Shop (open September to December). Fresh home-cooked food in the Granary Tea Shop, River Bar and the Plough and Sail pub. Open all year, daily 10am-6pm (10am-5pm in winter). Snape Maltings, near Saxmundham, Suffolk IP17 1SR. Telephone (0728) 688303/5

Suffolk Craft Society

The Suffolk Craft Society represents the best professional craftsmen in Suffolk. Details of the 140 members - Basketmakers, Bookbinders, Calligraphers, Furniture-makers, Glass engravers, Jewellers, Musical instrument makers, Potters, Print makers, Sculptors, Textile artists, Wood carvers & turners - can be found in its new book **Living Crafts in Suffolk**, £3.50 from East Anglian bookshops. The Annual Exhibition at the Peter Pears Gallery, Aldeburgh, from the last week in July until the end of August, attracts over 10,000 visitors. You will find good craftsmanship, modestly priced and beatifully displayed. Or you could telephone an individual maker to arrange a studio visit and place an order. For further details (Or the book at £4.25 inc postage): Wendy Hughes, Fairfield House South, Saxmundham, IP17 1AX. Tel: (0728) 602060.

Craft at the Suffolk Barn

Margaret and Geoffrey Ellis restored an old Suffolk barn to sell East Anglian crafts, country books, herbs, alpines, garden plants and wild flowers. Herb, wild flower and ornamental gardens. Free entry (charity box) Home-made refreshments, light lunches. Car park. Open mid March to Christmas; Wed, Thurs, Fri, Sat and Bank Hols 10-5.30, Sun 12-5.30. Fornham Rd, Gt Barton, Bury St Edmunds. Tel: Gt Barton (028487) 317.

Ascot House Crafts
Earl Stonham – Norwich Road A140

1000 square feet of attractive and fragrant display welcomes visitors who browse our selection of Pottery, Objets D'Art, Turkish Copperware, Craft Jewellery, Colour Box Miniatures, Collectibles, Pictures, Corn Dollies, Dried Flowers, Toys, Cards and Giftwrap. Pine furniture is also featured. Sensible prices and well worth a visit. Situated on the main A140 Ipswich to Norwich road at the crossing with the A1120 Stowmarket/Yoxford road. Good parking and only 15 minutes from Ipswich. Jan-July open daily except Mon/Tues. July-January open daily except Mondays. Hours 10-5.30. Open Bank Holiday Mondays. Tel Stowmarket (0449) 711495.

Butley Pottery

The Pottery housed in restored thatched barns is situated in Mill Lane, Butley. 8 miles North of Woodbridge, 4 miles from Orford on the 1084 and is signposted from The Street in Butley. Here a wide range of Majolica ware can be seen in production and on sale in the showroom. The Pottery is highly decorative displaying attractive floral and fruit designs. Terracotta garden pots are also available in a variety of sizes. Paintings and Artists' prints can be viewed in the Gallery and Special Exhibitions occasionally held. The Tea Room serves coffee, lunches and teas. On Sunday midday there is usually live music. Evening parties can be catered for by appointment. Open daily 10.30-5.00. For tea room opening hours refer to 'Afternoon Teas' section. Tel: (0394) 450785.

Watson's Potteries

Earliest record of Wattisfield potters is 1646. The Watson family have perpetuated the craft for more than 170 years. Original Suffolk Collection of printed terra-cotta ware includes kitchen and gift items, unique terra-cotta wine coolers, herb, spice and storage jars, lasagne dishes, bread bakers, etc. See original kiln, tour factory by appointment, visit shop selling quality seconds. Wattisfield (A143 between Bury and Diss). Tel Stanton (0359) 51239.

Sutton
Pottery

Sutton Windmill Pottery

Sutton is a small Broadland village 17 miles north-east of Norwich via the A1151, and 16 miles north of Great Yarmouth just off the A149. Malcolm Flatman makes and designs a large range of microwave and dishwasher safe stoneware pottery and tableware items in a selection of glazes. Many lamps and decorative pieces are "one-offs", and Malcolm will produce items to customers' own designs. Visitors are welcome in the workshop to see work in progress and to purchase from a selection of finished pottery. Please telephone at weekends, and before a long journey. A price list is available on request, and telephone and postal enquiries are welcome. Pottery can be posted to customers if required. Sutton Windmill Pottery, Church Road, Sutton, Norwich, Norfolk. Telephone Stalham (0692) 580595.

BRUISYARD
VINEYARD & WINERY
HERB & WATER
GARDENS

Bruisyard Vineyard & Herbs Centre

10-acre vineyard and winery producing the estate-bottled Bruisyard St Peter wine, situated west of Saxmundham. Wines, vines, herbs, souvenirs, etc for sale. Open 2nd January to 24th December, daily, 10.30-5. Conducted tours. Parties of 20 or more by appointment. Large herb and water gardens, shop, restaurant, children's play area and picnic area. Free wine tasting for vineyard and winery visitors. Bruisyard Wines, Church Road, Bruisyard, Saxmundham, Suffolk IP17 2EF. Tel: Badingham (072875) 281.

The National Horseracing Museum

Horseracing is part of British history. Explore this fascinating story at the National Horseracing Museum. A beautiful collection of racing art, personalities, objects and history, to interest both racing enthusiasts and casual visitor alike. Fine gift shop, gardens, licensed cafeteria. Open: Tues 30 Mar-Sun 5 December, Tues-Sat 10-5, Sun 2-5, closed Mons except Bank Hols. July and August Mon-Sat 10-5, Sun 12-5. Adults £2.50, OAP £1.50, Child 75p. 10% Reduction for adults and over 60's in group of 20 or more. Equine tours available, charges on request (booking essential). The National Horseracing Museum, 99 High Street, Newmarket, CB8 8JL. Tel 0638 667333.

Aldringham Craft Market

Aldringham Craft Market
Established in 1958. Wide selection of British craft products. Studio, domestic and garden pottery, wood, leather, glass, jewellery and metalwork. Original paintings, drawings, etchings and prints. Sculpture. Toys, ladies clothes, toiletries, books, maps, etc. Frequent exhibitions. Light refreshments. Children's play area. Easy car parking. Open Mon-Sat 10- 5.30, Sun 10-12, 2-5.30. Evening party visits by arrangement. Aldringham, Nr Leiston, Suffolk. Tel Leiston (0728) 830397.

MILESTONE·HOUSE·POTTERY

HIGH·STREET·YOXFORD·SUFFOLK

Milestone House Pottery
Turn off the A12 into Yoxford High Street to find this pottery with its attractive Trafalgar balcony. We make our stoneware domestic pottery on the premises and import a selected few from Africa. Also available are greeting cards, kites, jam made in the village and many other things to make a visit worthwhile and interesting. Open Easter-Christmas, 10-5. Closed Weds 1pm and Sunday. Winter opening Thurs-Sat, 10-5. Milestone House Pottery, High Street, Yoxford, near Saxmundham, Suffolk, IP17 3EP. Tel: (072877) 465

For all who love Flowers

Swan Craft Gallery
Welcome to the restored stable of a former 17th century Inn. Enjoy browsing amid a carefully selected collection of quality Creative Crafts and an unique mix of new and traditional hand decorated accesories and gifts. The whole range is displayed in such an imaginative style that it will make your visit a sheer delight. From our own Workshops, flower designer and author Mary Lawrence, produces original Real Flower jewellery which is sold worldwide.We are situated on the main A1120 at Ashfield between Stowmarket and Yoxford. Open from April to Christmas on Tuesdays to Saturdays and Bank Holidays 9.30-5.00. On Sundays from 2-5. Tel: (0728) 685703.

CRAFT SHOP - TEA ROOM

Corncraft
At Monks Eleigh, in the heart of the Suffolk countryside between Hadleigh and Lavenham, Corn Craft specialise in growing and supplying corn dollies and dried flowers for the gift trade. A wide range of their own products, along with an extensive selection of other British crafts is available from their craft shop, beautifully set amongst the farm buildings. Coffee, cream teas, home made cakes and other light refreshments are served in the converted granary adjoining the shop. Ample space and easy parking. Evening demonstrations of corn dolly making are given by arrangement. Contact Mrs Win Gage. Open every day throughout the year from 10-5. Bridge Farm, Monks Eleigh, Suffolk. Tel: (0449) 740456.

NURSEY & SON LTD
The Sheepskin Clothing Specialists

Nursey & Son Ltd
Established 1790. Specialist in Sheepskin and Leather Clothing. Sheepskin Hats, Gloves, Mittens, Moccasins, Rugskins etc. The Factory shop has a good selection especially for Gifts, also a wide variety of sub-standard Products and Oddments. Mon - Fri 9-1, 2-5. Closed 24 July. Reopen 9 August. Access, Visa. 12 Upper Olland St, Bungay. Tel: (0986) 892821

The PARISH LANTERN | **Original Crafts, Gifts, Pictures, and Teas**

on the Village Green at Walberswick

I am sure you will agree that there is something for everyone at the Parish Lantern including delicious light refreshments and a warm and friendly welcome. Before the advent of streetlamps the only light in the village was provided by the moon which was called The Parish Lantern. Walberswick is one of the few villages still using the moon in this way. Open daily, 10-5.30. Friday, Saturday & Sunday only during January, February and March . Tel: Southwold (0502) 723173.

Gifford's Hall
Hartest, near Bury St Edmunds. 33 acre small country living. For full desciption see advertisement on page 10.

Lavenham Taxidermy Studio and Wildlife Park

The Lavenham Taxidermy Studio and Wildlife Park, situated 1 ½ miles south-east of Lavenham at Brent Eleigh, is set in 12 acres of the beautiful Brett valley. See exhibitions of the art of taxidermy and displays of finished work. The Wildlife Park has many animal attractions including falconry displays at the owl and bird of prey centre with eggs hatching most days. Most of the animals are handleable. Take time to visit the deer park or to go on the picturesque river walk, and there is also a shooting range. Cream teas and other refreshments available. There is also a large car park and picnic area. Open all year from 9am to dusk. Admission: adults £3.25 and children £1.75. Telephone Lavenham (0787) 248290. *Opens spring 1993 subject to planning permission.*

HERTFORDSHIRE

WESTON BARNS

Weston Barns
Weston Barns is a craft centre in the middle of the attractive village of Weston in the rural hills of North Hertfordshire. It offers a collection of working crafts including an extensive pottery producing a wide range of stoneware for houses and gardens. Visitors can watch and learn about the various crafts at the centre, buy craft made items in the shop and enjoy morning coffee, lunches and teas in the tearoom. Picnic site available. Ample free parking and free admission. Just two minutes off the A1(M) near Baldock. Open 7 days a week, 10am to 5pm. Closed Christmas and New Year. Telephone (046279) 771.

Suffolk Craft Society exhibition

PEOPLE TO HELP YOU EXPLORE THE AREA

GUIDED TOURS BY REGISTERED BLUE BADGE GUIDES

Each registered Guide has attended a training course sponsored by the East Anglia Tourist Board and can be identified when wearing the "Blue Badge". Regional Blue Badge Guides are further qualified to take individuals or groups around the region for half day, full day or longer tours if required. For a list of these Guides and an information sheet on Guiding Activities, please contact the East Anglia Tourist Board. The 9 towns/cities listed below support registered Guides. *Please contact the Tourist Information Centre (see pages 100-101) in the town/city for further information unless otherwise indicated.*

BURY ST EDMUNDS

Regular Town Tours: Tours lasting 1 1/2 hours leave from the Tourist Information Centre on Tue and Thu afternoons mid May-Sept and also Sunday mornings in July & Aug. Tickets can be purchased in advance, or on the day.

Tours for Groups: Guides can also be arranged for groups at any time. Please give at least one week's notice.

CAMBRIDGE

Regular College Tours: Individual visitors may join tours which leave the Tourist Information Centre daily and up to 5 times a day in summer.

City Centre Tours: These tours do not go into the colleges, but explore the street scenes and the historic past of the city. Evening tours take place during mid summer, including drama tours.

Tours for Groups: Guides are available at any time for private groups. Each tour lasts about 2 hours. One guide can escort up to 20 people. Guides for the whole of East Anglia also available. Tel: (0223) 463290.

College Tours for Groups: All parties of 10 or more who intend to tour the colleges must be accompanied by a Cambridge registered Blue Badge Guide. Please note that most colleges are closed to the public during examination time (May-mid June).

Fitzwilliam Museum, Trumpington Street. Regular tours take place during the summer and last about 1 1/4 hours. Groups may also book tours during museum opening times. Tel: (0223) 332900.

COLCHESTER

Regular Town Tours: Individuals may join the tours leaving the Tourist Information Centre daily during the summer, Mon-Sat 2pm, Sun 11am. The tour takes about 1 3/4 hours and ends at Colchester Castle.

Group Tours: May be booked at any time of year. Please give at least four days notice.

ELY

Cathedral & City Tours: Guides are available for pre-booked groups all year and tours may include the Cathedral and city, or just the city.

Cathedral Only Tours: Groups may book a special guided tour of Ely's magnificent Cathe-

dral. Contact The Chapter Office, Tel: (0353) 667735 Mon-Fri, 9-4.

Regular Tours: Individuals may join these tours on Thu and Sun in Jul and Aug. Tours include the city and either the Cathedral or Oliver Cromwell's House.

Oliver Cromwell's House Tours: available for pre-booked groups all year round. The tour may be combined with a city tour.

Theme Tours: Tours can be arranged on a particular theme as required. For example, local pubs, ghosts, haunted places, the fens drainage story, photographic spots. For pre-booked groups only.

IPSWICH

Regular Town Tours: Individuals may join the tours which leave the Tourist Information Centre, May-Sept, Tue 2.15. Tours take about 1 hour.

Tours for Groups: Tours can be arranged for groups throughout the year. Please give at least one week's notice.

KING'S LYNN

Regular Town Tours: Individuals may join the tours which leave the Tourist Information Centre at 2.00pm Wed & Sat, May-Sept, Sun in Aug and each afternoon during Festival Week. The tour takes about 1 hour.

Group Tours: Guided tours can be arranged for groups by contacting the King's Lynn Town Guides Tel: (0553) 671925, 6-9pm weekdays.

NORWICH

Regular City Tours: Historic Norwich walking tours leave from the Tourist Information Centre, lasting 1 1/2 hours: Easter Sun & Mon, 10.30; Apr & May, Sat 2.30; 24 May-30 Oct, weekday tours 2.30; Jun-end Sept, Sun 10.30. Bank hol tours, 10.30. Guided coach tours of Norwich, Jul & Aug, Mon, also Wed in Aug, at 2pm.

Tours for Groups: Walking tours can be arranged for groups all year on a variety of themes.

Coach Tours for Groups: Guides can be arranged to accompany a day or half day coach tour of East Anglia and Norwich. Assistance with itineraries.

PETERBOROUGH

Group Tours: (min 10) need to pre-book for guided walks. Duration 1 1/2 to 2 hours.

SAFFRON WALDEN, DUNMOW & UTTLESFORD DISTRICT

Guided walking tours of Saffron Walden on Sun 2.30, leaving from outside the Tourist Information Centre. Specialist tours by arrangement. Tel: (0799) 526637.

British Thoroughbred Tours. Professional tours of Newmarket, HQ of racing, organised to suit the individual. Travel in comfort, visit a top trainer's yard, see beautiful racehorses at exercise and watch mares and foals at a nearby stud. Tel: (0638) 660212.

Cambridge and East Anglia Guided Tours - Half, full day or short break tour itineraries. Also specialist tours arranged to order. All tours accompanied by East Anglia Blue Badge Guides. Contact the Tours Organiser, Tourist Information Centre, Wheeler Street, Cambridge CB2 3QB. Tel: (0223) 463290/322640, Fax (0223) 463385.

Cycle Hire Centre. Byways Bicycles has a choice of cycles for hire, to suit all ages. Follow a planned route showing you local places of interest, pubs, tea rooms or picnic places, or choose your own. Cycling holidays also arranged. Byways Bicycles, Darsham, Nr Saxmundham, Suffolk IP17 3QD, Tel: (072877) 764 or 459. Open Easter and May-Oct, 10-6 (at other times by appointment). Closed Tuesdays.

Minsmere Cliffs

Hoofbeats tours of Newmarket, headquarters of British racing. Tours available by arrangement for individuals or groups, of the historic town, gallops, trainers yard, National Stud and other places of interest. Price on application. Ring Jean on (0638) 668455 or write to Hoofbeats, 66 Old Station Road, Newmarket, Suffolk CB8 8AA.

Just Pedalling. Well known for their cycling holidays. Also day or weekly hire of 3 speed and mountain bikes. Conveniently situated in the Broads area where cycling is easy and interesting. Open all year. Contact: Alan Groves, Just Pedalling, 9 Church Street, Coltishall, Norfolk NR12 7DW. Tel: (0603) 737201.

The National Stud, Newmarket. The 75 minute conducted tours will delight all animal lovers. The 8 horse stallion unit and up to 100 mares and foals are included in the visit. The guides give a full insight in to the workings of a modern thoroughbred stud. Open late Mar-Oct. Booking essential Tel: (0638) 663464.

Newmarket Equine Tours/National Horseracing Museum. Tour historic Newmarket with an expert guide. Watch racehorses exercising on the gallops and in the swimming pool. Visit a training yard and stud. Combine old and new at the museum. Booking essential. Charges on request. Tel: (0638) 667333.

Rockingham Forest Tourism - Can help you discover Northamptonshire's countryside. Stately homes, where to stay, leisure drives, list of guides, walks, what's open. Contact them at: c/o Civic Centre, George Street, Corby, Northants NN17 1QB.

Windmill Ways Walking and Cycling Holidays in Norfolk. Leisurely breaks to suit individual tastes. Start and finish when you choose, travel at the pace you wish, complete personal service. Accommodation booked in quality guesthouses and hotels; maps, routes and local information provided; baggage transported; excellent touring, mountain or tandem bikes with back-up service. Colour brochure available. Windmill Ways, 50 Bircham Road, Reepham, Norfolk NR10 4NQ. Tel: (0603) 871111.

FAMILY FUN

ADVENTURE PLAYGROUNDS

Activity World, Longmead, Birchwood, Hatfield, Tel: (0707) 270789: Indoor adventure playground for children under 4ft 9in, covering 6,000 sq feet on three levels. Wide range of play equipment, birthday parties provided. *All year (ex 25 & 26 Dec), daily 10-8. From £1.60.*

ARTIFICIAL SKI SLOPES

Aylsham
Ski Barn, Aylsham, Norfolk, Tel: (0263) 733893. All sessions must be booked in advance. Ski tuition for beginners.

Hemel Hempstead
Hemel Ski Centre, St Albans Hill, Tel: (0442) 213755 for brochure.

Ipswich
Suffolk Ski Centre & Golf Driving Range, Bourne Terrace, Wherstead, Tel: (0473) 602347 for details of opening times.

Norwich
Norfolk Ski Club Ltd, Whitlingham Lane, Trowse, Tel: (0603) 620851 for details and practice times.

ICE SKATING

Chelmsford
Riverside Ice and Leisure Centre, Victoria Road, Tel: (0245) 269417: Ice rink, 3 pools, 6 court sports hall, gymnasium, squash courts, snooker hall and health suite. *Daily (ex 25 Dec), 6.30am-11pm (Fri opens 7.30am).*

Peterborough
Peterborough Ice Rink, Mallard Road, Bretton, Tel: (0733) 260222: Full size ice skating rink offering public skating sessions most days. Ice hockey, speed skating and other ice related activities.

Stevenage
The Ice Bowl, Roaring Meg, London Road, Tel: (0438) 740750: Ice rink, ice hockey, cafe. *All year, daily (ex 25 Dec).*

LEISURE CENTRES

BEDFORDSHIRE
Oasis Beach Pool, Cardington Road, Bedford, Tel: (0234) 272100: Waterslides, fountains, bubble burst, outside river ride, quiet pool, spa baths. Conditioning gym, sauna and sunbeds. *All year.*

ESSEX
Bramston Sports Centre, Bridge Street, Witham, Tel: (0376) 519200/517620: Indoor 25m pool, teaching pool and diving pool, 4 squash courts, multi-purpose sports hall, gymnasium,

conditioning gym, projectile room, sauna and solarium suite, toning table salon, outdoor area with bowling green. Cafeteria and bar. Sports shop. *Reception opening times: Mon-Fri, 9.15am-10.45pm, Sat & Sun, 7.45am-9.45pm. Bank Hols, closes at 5.*

Harlow Pool, First Mandela Avenue, Tel: (0279) 446420: Twin pools, health suite, beauty clinic, dance studio, trimnasium, cafe and creche. *Mon-Wed & Fri 7am-10pm; Thu 7.15am-10pm; Sat & Sun 7-6.*

HERTFORDSHIRE
Lee Valley Leisure Pool, Old Nazeing Road, Broxbourne, Tel: (0992) 446677: Wavemakers, waterslide, fountain, simulated beach and health spa. Cafeteria. Set in a tropical atmosphere. *All year.*

NORFOLK
Great Yarmouth Marina Leisure Centre, Marine Parade, Gt Yarmouth, Tel: (0493) 851521: Leisure pool with waves and aquaslide. Multi sports hall, polygym, table tennis, snooker, pool, squash courts, sauna/solarium, restaurants, bars, children's play area, entertainment, multi-gym and indoor bowls hall. Indoor roller-skating rink. *Daily ex 25 & 26 Dec, 10-10.*

Hunstanton Oasis (Promenade), Tel: (0485) 534227: Exciting family leisure centre on seafront. Indoor and outdoor leisure pools (Easter-Nov), aquaslide, toddler pools, whirlpool spa, soft play area with toddler slides, swings and see-saw, indoor bowls (Sept-Apr), squash courts, cafeteria, bar, sun lounge.

Norwich Sport Village & Broadland Aquapark, Drayton High Road, Hellesdon, Tel: (0603) 788912: Indoor and outdoor tennis, squash, multi sports hall, health & fitness centre including gymnasium, sauna/steam rooms, plunge & spa pool, bars, restaurants and hotel. The Aquapark is a 6 lane, 25m competition pool and has 2 giant water flumes. *Daily, 7am-11pm.*

Sheringham Pool, The Splash, Weybourne Road, Sheringham, Tel: (0263) 825675: Giant waterslide and splash pool, wave pool, childrens paddling pool and walrus slide. Health and fitness club. Ice-cream parlour, poolside bar and fast-food. Shop. *Summer, daily 10-8. Winter, Wed-Sun 12-8.*

SUFFOLK
Bury St Edmunds Sports & Leisure Centre, Beetons Way, Tel: (0284) 753496/7: 33m pool, 20m learner pool, leisure pool with flumes. Sports hall, 2 ancillary halls, 3 squash courts, climbing wall, weight and fitness training, sporturf all weather pitches, saunaworld. Cafe and bar.

Felixstowe Leisure Centre, Undercliff Road West, Tel: (0394) 670411. Features include leisure swimming pool, learner pool, impulse pool, sauna, sunbeds, bowls hall, fully licensed lounges and bars, multi-purpose entertainment and conference hall, amusement area, cafe and refreshment facilities, tourist information centre. *Daily ex 25 Dec & 1 Jan, 7.30am-10pm (24, 26 Dec & 1 Jan, 9-6).*

Crown Pools, Crown Street, Ipswich IP1 3JA. Tel: (0473) 219231. Award winning 3 pool complex, 8-lane 25m competition pool, beach entry free-form leisure pool with wave making machine, waterfall fountains, inflatable slide and teaching pool, surrounded by an oasis of tropical plants. Full theatrical lighting system. Bar, restaurant and cafeteria. *Open Mon-Fri, 7.15am-9.10pm. Sat-Sun 7.45am-4.55pm.*

Kingfisher Leisure Pool, Sudbury, Friars Meadow, Tel: (0787) 75656. Leisure pool including 25m pool, 55m flume ride, wave machine, water cannon, health suite and gymnasium.

ROLLER SKATING

Bury St Edmunds
Rollerbury, Station Hill, Tel: (0284) 701216: Roller-skating, skating lessons, cafe and bar. *Tues-Sun.*

Skating at Rollerworld, Colchester

Colchester
Rollerworld, Eastgates, Tel: (0206) 868868: Great Britain's largest roller-skating rink, 25m x 50m maple floor. Roller hire, roller cafe, roller bar. Sound and lightshow. Quasar at Rollerworld -serious fun with a laser gun. *All year, ex 25 Dec. Tel for session times and prices.*

Southend-on-Sea
Roller City, Aviation Way, Tel: (0702) 546344: Roller rink, skate hire, shop, snacks available. *Fri-Sun.*

Welwyn Garden City
Roller City, The Campus, Campus West: Roller rink, skate hire, snacks available. *All year, Wed-Sun.*

BIG FUN. BIGGER VALUE.

In East Anglia, **big** means Pleasurewood Hills. Acre upon acre of big rides, shows and attractions - more than 50, in fact, including **the spectacular Wild Water Falls log flume**. Not to mention the Big Top of our new Superhuman Circus Show,

mounds of big American food - and Woody, the biggest-hearted bear this side of the Rockies.

But biggest of all is the sheer value of a family day out at Pleasurewood Hills. Because once you're in, it's **all** in*. You only pay once and all the main rides, shows and attractions are **FREE** - as many times as you like! And you'll get a voucher to come back at a huge discount. How's that for value?

To find out more about your Big Day, call us right away on **0502 508200**.

RIDES OPEN: 10am-5pm or 6pm According to season	
APRIL	9 to 18 April (Easter) 24/25 April
MAY TO SEPTEMBER	1 to 3 May (Bank Holiday) 8/9 May DAILY: 15 May to 19 September 25/26 September
OCTOBER	2/3 October

*Excluding coin-operated amusements

Please mention East Anglia Guide when replying to advertisements

Breathtaking ride at Great Yarmouth Pleasure Beach

SEASIDE FUN

ESSEX

Clacton

Clacton Pier: 23 rides, including rides suitable for young children. 2 acres under cover. British marine life aquarium and sea-lion show. Gift shops, cafes, side shows and attractions. Roller rink, pub and night club. *All year. Pier rides 1 Mar-30 May, weekends plus school hols. 30 May-30 Sept, daily. Weekends in Oct. Option to pay one price or individual ride tickets.*

Southend-on-Sea

Never Never Land, Western Esplanade near Southend Pier: Set in two acres of magical illusionary scenery, Never Never Land is a unique and original children's adventure park where fantasy becomes living, animated reality with many fairytale features and special effects, including the familar stories of Jack and the Beanstalk, Merlin the Magician, fairy castles and futuristic themes such as "Masters of the Universe", Badger's house from "Wind in the Willows", "Snow White's Cottage" and the "Old Woman who Lived in a Shoe". *Easter-end Oct, Sat, Sun & all local school holidays; 11-10 (Good Fri opens 4.30). £1.40/90p/90p.*

Peter Pan's Playground, Sunken Gardens West. Right on the seafront: Over 20 rides and attractions including Roller coaster, big wheel etc. Souvenir shop. *Jan, Feb, Mar & Nov, weekends. Easter-end Sept, daily. 10-10 (until dusk in winter). School half terms open daily. All times are weather permitting.*

Southend-on-Sea Pier, Western Esplanade: Take a train ride or walk the Pier, approx 1 1/3 miles long. Pier Museum at the North Station. Amusements, shop, restaurant at South Station. Also guided tours of lifeboat house. *Daily, ex 25 Dec. Admission charge for train and walkway.*

Ten Pin Bowling, Pavilion Lanes, The Pier. Tel: (0702) 463081 for reservations. Fun for everyone. Amusement area, licensed bar, fast food service. *Open daily, 10am-midnight.*

NORFOLK

Great Yarmouth

Great Yarmouth Pleasure Beach: Over 70 combined rides, sideshows and attractions. Restaurant and fast food outlets. *Mar-May, Sun & Bank Hol 1-6. 22 May-19 Sept, daily. 1-6 (11-10 high season).*

House of Wax, 18 Regent Street: Waxworks exhibition, torture chambers, chamber of horrors, hall of funny mirrors and family amusement arcade. *Open Apr-Oct, daily, 10.30-7.30, £1.50*

World of Wax, Regent Road/Marine Parade: Waxworks include Fairyland, horrors, crown jewels, pop stars and royalty. *Easter-end Sept, 9am-10pm. Mar, Oct, weekends and school hols, inc Christmas (ex 25 Dec), 11-5. £1.90/£1/£1.*

Merrivale Model Village, Marine Parade: Over 200 models in an acre of landscaped gardens. *Easter-31 Oct, daily 9.30-6 (opens 10am Easter-Jun). £2.50/£1.20/£2.*

Ripley's Believe It or Not, The Windmill, Marine Parade: A weird and wonderful collection of oddities. Interactive displays, illusions, videos and special effects. *1 Apr-31 Oct, daily. £2.99/£1.99/£2.20.*

Treasure World, Marine Parade: Museum of diving, treasure and the history of diving. Restaurant and shop. *All year, daily 10-dusk. Tel to check (0493) 330444. Adm charge.*

SUFFOLK

Felixstowe

Charles Mannings Amusement Park, Sea Road: Traditional amusement park with numerous rides and attractions featuring "The Log Splash", dodgems, waltzer, crazy house etc and including "Tenderfoot Territory" for the younger adventurer. Amusement arcade, bingo, cafes and kiosks. *Arcade: all year, daily ex 25-26 Dec. Rides: Easter-end Sept, weekends and school hols, Mon-Sat 1-9.30, Sun & Bank Hols 11.30-9. (Times vary with the season).*

THEME PARKS

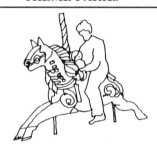

Pleasurewood Hills American Theme Park, Lowestoft: Take a holiday in East Anglia and you will be ideally placed for a visit to one of Britain's major Theme Parks. Offering hours of American-style magic every day in summer, you pay only once and then everything's free. Everything you climb and ride on, all the hairy scarey rides and all the shows – as many times as you like. And there are over 50 to choose from! Definitely 'YOUR BIGGEST DAY OUT EVER'. *9-18, 24-25 Apr; 1-3, 8-9 May; daily from 15 May-19 Sept; 25-26 Sept; 2-3 Oct. 10-5 or 6 depending on season. £8.50/children under 4 free.*

WATERSPORTS

CAMBRIDGESHIRE

Tallington Windsurfing Club, Tallington Lakes Leisure Park, Tallington, nr Stamford, Lincs. Waterbase Tel: (0778) 346342. Waterski and jetski Tel: (0778) 347000. Dry ski slope Tel: (0778) 344990. Windsurf, canoe and dinghy hire Tel: (0788) 380002.

ESSEX

Bradwell Field Studies and Sailing Centre, Bradwell Waterside, nr Southminster, Tel: (0621) 776256. Offshore cruising, dinghy sailing, canoeing, windsurfing. RYA Centre. Apr-Oct.

Channels Windsurfing, Mountain Bike and Canoe Centre, Belstead Farm Lane, Little Waltham, Chelmsford, Tel: (0245) 441000. Also at 42 The Ridgeway, Westcliff-on-Sea, Tel: (0702) 713389.

Chalkwell Windsurfing Club, Chalkwell Beach, Leigh-on-Sea, Tel: (0702) 79896. Car parking, toilets. Tuition can be arranged. Regular racing.

Gosfield Lake & Leisure Park, Church Road, Gosfield, Halstead, Tel: (0787) 475043: Water skiing and speed boat rides. Pitch 'n' Putt, fishing, restaurant and snack bar. *Apr-Sept, daily.*

Southend Marine Activities Centre, Eastern Esplanade, Southend, Tel: (0702) 612770. Tuition in sailing, canoeing, windsurfing and power boat driving during evenings, weekends and school holidays.

NORFOLK

Surf 55, 55 St James's Street, King's Lynn, Tel: (0553) 764356. Waterbase: Leziate Park, Brow of the Hill, Leziate, King's Lynn. Windsurf, mountain bike and kite centre.

SUFFOLK

Windsurfing Seasports, The Beach, Sea Road, Felixstowe, Tel: (0394) 284504. Car park, club, changing facilities, toilets, comprehensive rescue facilities. Shop, hire, tuition.

Alton Water Sports Centre, Alton Water, Stutton, Ipswich, Tel: (0473) 328408: Windsurfing, sailing and canoeing. Tuition and equipment hire. Cafeteria, chandlery, changing facilities, toilets.

Suffolk Water Park, Bramford, Ipswich, Tel: (0473) 830191 : Windsurfing and canoe hire, tuition, sales, changing rooms, snack bar, licensed bar.

Windsurfing at Alton Water

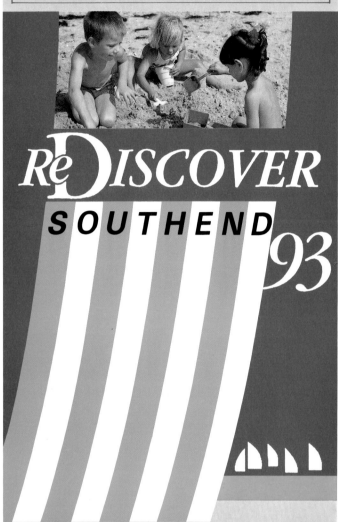

BESIDE THE SEASIDE

ALDEBURGH

The wide High Street, with its cottages and shops, runs north-south just a stone's throw from the shingle beach where the lifeboat is always ready. Fishermen draw up their boats on to the beach and sell their fish. The Moot Hall, the Tudor centre of the town, stands exposed only yards from the sea, which over the centuries has whittled away the shoreline. Benjamin Britten and Peter Pears began the Aldeburgh Festival in 1948 and it has developed into a year-round programme of music and arts, shared between Aldeburgh and Snape Maltings concert hall. The Aldeburgh Festival is in June, the Maltings Proms in August. Thorpeness village, a seaside village created in 1910 is just two miles up the coast. *TIC.*

BRIGHTLINGSEA

Once an important fishing town, Brightlingsea is now a yachting centre with one of the best stretches of sailing on the East Coast. Superb walks along the banks of Brightlingsea Creek and the River Colne offer the naturalist a chance to study birdlife on the saltings. *Holiday guide to the Essex Sunshine Coast from Council Offices (EDU), Thorpe Road, Weeley, Clacton-on-Sea, Essex, CO16 9AJ. Tel: (0255) 256161.*

CLACTON-ON-SEA

Clacton-on-Sea's south facing seven mile long sandy beach forms the sunshine holiday coast of Essex. It is a strikingly clean town with tree-lined streets and colourful gardens. An everyday holiday programme of entertainments, events, leisure centre, sports and recreation, also coastal trips and coach excursions, is planned to provide a variety of interests to suit most tastes. The town is an ideal centre for visiting a number of historic houses and castles. The beach has gently sloping sand. The Princes Theatre and West Cliff Theatre, pier, and various amusement centres provide a wide range of exciting attractions. *TIC. Holiday guide to the Essex Sunshine Coast*

from Council Offices (EDU), Thorpe Road, Weeley, Clacton-on-Sea, CO16 9AJ. Tel: (0255) 256161.

CROMER

Dominated by its parish church the town of Cromer stands in a cliff top setting, with wide sandy beaches running down to the sea. It is famous for its fishing boats that still work off the beach and offer freshly caught crabs. The town boasts a fine pier theatre, museums and lifeboat station along with the usual seaside attractions. A week not to be missed is carnival week held in August. *TIC. For a free guide write to Coast and Countryside, Dept EG93, Brochure Despatch Centre, Mackintosh Road, Rackheath Industrial Estate, Norwich, Norfolk, NR13 6LH. Tel: (0603) 721717 (24 hours).*

FELIXSTOWE

Felixstowe is a popular resort town between the estuaries of the rivers Deben and Orwell in a sheltered position on the Suffolk coast. It is popular as a family resort with a playground, boating lake, model yacht pond, miniature railway, amusement park and the beach itself which is safe at all states of the tide and is a mixture of sand and shingle. The Spa Pavilion Theatre presents a lively and wide-ranging programme of entertainment throughout the year and the Leisure Centre has three swimming pools and a sauna, fitness area and lounge bars. Felixstowe is justly proud of its cliff gardens which provide a floral welcome all year. The resort is an ideal centre from which to tour the lovely and historic Suffolk countryside. Sea and river cruises, and ferries across the River Orwell to Harwich. Events: May Folk Festival, Championship Driving Tests, Drama Festival; July High Season Entertainment at Spa Pavilion begins, East of England Lawn Tennis Championships, Deben Week Regatta; Aug Felixstowe Carnival; Nov Fishing Festivals. *Guided tours in season. TIC.*

FRINTON-ON-SEA AND WALTON-ON-THE NAZE

Frinton, sited on a long stretch of sandy beach, is quiet, secluded and unspoilt. Its main shopping street has been named the "Bond Street of East Anglia". Summer theatre and other open-air events take place during the season. A variety of attractive hotels and guest houses face the magnificent greensward on the clifftop. Frinton also has excellent golf and tennis clubs. Walton is more fun of the fair. It is a jolly, quaint little resort which focuses on the pier with all its attractions. The sea front has good sand and to the rear of Walton are the Backwaters, a series of saltings and little harbours leading into Harwich harbour. New indoor swimming pool on the seafront. *TIC. Holiday guide to the Essex Sunshine Coast from Council Offices (EDU), Thorpe Road, Weeley, Clacton-on-Sea, CO16 9AJ. Tel: (0255) 256161.*

GREAT YARMOUTH

Is one of Britain's most popular seaside resorts with wide sandy beaches and the impressive Marine Parade which has colourful gardens and almost every imaginable holiday attraction and amenity. The award-winning multi-million pound leisure complex, the Marina Centre, offers a huge variety of all-weather sports and entertainment facilities, including a swimming pool with waves! Gorleston has a wide promenade lined with flower gardens and old streets dating from the days when it was an important sea port. The sandy beaches outside the town are unspoilt. Great Yarmouth is also an interesting historical centre, sections of the old walls remain and there are numerous museums and other places of historic interest to be explored. Boating: Yacht Station and Port of Yarmouth Marina; day cruises to the Broads, Broads sailing and day boats for hire. Entertainment: Huge variety at various theatres and venues including Britannia Theatre (Tel: 0493 842209), early July-mid Sept. Summer season top star live show. Gorleston

Pavilion (Tel: 0493 622832) early June-end Sept. Summer show. Hippodrome (Tel: 0493 844172), early July-Sept. Circus with water spectacle, Oct-May, occasional concerts, etc. Wellington Pier Theatre (Tel: 0493 843635 or 842244), early June-mid Sept, various summer shows and concerts. Winter Garden (Tel: 0493 844945), early June-late Sept, variety family entertainment all day. Royalty Theatre (Tel: (0493) 842043), early July-mid Sept, summer show or latest film presentations. St Georges Theatre (Tel: (0493) 858387) June-Sept, summer show; remainder of year, concerts, recitals, plays etc. Marina Centre Piazza (Tel: 0493 851521) entertainment nightly, late June-late Sept. Also horse racing and numerous other holiday attractions including 'Kingdom of the Sea' Sealife Centre, Ripley's 'Believe it or Not' exhibition, 'Treasure World' underseas exhibition and a huge Pleasurebeach with all the latest rides. *Full details of all facilities and accommodation included in Holiday Guide available from TIC, price 50p (in advance by post, free).*

HUNSTANTON

Hunstanton possesses two quite distinct physical features: it is famous for its striped cliffs, made of successive layers of carr stone, red chalk and white chalk; and unlike any other resort in East Anglia, the town faces west. Winner of the Tidy Britain Group Seaside Award for cleanliness of beach and water. Hunstanton's wide sandy beaches are excellent for bathing, and it is also popular with boating, windsurfing and water-skiing enthusiasts. Hotels and guest houses are bounded to the south by well laid out caravan sites and holiday centres and to the north, cliffs slope away to the dunes and quiet sandy beaches. The focal point of the town is the large, open greensward known as "The Green", and there are the lovely Esplanade Gardens sloping gently down to the sea. The Oasis all weather leisure centre, Princess Theatre and the Kingdom of the Sea are favourite attractions for visitors. *Free brochure from TIC.*

LOWESTOFT AND OULTON BROAD

Lowestoft successfully combines its role as a leading holiday resort with that of a modern fishing and commercial port. Lowestoft South Beach and North Beach are winners of the Tidy Britain Group Seaside Award for cleanliness of beach and water. Oulton Broad, one of the finest stretches of inland water in England, offers the chance to get afloat in a range of craft from modern cruiser or day boat to sailing dinghy or rowing boat. Add to the natural amenities such facilities as theatre, seafront indoor Tourist Complex, indoor and outdoor swimming pools, attractive parks, putting and bowling greens, tennis courts, boating lakes, sports centre, American theme park, museums, high speed motor boat racing, and concerts, naturist beach, and you have the making of an ideal family holiday. The staff of the tourist information centre on the seafront will do all they can to make your stay a happy one. They will offer help in

finding accommodation, and suggest things to do and places to visit, and arrange a tour of the fishing industry or book a theatre seat. Lowestoft and Oulton Broad is a fine holiday centre where a warm welcome is assured. *TIC. Free Waveney Guide available from Room 2, District Technical & Leisure Services Dept, Mariners Street, Lowestoft NR32 1JT. Tel: (0502) 565989 (answerphone).*

SHERINGHAM

Sheringham is a mixture of Victorian and Edwardian houses which has grown up around its fishing traditions. The original village is still the haunt of seafarers who carry on the brave tradition of manning the lifeboat. Sandy beaches and a range of amusements and activities are to be found in and around Sheringham. Attractions include the North Norfolk Steam Railway, museums, theatre and the Splash Fun Pool. *TIC. For a free guide write to Coast and Countryside, Dept EG93, Brochure Despatch Centre, Unit 28, Mackintosh Road, Rackheath Industrial Estate, Norwich, Norfolk, NR12 6LH. Tel: (0603) 721717 (24 hours).*

SOUTHEND-ON-SEA

Southend-on-Sea invites you to spend a family day beside the sea. This major resort can offer all the traditional fun of the seaside and all the excitement of many special events. Seven miles

of coastline from East Beach to the the fishing village of Old Leigh, popular for waterside pubs, fresh seafood stalls, Art Gallery and Heritage Centre, it has a unique atmosphere of its own. A visit to the town must include the world famous pier, over 100 years old, a mile and a quarter of bracing fresh air. For the less energetic a ride on the pier train can be an enjoyable experience. Shopping has now become a very important part of seaside life, with the excellent High Street shops, boutiques and street markets. Relax for a while in one of the many parks and gardens and enjoy a stroll along the Cliff Gardens. Many special events throughout the year including Air Show, Barge Race, Open Air Concerts. Opening for the '93 season - Sealife Centre, Victorian Pavilion on the pier for family entertainment, and the completely refurbished Cliffs Pavilion. Free guide and events list with all the details of what's on. *TIC. Contact the Marketing Department, E.A. PO Box 6, Southend-on-Sea, SS2 6ER. Tel: (0702) 355118.*

SOUTHWOLD

Southwold is an elegant and attractive town standing on the cliff top facing the sea, with its mixture of sand and shingle beach. Winner of Tidy Britain Group Seaside award for cleanliness of beach and water. Fishermen's cottages, pleasant old streets and green open spaces give it much character. Discreetly fashionable as a Victorian bathing place, there is still an atmosphere of old-fashioned charm. Trade with northern Europe has left its mark on many buildings in Southwold, which show a marked Dutch influence, although the battle of Sole Bay between the Dutch and English fleets was just off the coast here (and commemorated in the local brewery's Broadside Ale). *TIC. Free Waveney Guide available from Room 2, District Technical & Leisure Services Dept, Mariners Street, Lowestoft, Tel: (0502) 565989 (answerphone).*

WELLS-NEXT-THE-SEA

A small but busy port for coasters and the local whelk and shrimp boats. Wells is a town of narrow streets and flint cottages with interesting shops and two narrow gauge railways. Sandy beaches, nature reserves and miles of footpaths make Wells-next-the-Sea an ideal holiday town. Winner of the Tidy Britain Group Seaside Award for cleanliness of beach and water. *TIC. For a free guide write to Coast and Countryside, Dept EG93, Brochure Despatch Centre, Mackintosh Road, Rackheath Industrial Estate, Norwich, Norfolk, NR13 6LH. Tel: (0603) 721717 (24 hours).*

YOUR 1993 GOOD BEACH GUIDE

On the north Norfolk coast there are wonderfully big beaches where the sea goes out for miles and where it is possible to get away from everything. On the East Coast beaches tend to be narrower, and shelve steeply. Suffolk beaches are always safer and more attractive at low tide when there is normally a strip of clean sand and the beaches shelve less steeply. (Tide tables can always be found in the East Anglian Daily Times.) At Hunstanton the high tide comes right up to the promenade as it does at Clacton, ensuring a clean beach but restricted space as high water approaches. Beware undercurrents particularly where beaches shelve steeply, and remember that the current flows south on the flood and north on the ebb and can run quite strongly, especially when the wind is in the same direction. Although East Anglia has more sunshine than most parts of the country there can be onshore easterly winds so a windbreak can be useful. Groynes constructed to stop erosion also make useful shade and shelter for picnics. Beware of strong offshore winds; these take effect 50 to 100 metres from the beach, air beds and small inflatables are very vulnerable.

Fishing boats at Old Leigh, near Southend

NORFOLK

1 Hunstanton (see p 77)

Winner of the Tidy Britain Group Seaside Award (Resort Beach category). Sandy beaches make an ideal playground for children, whilst windsurfers find the Wash an excellent location for their sport. To the north there are red and white cliffs and then sand dunes and a quieter beach at Old Hunstanton. The beach is very gently shelving and when the tide goes out it makes a pleasant walk for a swim. Deck-chairs. Pony rides. Pitch and putt and crazy golf courses. Specially designed route for wheelchairs along the seafront. Car parking. Toilets. TIC.

2 Holme-next-Sea

A long unspoilt sandy beach with a wild area of dunes and marshes at Gore Point. Nearby 400-acre nature reserve. Approached via Holme village (approx 2 miles). Car parking. Toilets.

3 Brancaster

Very quiet broad sandy beach with dunes. Approached by lane leading north from the village. The tide retreats for more than a mile to the east, but not so far to the west. Car parking. Toilets.

4 Holkham

A huge private sheltered sandy beach with dunes backed by pine trees. A favourite spot for picnics and swimming. The tide goes out for miles. Car parking along Lady Anne's Drive on payment of fee in summer, but free in winter.

5 Wells-next-the-Sea (see p77)

The wide spacious beach is a mile from the town, and is reached across dunes, or by the narrow gauge railway. Consisting of sand and shingle, the beach has a large boating lake known as Abraham's Bosom and pine trees on one side with the harbour channel on the other side. Winner of the Tidy Britain Group Seaside Award (Rural Beach category). Car parking. Toilets. Wells is famous for its cockles, whelks and shrimps. TIC.

6 Sheringham (see p 77)

A beach of sloping pebbles and shingle above sand. Rocks and groynes with shallow pools at low tide. Low cliffs. Fishing boats are hauled up on the beach. Amusements and refreshments. Deck-chairs. Car parking. Toilets. TIC.

7 East Runton & West Runton

Gently shelving sand and shingle beaches backed by low crumbling cliffs. Groynes. Rocky at low tide. Car park. Toilets.

8 Cromer (see p 75)

Gently shelving sandy beach with shingle and pebbles, the west beach is more shingly than the east one. Shallow pools at low tide. Cliffs. Pier with entertainment. Famous lifeboat. Crab fishing. Deck-chairs. Car parking. Toilets. TIC.

9 Overstrand

Gently shelving sandy beach with pedestrian access. Groynes, pleasant cliff-top walks. Small car park. Toilets.

10 Mundesley

Quiet holiday resort built in a dip in the coast line. Cliff path access to a smooth sandy beach between groynes. Deck-chairs. Car parking. Toilets. TIC.

11 Winterton-on-Sea

Very wide sandy beach backed by extensive sand dunes. Pools at low tide. Nature reserve. Car park. Toilets. TIP.

12 Hemsby

Wide sandy beach scattered with stones and backed by grassy dunes. Amusements and deck-chairs. Boat trips. Car parking. Toilets. TIP.

13 Scratby/California

Low cliffs and long track down to wide sandy beach. Shallow pools at low tide. Amusements on cliff top at California. Car park at Scratby. Toilets. TIP.

14 Caister-on-Sea

Wide sandy beach which shelves steeply in some places. At the north end, towards California, there are low sandy cliffs. Low sea wall with dunes behind. Boat trips. Volunteer Lifeboat Station. Deckchairs. Car parking on Beach Road (central beach). Toilets. Picnic area. TIP.

15 Great Yarmouth (see p 75)

Very long sandy beach lined by the Marine Parade with its colourful gardens and countless attractions and amenities. Dog ban between Wellington and Britannia Piers from 1 May to 30 Sept. Two piers with entertainment. Dunes at North beach. Boat trips, trampolines, and numerous refreshment stalls. Marina Centre. Deckchairs. Beach huts and tents. Car parking. Toilets. TICs.

Mundesley beach

16 Gorleston

Quieter than nearby Great Yarmouth. Flat sandy beach with some pebbles. Dog ban on northern section from ravine to harbour. Pier, forming part of harbour entrance. Amusements. Low cliffs between sea wall and promenade. Beach chalets. Deck-chairs. Car parking. Toilets. TIP.

17 Hopton

Flat sandy beach with some shingle beneath low cliffs. TIP.

SUFFOLK

18 Corton

Sand and shingle beach, with southern area available to naturists. Car parking in official car park. Water meets EEC standards.

19 Lowestoft (see p77)

South Beach is the sandy pleasure beach with two piers. It has been awarded the Tidy Britain Group Seaside Award (Resort Beach category). Punch and Judy. Deck-chairs. Amusements. Ness Point is Britain's most easterly point. The North Beach, also winner of the Tidy Britain Group Seaside Award (Rural Beach category), is somewhat quieter and sandy with cliffs and sand dunes. Car parking. Toilets. TIC.

20 Pakefield

Sandy beach scattered with shingle below low grassy cliffs. Car parking. Toilets.

21 Kessingland

Easy access to pebble and shingle beach with some sand. Low cliffs. River. Suffolk Wildlife & Country Park nearby. Winner of the Tidy Britain Group Premier Seaside Award (Rural Beach category).

22 Southwold (see p 75)

Part sand, part shingle beach depending upon tides, with some dunes for sheltered picnics. Uncommercialised, but pots of tea are available on the beach. Short pier with amusements and refreshments. Deck-chairs and beach huts. Parking. Toilets. TIC. Winner of the Tidy Britain Group Seaside Award (Rural Beach category).

23 Walberswick

Approached over The Flats, the beach is sand and shingle with sand dunes. It becomes steeper and more shingly to the south with some pebbles. Popular with painters and birdwatchers. Stall selling fish on beach. Winner of the Tidy Britain Group Premier Seaside Award (Rural Beach category). Car parking. Toilets.

24 Dunwich

Short walk to shelving sand and shingle beach above sand. High eroding cliffs should be avoided. There is marsh, dunes and more sand to the north. Nature reserve at nearby Dunwich Heath. Occasional underwater exploration of old submerged town destroyed by storms – they say you can hear the church bells from beneath the waves! Car parking. Toilets.

25 Thorpeness

Steeply shelving shingle beach with some sand at low tide. Dunes and low cliffs starting to the north. Curious holiday resort developed in early 1900s with varied architectural styles. Car parking limited. Toilets.

26 Aldeburgh (see p 75)

Quiet unspoilt resort. Long steeply shelving shingle beach with groynes. Lifeboat. Fishing boats hauled up, with stalls selling fresh fish daily. Car parking. Toilets. TIC.

27 Shingle Street

As its name suggests, a steep shingle beach particularly good for bracing walks and beach-combing (sometimes you can find amber). Popular for offshore fishing. Very limited car park.

28 Felixstowe (see p 75)

Popular south-east facing holiday resort with Leisure Centre (three swimming pools), seafront gardens, pier, museum, amusements and entertainment. Shelving sand and shingle beach with little tidal movement. Some groynes down to pebbles and sand. Low cliffs to the north. Deck-chairs and beach huts. Car parking. Two-mile long promenade with public seating. Toilets. TIC.

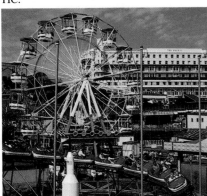

Southend on Sea

ESSEX

29 Walton-on-Naze (see p 75)

Traditional resort with a gently shelving sandy beach. Groynes, cliffs and dunes at The Naze a grassy area on low cliffs giving excellent views of the busy shipping lanes around Harwich and Felixstowe. Nature trail. Pier and groynes. Donkey rides, deck-chairs. Speedboat trips. Putting and tennis. Refreshment kiosks at regular intervals along the seafront. Car parking. Toilets. TIC.

30 Frinton-on-Sea (see p 75)

Wide expanse of greensward on top of low cliffs above a wide gently shelving sandy beach. A first-class golf course plus excellent cricket, tennis and squash facilities. A resort of peace and tranquility. Deck-chairs. Toilets. Car parking.

31 Holland-on-Sea

Good sandy beaches which are usually quieter and less crowded than nearby Clacton. Groynes. Deck-chairs. Adjoining is the Holland Haven Country Park. Car parking. Toilets.

32 Clacton-on-Sea (see p 75)

Gently sloping long sandy beach. Amusements and entertainments. Pier featuring spectacular rides, roller skating rink, living ocean, fourth dimension and night spot. Magic City the latest childrens fun filled attraction. Leisure centre and children's adventure world. Pavilion Entertainment Centre. Deck-chairs. Car parking. Toilets. TICs.

33 Southend-on-Sea (see p 77)

Seven miles of sea and foreshore with sand and shingle beach. Expanse of seaside provides walks, traditional seaside entertainment, boat trips, water sports. Longest pleasure pier in the world with pier trains, Peter Pan's Adventure playground, Never Never Land Fantasy Park, colour illuminations. Popular beaches include East beach at Shoeburyness which has recieved a Seaside Award from the Tidy Britain Group (Rural Beach category). This stretch of the coast has a wide expanse of grass, as well as a shingle beach ideal for young children to play. Additional beaches include Three Shells Beach (valeted daily), Thorpe Bay and Chalkwell. Look out for the colourful information boards on the seafront keeping you up to date on the bathing water quality. Restaurants, refreshment kiosks, archway cafes, deckchairs, boat trips, car parking, toilets, TIC.

TIC=Tourist Information Centre
TIP=Tourist Information Point

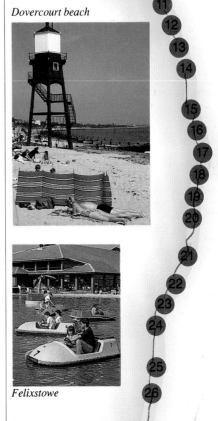

Dovercourt beach

Felixstowe

SEASIDE AWARD FLAG

Look out for the blue and yellow Seaside Award Flag. Wherever you see it you can be assured that both the beach and bathing water meet certain standards. The beach must be free of litter, industrial waste, sewage related debris, oil pollution and large accumulations of rotting seaweed. The water quality must meet the mandatory standard of the EC Bathing Water Directive, and a Seaside Award pale blue and yellow flag confirms this.

The water must be sampled and tested at least 20 times a year. Your peace of mind is guaranteed because if any of these criteria lapse, the flag must come down until the problem is solved.

Seaside Award Beaches in East Anglia include Hunstanton, Lowestoft North and South beaches, Snettisham, Wells next the Sea, Kessingland, Southwold, Walberswick, and Shoeburyness (Southend).

BOAT HIRE

CRUISER HIRE

Blakes Holidays Ltd, Wroxham, Norwich: Cruisers, yachts and houseboats on the Norfolk Broads. Narrowboats on the Cambridgeshire waterways. Choose from a wide selection of types from 2-12 berth. Tel: (0603) 782911 (instant bookings/general enquiries). East Anglian Cottages Tel: (0603) 783221. Free colour brochure Tel: (0603) 782141 or 783226 (Recorded message).

Broads Tours Ltd, Tel: (0603) 782207. Broads cruiser hire and self drive day boats. *Daily, Apr-Nov.*

Harbour Cruisers, Riverside, Brundall, Norfolk, Tel: (0603) 712146: Motor cruisers, craft launching facilities and repair facilities.

Horning Pleasurecraft Ltd, Ferry View Estate, Horning, Norwich, Tel: (0692) 630366/630128. Self drive holiday cruisers 2-10 berths available.

Hoseasons Holidays Ltd, B13, Sunway House, Lowestoft, Suffolk: Norfolk Broads & Cambridgeshire, motor cruisers and houseboats. Instant bookings, Tel: (0502) 501010. Free colour brochure, Tel: (0502) 501501.

Moore & Co, Hotel Wroxham car park, Tel: (0603) 783051: All weather diesel self-drive day launches and luxury motor cruisers. Other facilities include self-catering riverside properties, moorings and indoor swimming pool. Boat building and repairs.

Richardsons Boating Holidays, The Staithe, Stalham, Tel: (0692) 581081: Cruisers on the Broads. 2-10 berth boats for hire, weeks/part weeks.

Stalham Yacht Services Ltd, The Staithe, Stalham, Tel: (0692) 580288: Motor cruisers, launches, houseboats, canoes for hire 1 Mar-1 Nov. Cottage for hire all year.

Two Tee's Boat Yard, 70 Water Street, Chesterton, Cambridge, Tel: (0223) 65597. Cruisers on the Cambridgeshire waterways incorporating the Fens. Weekly and part week hire. *Apr-Nov.*

Westover Boat Company Ltd, PO Box 43, Hemingford Grey, Huntingdon, Tel: (0860) 516343. Week long cruises in 2 barges on River Ouse. Full board and excursions to places of interest are provided.

NARROWBOAT HIRE

Blackwater Boats, Croft End, Bures, Suffolk, Tel: (0787) 227823: 4 berth steel narrowboats on the Chelmer and Blackwater Canal for short breaks or longer holidays. Luxurious self-drive boats or skippered cruises by arrangement.

Lee Valley Boat Centre, Old Nazeing Road, Broxbourne, Herts, Tel: (0992) 462085: 6 berth narrowboats for weekly or 3 day hire.

DAY BOAT HIRE

CAMBRIDGESHIRE

Cambridge
Scudamores Boatyards, Mill Lane, Granta Place, Tel: (0223) 359750: Punts and rowing boats for hire on "the backs" and River Granta.

Tyrrell's Marine Ltd, 23-27 Bermuda Road, Tel: (0223) 352847/63080: Boat, engine, chandlery sales. Punts, rowing boats, canoes. Hire at Quay Side, Magdalene Street.

Huntingdon
Huntingdon Marine & Leisure Ltd, Bridge Boatyard, Tel: (0480) 413517. Day boat hire. Boat engine, chandlery & inflatable sales.

Purvis Marine Boatyard, Hartford Road, Tel: (0480) 453628. Canoes, row boats, motor launches and day boats.

ESSEX

Dedham
D. E. Smeeth, The Boatyard, Mill Lane, Tel: (0206) 861748: Rowing boats and canoes. Evening bookings for parties. Teas, ices, snacks etc.

Mersea Island
Eastcoaster Sailing, 5, Prince Albert Road, Tel: (0206) 382545: Specialises in sailing holidays, sail training, charter and can also offer a unique day's sailing for business entertaining.

HERTFORDSHIRE

Lee Valley Boat Centre, Old Nazeing Road, Broxbourne, Tel: (0992) 462085: Rowing boats and motor boats for hourly hire. Electric 8 person day boats for 1 or 1/2 day hire. 6 berth narrowboats for weekly or 3 day hire.

NORFOLK

Acle
Anchor Craft, Acle Bridge, Tel: (0493) 750500: Day launches, cruisers and riverside bungalows.

Denver
Daymond Services, "Frojo" Fleet of Hire Craft, Frojo Fleet Quay, Denver Sluice, Tel: (0366) 383618 (24 hr answering service) 384404 (Quay heading). For rowing boats, 6 person day cabin launch, 10 person day boat, 4/5 berth family, weekly and weekend hire craft. *All year.*

Hickling
Whispering Reeds Boatyard, Tel: (069 261) 314: Rowing boats, sailing boats, motor launches, cruisers, houseboats for hire. Slipway facilities available. *All year, daily.*

Horning
Ferry Boatyard Ltd, Ferry Road, Tel: (0692) 630392: Selection of waterside properties with moorings. Cruisers and day launches. Modern workshop facilities with electric hoist, boat sales and marina moorings. *All Year.*

Norwich
Highcraft, Griffin Lane, Thorpe St Andrew, Tel: (0603) 701701. Motor cabin cruisers, day and picnic boats.

Potter Heigham
Maycraft Ltd, River Bank, Tel: (0692) 670241: 30 motor launches, row dinghies, half-decker sailing boat, 4 cruisers 2 to 5 berth.

Wroxham
Faircraft Loynes, The Bridge, Tel: (0603) 782280: 32 all-weather cabin-type day launches. Hire cruisers available for weekly cruises. Passenger boats make regular trips to visit various

'Arcturus' Day Cruises

Broads. Special facilities on certain boats to accommodate wheelchairs.

Moore & Co, Tel: (0603) 783311: 2-9 berth modern motor cruisers and self drive day launches.

SUFFOLK

Brandon
Bridge House, Tel: (0842) 813137: Rowing boats and canoes. *All year, daily.*

Bungay
Outney Meadow Caravan Park, Tel: (0986) 892338: Rowing boats, skiffs and canoes. Hourly or daily hire.

Lowestoft
Waveney River Tours Ltd, Mutford Lock, Bridge Road, Oulton Broad, Tel: (0502) 574903: Inboard motor launches. *Easter-end Sept.*

REGULAR EXCURSIONS

ESSEX

Harwich
Orwell & Harwich Navigation Co Ltd, The Quay, Tel: (0255) 502004: Pleasure steamer M/S Brightlingsea carrying up to 150. Morning and afternoon cruises with commentary on Rivers Stour and Orwell, and Harwich Harbour. Cruises, discos, folk nights. Booking advisable. Also 12-seater covered launch available for hire. Ferry service to Felixstowe.

Maldon
Ostrea-Rose, Tel: (0245) 261362. Traditional charter day trips and cruises from Maldon on the River Blackwater's last commercial oyster smack, now fitted out to a high Edwardian yacht standard. Also Gaff Rig tutorial.

Southend-on-Sea
Pleasure cruises from Southend Pier including regular service on M V Clyde from Southend to Rochester. Special paddle steamer trips on P S Waverley and Kingswear Castle. *For details contact the TIC.*

HERTFORDSHIRE

Sawbridgeworth
Adventuress Cruises, Unit X, The Maltings, Station Road, Tel: (0279) 600848. "Adventuress" offers scheduled passenger trips and hosts outings and various functions on the Essex/Herts border. Full catering and bar service available. *Charter all year, public trips Easter-Sept.*

Watford
'Arcturus' Day Cruises, Cassio Wharf, Tel: (043 871) 4528: Famous Star Class, wooden boat built 1934. Public trips from Ironbridge Lock in Cassiobury Park. *Easter-Oct, Sun & Bank Hol 2.30-4; also Tue & Thu in Aug 2-3.30.*

NORFOLK

Burnham Overy Staithe
William Scoles, The Old Rectory, Gt Snoring, Fakenham, Tel: (0328) 820597: Trips to Scolt Head Bird Sanctuary and Overy Beach.

Horning
Mississippi River Boats, The Little House, Irstead, Tel: (0692) 630262: 1-2hr Broadland trips on 100-seater double-decked Mississippi paddle boat. Bar, meals for up to 80 by arrangement. *Easter-end Sept. Apr-May party bookings only.*

Norwich
Southern River Steamers, Elm Hill & Thorpe station, Tel: (0603) 501220: Two river boats seating 84 & 92 for 1 1/2 and 3 hour Broadland river cruises and city cruises. Also available for private hire to groups.

Hunstanton
Searle's Hire Boats, South Beach Road, Tel: (0485) 534211: July-Sept: Motor launch carrying up to 60. Cruises to Seal Island viewing the seals of the Wash. Also 1/2 hour coastal cruises. Fishing trips. Speedboat rides. Located opposite Sea Life Centre.

Potter Heigham
Stalham Water Tours, 28 St. Nicholas Way, Tel: (0692) 670530 answerphone: All weather luxury cruiser for 1-2 1/2 hour Broads cruises. Light refreshments. Departs Richardson's Boatyard, Stalham. Visit to How Hill Gardens, *Mon-Fri & Sun afternoons.*

Wroxham
Broads Tours Ltd, Tel: (0603) 782207: 1 1/4, 1 1/2, 2 and 3 1/2 hour Broadland tours in all-weather motor launch. Largest boat takes 170. *10 May-26 Sept, daily.*

Harwich/Felixstowe passenger ferry

SUFFOLK

Orford
Lady Florence, 50 ft motor vessel cruising rivers Alde and Ore. Maximum 12 passengers. Special days for individuals. Food and Bar. Daily. For booking and details Tel: (0394) 450210, 9.30-5.30.

Oulton Broad
Waveney River Tours Ltd, Mutford Lock, Bridge Road, Tel: (0502) 574903: "Waveney Princess", with licensed bar, up to 125 passengers. "Enchantress", up to 92 passengers. Light refreshments. Broads trips. *Easter, end May-end Sept.*

Snape
Snape Maltings, Tel: (072888) 303: One hour trip on the River Alde aboard Edward Alan John, a covered boat carrying up to 70 passengers or Lady Moyra an open launch carrying up to 35 passengers. Departure times dependent on tides. Reduction for children (must be supervised). Bookings for groups. Details on request.

Sudbury
Stour Steam Navigation, The Granary, Quay Basin, Sudbury: "Firebird" is a traditional steam launch and can carry up to 12 passengers. *Easter-end Sept, Sun 2-5.30, 1/2 hr trips. Private hire at other times, Tel: (0787) 310018.*

Waldringfield
Waldringfield Boat Yard, cruises on River Deben, morning, afternoon and evenings. Reservations must be made. Tel: (047 366) 260

BOAT HIRE FOR GROUPS

ESSEX

Chelmsford
Chelmer & Blackwater Navigation Ltd, Paper Mill Lock, Little Baddow, Tel: (0245) 225520: Modern pleasure barge, with bar and refreshments. Charter by groups of up to 48. Individual trips Sun and Mon of Bank Hol weekends. *Apr-Oct.*

Maldon
Anglian Yacht Services, The Hythe, Maldon, Tel: (0621) 852290: Thames sailing barge "Reminder" for individuals or for groups of up to 12.

HERTFORDSHIRE

Leighton Buzzard
Leighton Lady Cruises, Bramptoms Wharf, Tel: (0525) 384563: 70 foot narrow boat. Heated passenger saloon with cushioned seats, seating up to 54. Cream teas and buffet available on request. Tel for public trips list. *All year.*

NORFOLK

Norwich
Norfolk Wherry Trust, 14 Mount Pleasant, Tel: (0603) 505815: The Trust owns "Albion" which may be chartered for up to 12 people. Membership available with special members' cruises.

Wherry Yacht Charter, Barton House, Hartwell Road, The Avenue, Tel: (0603) 782470: Broadland cruising on historic wherry yachts "Olive" and "Norada", and pleasure "Hathor". For groups of up to 12 on each.

SUFFOLK

Ipswich
P & Q Saling Centre & Holiday Charter, Deer Park Lodge, Mannings Lane, Woolverstone, Tel: (0473) 780293: Two cruising yachts for parties of up to 5 per yacht, Also sailing tuition. *Apr-Oct.*

The river Deben runs through 10 miles of lovely wooded countryside from its estuary at Felixstowe Ferry. Cruises start from Waldringfield to Felixstowe or Waldringfield to Woodbridge. The MV Jahan is licensed to carry 54 passengers (up to 12 disabled in wheelchairs) with toilet, bar and galley for meals & snacks. Cruises for individual groups: mornings 11.00, afternoons 2.30, evenings 6.30 or by special arrangements.

Waldringfield Boatyard Ltd. The Quay, WALDRINGFIELD, Woodbridge, Suffolk IP12 4QZ Telephone: Waldringfield 047336 260

BY APPOINTMENT ONLY

SNAPE MALTINGS

Riverside Centre for Arts & Activities

This remarkable collection of old maltings buildings is set on the banks of the River Alde. Many interesting shops, galleries and restaurants offer quality products and fresh home cooked food. There is a programme of painting and craft weekends, river trips in summer and unusual self-catering accommodation.
OPEN ALL YEAR, EVERY DAY, 10-6 (5 in winter)
Snape Maltings, nr Saxmundham, Suffolk IP17 1SR
Tel: (0728) 688303/5

Snape Maltings Concert Hall

Home of year-round programme of events, including Aldeburgh Festival (11-27 June 1993), Snape Proms (1-31 August), Britten Festival (October), Easter, Christmas and New Year.
Also Britten-Pears School for Advanced Musical Studies (public master classes February - October). Guided tours for groups by arrangement.
Tel: (0728) 452935, Box Office (0728) 453543

Please mention East Anglia Guide when replying to advertisements

EVENTS

SHOWS AND DISPLAYS

4-7 Feb	Springfields Horticultural Exhibition, Spalding, Lincs
20 Mar	National Shire Horse Show, East of England Showground, Peterborough
14 Mar	Dolls Fair Woburn Abbey, Beds
3-4 Apr	Thriplow Daffodil Weekend, Thriplow, Cambs
1 May	Spalding Flower Parade 92, Spalding, Lincs
1-3 May	Spring Craft Show Woburn Abbey, Beds
1-3 May	Tudor May Day Celebrations Kentwell Hall, Long Melford Suffolk
3 May	Ickwell May Day Festival, Ickwell Green, near Biggleswade, Beds
6-9 May	Living Crafts Working Exhibition Hatfield House, Herts
8 May	South Suffolk Show, Ingham, Bury St. Edmunds, Suffolk
15 May	Hadleigh Agricultural Show, Hadleigh, Suffolk
15-16 May	Fighter Meet Air Show, North Weald Airfield, Essex
21-23 May	Rickmansworth Canal Festival Rickmansworth, Herts
29-30 May	Air Fete '93, RAF Mildenhall, Suffolk
29-30 May	Hertfordshire County Show, The Showground, Redbourne, Herts
29-31 May	East Anglian Home and Garden Festival, Rowley Mill Racecourse, Newmarket
30-31 May	Southend-on-Sea Airshow, Southend-on-Sea, Essex.
2-3 June	Suffolk Show, Suffolk Showground, Ipswich, Suffolk
12-13 June	East Anglian Daily Times Country Fair, Melford Hall, Long Melford, Suffolk
18-20 June	Essex County Show Essex County Showground
19-20 June	Great Amwell Steam Rally, Ware, Herts
20 June-18 July	Historical Re-Creation of Tudor Life, Kentwell Hall, Long Melford, Suffolk - Sat, Sun & 16 Jul
19 June	Flitwick Carnival, Flitwick, Beds
26 June	The Bentley Drivers' Club Concours, Hatfield House, Herts
30 June-1 July	Royal Norfolk Show, The Showground, Norwich
3-4 July	Duxford's Classic Fighter Display, Duxford Airfield, Cambs
3-10 July	Ware Week, Ware, Herts
7-10 July	Rose Fair, Wisbech, Cambs
10 July	Tendring Hundred Show Manningtree, Essex

10-11 July	Wings n Wheels Spectacular, North Weald Airfield, Epping, Essex
10-11 July	South Bedfordshire Show, Toddington, Beds
20-22 July	East of England Show, East of England Showground, Peterborough
28 July	Sandringham Flower Show, Sandringham House, Norfolk
14-21 Aug	Southend-on-Sea Carnival, Southend-on-Sea, Essex

Flower Festival, Southend-on-Sea

21-22 Aug	Southend Show and Flower Festival, Priory Park, Southend-on-Sea, Essex
28-30 Aug	National Waterways Festival 1993, Peterborough, Cambs
30 Aug	Aylsham Show, Blickling Park, Blickling, Norfolk
2-5 Sept	Burghley Horse Trials, Burghley Park, Lincs
5 Sept	Luton and Dunstable Countryside Day, Beds
18-19 Sep	Roxton Traction Engine Rally, Roxton, Beds

MUSICAL EVENTS

3-14 Mar	Norfolk County Music Festival, Norwich, Norfolk
1-22 May	Beccles Festival, Beccles, Suffolk
15-22 May	Chelmsford Cathedral Festival, Chelmsford, Essex
11-27 June	46th Aldeburgh Festival of Music and the Arts 1993, Snape Maltings (and other venues), Suffolk

2-10 July	Peterborough Cathedral Festival, Peterborough
2-11 July	Cambridge Festival, Cambridge
7-17 July	International Organ Festival, St Albans Cathedral, Herts
17-31 July	King's Lynn Festival, King's Lynn, Norfolk
30 July-1 Aug	Cambridge Folk Festival, Cherry Hinton Hall Gardens, Cambridge
1-31 Aug	Snape Proms, Snape Maltings, Snape, Aldeburgh, Suffolk
7-8 Aug	Southend Jazz Festival, Southend-on-Sea, Essex
7-17 Oct	Norfolk and Norwich Festival, Norwich, Norfolk

EAST ANGLIA CUSTOMS

8-10 Jan	Whittlesey Straw Bear Festival, Whittlesey, Cambs
3 May	Stilton Cheese Rolling, Stilton, Cambs

HORSE RACING

Racing at Newmarket	*Tel (0638) 663482*
Racing at Fakenham	*Tel (0328) 862388*
Racing at Great Yarmouth	*Tel (0493) 842527*
Racing at Huntingdon	*Tel (0480) 453373*

This is just a selection of events in the region. Please contact the East Anglia Tourist Board Tel: (0473) 822922 for details of these and other events.

AFTERNOON TEAS

What can be more tempting then a traditional English cream tea? You can be sure of a delicious selection of home made goodies at any of the following tea rooms, so forget about your waist line, and treat yourself!

To help you find the tearooms nearest to you we have marked the locations with a teacup symbol on the maps on pages 108-111. Establishments which are members of the Tourist Board have a * after the text.

CAMBRIDGESHIRE

ELY
Steeplegate Ltd
16/18 High Street.
Tel: Ely 664731
Proprietor: Mr J S Ambrose
Seats: 40
Open: Daily except Sunday
Home-made cakes, scones and fresh cream teas served in historic building backing onto cathedral. Medieval vault on view. Craft goods also sold. Small groups welcome.*

ST IVES
The Cafe Upstairs
Crown Place (situated beside Woolworths)
Tel: 0480 494214
Proprietor: Mrs S Summerside
Seats: 34
Open: Monday-Saturday from 10.00, Sunday afternoon (Jun-Sep)
Morning coffee, wide range of homemade light hot and cold meals, sandwiches, homemade cakes and scones served all day. Ice-creams a speciality. Large no smoking area. Young children welcome! Parties, especially for cream teas, welcome by prior appointment. *

ESSEX

DEDHAM
The Essex Rose Tea House
Royal Square. *Tel: Colchester 323101*
Proprietors: Mr and Mrs Bower and Mandy
Seats: 80
Open: Daily
This pretty pink-washed 15c teahouse in the heart of Constable country serves morning coffee, salad lunches and sandwiches and of course traditional cream teas and special gateaux. Also a large selection of craft goods, paintings, homemade chocs and fudge.

THAXTED
The Cake Table Tea Room
4/5 Fishmarket Street, Thaxted
Tel: (0371) 831206
Proprietor: Mrs K M Albon
Seats: 30 inside plus extra 10 on patio
Open: Mon-Fri 11-5, Sat and Sun 11-5.30
The Cake Table Tearoom lies in the heart of this very pretty town, between its splendid old church and the recently restored John Webb's windmill. Winner of the Tea Council's Top Tea Place of the Year Award 1991, the tearoom has an old world charm rarely found today and is famous for its freshly baked cakes and scones.*

NORFOLK

BANHAM
Pantiles Bistro
The Appleyard, Banham, Near Attleborough
Tel: (095 387) 709
Seats: 35 + Courtyard seating (weather permitting)
Open: All year (except 25 & 26 Dec)
The beautifully restored timber framed barn and surrounding farm buildings provide an ideal setting for afternoon tea in a courtyard of crafts. Freshly baked cakes and pastries from the adjoining bakery, fresh milk and cream from a local farm, friendly service and free parking. Groups welcome by prior arrangement.*

ERPINGHAM
Alby Crafts-Barn Buttery
Cromer Road (on A140).
Seats: 60
Open: 14 March-19 December, daily except Mondays, 10-5.
Licensed Barn Buttery, situated in the centre of a working Craft Centre   serving real coffee, speciality teas, home made lunches, vegetarian specialities, cream teas and cakes. Coaches by appt. only.*

GREAT BIRCHAM
Great Bircham Windmill
Nr King's Lynn. *Tel: (048523) 393*
Proprietors: Mr and Mrs Wagg
Seats: 45
Open: Easter-20 May, Sun, Wed, and Bank Hol Mon, 20 May-30 Sept, daily (ex Sat), 10-6.
Tea rooms adjacent to the windmill. Cream teas, homemade cakes, free car park.*

HEACHAM
Norfolk Lavender Ltd
Caley Mill, Heacham.
Tel: Heacham (0485) 71965/70384
Seats: 38
Open: Daily, 10-5. Closed for Christmas holiday.
Average price: £1.65
Cakes and scones home-made, cream teas a speciality. Tea room in old millers cottage in the middle of lavender/herb gardens.*

Corncraft tea room at Monks Eleigh

The tea room at Butley Pottery

HORSHAM ST FAITHS
Elm Farm Chalet Hotel (Off A140 Cromer Road)
Nr Norwich. *Tel: Norwich 898366*
Proprietor: W. R. Parker
Open: All year, Monday-Saturday, 10-5
Situated in centre of picturesque village. Home-made cakes, scones, cream teas, fruit and cream served in garden or lounge. Light lunches. Parties welcome by prior appt.*

NORWICH
The Sue Ryder Coffee Room
St Michael-at-Plea Church, Redwell St
Tel: (0603) 666930
Seats: 55
Open: 9.30-4.30, Monday-Saturday
Light refreshments: cakes and pastries home-made. Coach parties welcome by appointment please write to the Manageress at the above address for details.

Norwich Cathedral Visitors Centre and Buffet
62 The Close, Norwich NR1 1EH
Tel: Norwich 626290
Seats: 68
Open: Monday-Saturday, 10.30-4.30
Refreshments served in an ancient room above the Cloisters, one of the earliest parts of the former monastery. Locally-baked cakes and scones; delicious light lunches, sandwiches etc. Tea, coffee, soft drinks. Open air terrace in summer months.

OVERSTRAND
The Pleasaunce
Overstrand, near Cromer
Tel: (026378) 212
Open: 3 May-28 Oct, Mon, Wed and Thu, 2-4.
Other times by appointment.
Ground floor of house designed by Luytens and gardens laid out by Gertrude Jekyll open to visitors. Admission includes cream tea.

SHERINGHAM WOODS
Pretty Corner Restaurant and Buttery with Tea and Coffee Gardens
Nr Pretty Corner Main Car Park, A148
Tel: Sheringham (0263) 822358
Open: All year, from 10.00 am
Buttery and Restaurant in creatively laid out Gardens with split-level and sheltered terraces. Home-made Dutch, Indonesian and English specialities, lunches and evening meals.*

THURSFORD
The Thursford Collection
Thursford, Fakenham,
Tel: (0328) 878477
Proprietor: Mr J. Cushing
Seats: 70 inside, 120 outside.
Admission: £4.20/£1.80/£3.30('92 prices)

Afternoon cream teas on the lawn served from our Garden Conservatory. Teas and light refreshments also served in our "Barn". Seats 70.*

WALSINGHAM
Sue Ryder Coffee Room and Retreat House
The Martyrs House, High St. *Tel: 032-872 622*
Seats: 35
Open: All year, 9-5.30.

Light refreshments: cakes and pastries home-made. Coach parties welcome by appointment. Bed & Breakfast accommodation available with evening meal if required.

SUFFOLK

ALDRINGHAM
Aldringham Craft Market, Aldringham, nr Aldeburgh.
Tel: Leiston (0728) 830397
Contact: Selina Huddle
Seats: Inside: 6, Outside: 30
Open: Spring-late Autumn, Mon-Sat 10-5.30, Sun, 10-12, 2-5.30.

Home-made cakes, scones, fresh coffee, etc, offered in our Coffee Shop. Adjacent lawn, climbing frame, etc, provides ideal venue for family break when visiting our extensive arts, crafts and gifts Gallery. Easy car parking.*

BRUISYARD
Vineyard and Herb Centre Restaurant
West of Saxmundham. *Tel: (072875) 281*
Seats: Inside: 25, Outside: 24
Open: 2nd January-24th December, daily 10.30-4.30

Morning coffees, light lunches, afternoon teas. Homemade cakes and scones, herbal and speciality teas. Winery tours and tastings, herb and water gardens. Vineyard shop with wines, vines, herbs, crafts and gifts.*

BURY ST EDMUNDS
The Angel Hotel
Angel Hill. *Tel: (0284) 753926*
Afternoon tea served daily, 3.30pm-5.30pm
Seats: 30
After soaking up the heritage and atmosphere of the historic town of Bury St Edmunds, enjoy traditional afternoon tea in comfortable, relaxing and historic surroundings of the Angel Hotel.*

BUTLEY
Butley Pottery and Tea Room
Mill Lane, Butley, Woodbridge
Tel: (0394) 450785
Seats: 30 plus outside
Open: Apr-Dec, daily; Jan-March, weekends only, 10.30-5.00
A selection of tasty lunches with salad; home made cakes and scones; tea and coffee. Served in the relaxed atmosphere of the renovated thatched barn in peaceful rural surroundings. Live music on most Sunday lunchtimes. Turn off the B1084 in Butley down Mill Lane. Evening parties can be catered for by appointment.

CAVENDISH
The Sue Ryder Coffee Room and Museum
High St,
Tel: 0787 280252
Seats: 110
Admission to museum: 80p/40p
Open: Daily, closed Christmas Day, 10-5.30.
Lunches and light refreshments: cakes and pastries home-made. Gift shop.

FELIXSTOWE
Ferry Cafe
Felixstowe Ferry
Tel: (0394) 276305
Proprietor: Laura Balsom
Seats: 48
Open: All year, 7 days a week

Teas with home made scones, cakes and pies, served in unique setting alongside mouth of River Deben with extensive fishing and boating activities. Also golf course nearby. Early breakfasts, superb fish and chips, and light meals all day. Parties catered for with free parking.

GREAT BARTON
Craft at the Suffolk Barn
Fornham Road, Great Barton, Bury St Edmunds.
Tel: Great Barton (028 487) 317
Proprietor: Margaret Ellis
Open: Mid March-Christmas, Wed, Thur, Fri 10-5.30, Sunday 12-5.30

Tea room housed in traditional renovated old Suffolk barn. Wide range of home cooking. Indian, Earl Grey or herbal teas. Light lunches. Local crafts, country books, plants and wild flowers for sale. Herb, wild flower garden and ornamental garden. Children welcome and coach parties by prior arrangement.*

HARTEST
Gifford's Hall
Hartest, on B1066, south of Bury St Edmunds.
Proprietors: The Kemp family
Seats: Indoors: 40, Outside: 50
Open: Easter-31 October
Cream teas and delicious homemade cakes are served in the delightful converted stable block which adjoins the farm shop of this 33 acre small country living. Visitors can also explore the smallholding, vineyard and winery. Coaches welcome by appointment.*

HELMINGHAM
Helmingham Hall
between Ipswich and Debenham on B1077
Tel: Helmingham 890363
Owner: Lord Tollemache
Open: 2 May-12 Sept, Suns only 2-6
Admission: £2.20/£1.20/£2.00

Home made cakes and scones served in the old Coach House or outside in the courtyard, make a welcome end to a visit to the gardens at Helmingham Hall.

KERSEY
The Bell Inn
The Street, Kersey, Nr Hadleigh, IP7 6DY
Tel: (0473) 823229
Open: Oct-Mar; weekends 2.30-5 & weekends by pre-booking only. Apr-Sept; daily 2.30-5.
Traditional cream and afternoon teas served between 2.30 and 5pm. Fresh cream only is used. Assam, Earl Grey, Darjeeling and traditional "3 star" tea. Parking for 50 vehicles. Groups over 10 please book in advance. Seats 80.*

LAVENHAM
Tickle Manor Tea Room
17 High St.
Tel: (0787) 248216
Proprietors: Mrs M Hartshorn
Seats: 35
Open for morning coffee, light lunch and afternoon tea, until 5.30pm. Home made cakes and scones with fresh cream from a local Jersey herd, served in a beautiful 16th century timber framed tea room in the centre of this famous medieval village. Speciality cakes include Sticky Toffee Pudding, Suffolk Honey Cake and Hot Chocolate Fudge Cake. Families, parties & bookings welcome. Licensed.

The Vestry Tea Rooms
The Centre, High Street, Lavenham.
Tel: (0787) 247 548
Proprietor: Mr K Morgan
Seats: 40
Open: All year, daily 10.30-5.30
This cosy tea room is set in a converted Victorian chapel which is now a shopping centre. Morning coffee, snacks, afternoon teas, home made cakes. Hot meals are available all day. Coach parties and groups welcome, by appointment if possible.

LONG MELFORD
Kentwell Hall
Lunches & Teas available to the public when visiting the Hall
Tel: Sudbury (0787) 310207
Owners: Mr and Mrs J P M Phillips
Seats: Old Kitchen 45, Undercroft 120

Home-made lunches plus cakes, scones and biscuits. Pre-booked coach parties welcome.
For admission prices and opening details please refer to Historic Houses entry.

MONKS ELEIGH
Corn-Craft
Bridge Farm, Monks Eleigh, Nr Lavenham
Tel: (0449) 740456
Seats: 40 inside, 30 outside
Open: All year, daily, 10-5
Corn-Craft serves morning coffee, cream teas, delicious home-made cakes and other light refreshments in a converted granary, beautifully set amongst farm buildings adjoining the craft shop. Ample parking. Coach parties welcome by appt. *For details of the craft shop refer to entry in Crafts section.*

ORFORD
The Old Warehouse
Quay Street. *Tel: Orford (0394) 450210*
Owners: Jean Bostock & Charles Jackson
Open: Easter-October, Mon-Sun; November-Easter, weekends.
Teas, coffees, home baked cakes and scones, full and varied lunch menu including local fish dishes, vegetarian meals and traditional Sunday roast. Terrace with superb views over Orford Ness. Full restaurant licence. Permanent art gallery, gift shop and yacht chandlers.*

STONHAM PARVA
Whistling Mouse Crafts & Tea Room
Norwich Road , Stonham Parva, Stowmarket
Tel: (0449) 711000
Proprietor: Cora Pullen
Open: All year, Wed-Sun & Bank Hols 10-5.30
Seats: 24 + 10 on patio
On the A140 at Little Stonham (near Magpie Inn) the Tea Room serves home made cakes and scones, coffee, assorted teas and locally made dairy ice cream. It adjoins the well stocked craft shop with ample parking next to house.

THORPENESS
Gallery Coffee Shop
Barn Hall. *Tel: Aldeburgh (0728) 453105*
Proprietors: Mr and Mrs J Strowger
Seats: 60 inside, 100 outside
Open: All year, 9.30-6

A licensed restaurant situated next to beach with pleasant garden overlooking boating lake. Specialising in cream teas, gateaux and ice cream desserts, with extensive craft and gift shop. Coach parties welcome by appointment.

WALBERSWICK
Mary's
The Street. *Tel: Southwold 723243*
Proprietors: Rob & Felicity Jelliff
Seats: 45
Open: April-October, daily (ex for Mondays, other than Bank Holidays. Open Mondays in August); November-March, Fri, Sat and Sun.

Morning coffee, lunch, afternoon and high teas, dinner Friday and Saturday. Home-made cakes and cream teas a speciality, served in the garden in fine weather. Parties welcome by appt. and lunch/dinner reservations advisable.

The Parish Lantern
on the Village Green
Tel: Southwold (0502) 723173
Proprietors: Mary Allen and Sarah Bellina
Open: Daily, April to December . January to March, Friday, Saturday and Sunday only.

Visit our tea room and garden where you can enjoy morning coffee, light refreshments, cream teas and home baked cakes. Also original crafts, gifts and pictures. We serve all day. You will be very welcome.*

THE SIGN OF REAL ALE

THE SIGN OF QUALITY
ELGOOD'S
The classical Georgian Brewery on Wisbech's famed North Brink was built in the 1790's on the riverside site of an "Oyl" Mill and Granary. Elgood's first brew was mashed in 1878 and since those early days Elgoods have brewed fine traditional ales for their houses throughout the Fens ... and for discerning free houses over an increasingly wide area. Most pubs will give you the choice of the full range of products – Elgood's Cambridge Bitter, Greyhound Strong Bitter, Fenman Special and Elgood's Mellow Mild. Elgoods also produce 3 bottled beers – Pale Ale, Russet Ale and Brown Ale. Brown LA, launched in 1989 and "Highway" Low Alcohol Bitter winner of the Food From Britain award in 1986. Elgoods have also won many international awards: Gold medal for Mellow Mild, Silver medal for Russet Ale, and the Power for Efficiency and Productivity for power saving technology used in the production of Elgood's low alcohol beers. Elgood's the only brewery in Cambridgeshire is still keenly independent and produces all its beers using the finest natural ingredients and ensuring the highest standards of excellence. Elgood's leading the way in bringing the art of Brewing into the 1990's.

STARSTON FAYRE

CRANES WATERING FARM SHOP
Starston, Norfolk. Home of Starston Fayre Farm Fresh Dairy Ice Cream made here on the farm from the milk of our own Jersey and Guernsey cows. Creams, cheeses and other dairy products are also made here, and we stock our own dairy fed pork and lots of other local produce such as jams, pies, cakes etc. Customers are welcome to picnic on the farmhouse lawn and stroll around the farm- maps available free from the shop. Open Tues-Fri 9-5.30, Sat 9-5 and Sun 9.30-12.30. Open all day Sun and Mon during June, July and August. On the road between Dickleburgh and Harleston. Tel (0379) 852387

Please mention East Anglia Guide when replying to advertisements

LOCAL - PRODUCE

CONGHAM HALL HERB GARDENS
Grimston, King's Lynn
At Congham Hall, one of East Anglia's highest rated Country House Hotels, the proprietors have created a unique Potager and Herb Garden which features around two hundred different herbs. The Potager is a vegetable garden based on XVII Century design and this supplies specialist vegetables and salads to the hotel kitchen who also make great use of the abundant supply of fresh herbs. Tours of the Gardens including a lunch based on the use of herbs and a talk by Mrs Forecast the proprietor and the Hotel Chef can be arranged. Gardens are open to the public April-October 2-4 daily except Sats. Regret no facilities for coaches. Please telephone Mrs C Forecast on Hillington (0485) 600250.

GIFFORD'S HALL

'A SMALL COUNTRY LIVING'
HARTEST • SUFFOLK

GIFFORD'S HALL, Hartest, on B1066 south of Bury St Edmunds – a small country living with 12 acres of vines and a winery producing delicious white and rosé wines, as well as country wines to traditional recipes. Vegetables are also produced in the organic vegetable gardens, free range eggs, honey and cut flowers. Home made cream teas and cakes are available in the converted stable adjoining the farm shop. Visitors are welcome between noon and 6, seven days a week from Easter-31 October and can explore the 33 acre smallholding, visit the winery and enjoy a free wine tasting. Groups welcome by appointment either daytime or evenings.

CHILFORD HUNDRED VINEYARD
Not just a vineyard, more a wealth of interest for all the family: art gallery with prints and sculpture; banqueting halls; farm and industrial artefacts; children's play area; picnic space and of course, the county's largest vineyard and winery, all in fascinating buildings featuring ornamental stonework from historic structures. Vineyard shop. Tour the winery and taste the wine. Visitors welcome 11-5, from 1 May-end Oct; also group visits arranged throughout the year. Take A11/A604 and follow Chilford Hall Vineyard signs from Linton to Chilford Hundred Vineyard, Balsham Road, Linton, Cambridge CB1 6LE. Tel: (0223) 892641

ILETT FARMS DAIRY PRODUCE
At Debach House we pride ourselves on our luxury Real Dairy Ice Creams made from our herd's own milk and using only natural ingredients. A selection of our flavours: Vanilla, Chocolate, Honey and Ginger, Marsala Rum & Raisin, Summer Pudding and Christmas Pudding. We also produce a range of pure fruit sorbets and low fat frozen yoghurts. The Farm & Shop are situated on the B1078 between Wickham Mkt. and Clopton at Debach. Visitors are always welcome and groups can be shown around the plant by arrangement. To assist with transport of our products we can also supply insulated containers to ensure they arrive home in perfect condition. We have mobile kiosks to book for your summer events and fetes. Open 7 days a week, 11-6. Telephone Simon Ilett on Charsfield 260. Fax: 0473 37755.

PULHAM VINEYARDS, PRODUCERS OF MAGDALEN FINE ENGLISH WINE
Pulham Vineyards are part of a wine making tradition that has featured in England's history since Roman times. Since then, much research has gone into identifying the best grape for our unpredictable climate, and Muller Thurgau and Auxerrois vines have produced award-winning vintages of Pulham's Magdalen wines. For an insight into the art and science of modern English wine making, visit Pulham Vineyards. You can explore the vineyard, winery, cellars and bottling plant in the company of an expert guide who'll introduce you to some of the secrets of the wine maker's art, and to the Magdalen wines themselves. Pulham Vineyards, Mill Lane, Pulham Market, Diss, Norfolk Tel: (0379) 676672 office, (0379) 676342 private. Tour charge £2.50 per person. Open daily except Mondays, strictly by appointment only.

DOWNFIELD WINDMILL
The mill dates from 1720, producing wholemeal, Brown 80%, Oatmeal, Rye, Barley and Maizemeal, and is one of the few windmills that produces flour all year. It has 3 pairs of millstones, 2 wind driven and one power driven. A dresser to sieve the wholemeal to make Brown Flour. The millstones are 4 feet to 4ft 6 ins diameter and driven slowly to avoid heat damage to the flour's nutritional benefits. Quality not quantity is our aim. The flours produced are sold at the mill and through shops. It is open to the public every Sunday 11-5. Downfield Windmill, Fordham Road, Soham, Cambs. Tel: Ely 720333 or 0533 707625

BRUISYARD VINEYARD & HERB CENTRE
10-acre vineyard and winery producing the estate-bottled Bruisyard St Peter wine, situated near Saxmundham. Wines, vines, herbs, souvenirs etc for sale. Open 2nd January to 24th December, daily, 10.30-5. Conducted tours. Parties of 20 or more by appointment. Large herb and water gardens, shop, restaurant, children's play area and picnic area. Free wine tasting for vineyard and winery visitors. Bruisyard Wines, Church Road, Bruisyard, Saxmundham, Suffolk IP17 2EF. Tel: Badingham (072875) 281

Please mention East Anglia Guide when replying to advertisements

RESTAURANTS

Editor, Ruth Watson, owner of Fox & Goose at Fressingfield.

Red herrings might not have been seen for years, and Suffolk cheese has always been regarded as a joke - Stilton was sold in Cambridgeshire, not made there - but East Anglians need feel no shame. Countless other glorious food stuffs are grown, caught, reared or produced in this fertile region.

With a long coast line that starts near Kings Lynn, bulges lavishly around Norfolk and Suffolk and finishes at Southend on Sea in Essex, fish and shellfish have always been a notable part of the East Anglian diet. Quotas may have brought anguish to the east coast fishing industry, but North Sea herring are still cured in Lowestoft to provide kippers, buckling and bloaters, and family-owned boats such as the Pinneys' in Orford, bring small catches of beautiful turbot, skate, cod and sole home each day.

As for shellfish, molluscs and the like, shifting sands might suspend the cockle harvest in Hunstanton from time to time, and Bonamia might have wrought devastating damage on the native oyster, but Cromer is still famous for its crabs, Leigh on Sea for its brown shrimps, Southwold to Felixstowe for divine, juicy lobsters, and Portuguese and Pacific oysters have taken quite happily to the beds left vacant in Colchester, Brancaster and Butley by their ill-fated brethren. Their flavour may not be quite as fine, but they do have one important advantage for the gastronome - they are available all year round - so no more having to remember where the R's occur in the calendar.

From the north Norfolk beaches too, comes a bright green, fern-like plant called samphire. Gathered in the late summer months, and tasting faintly of asparagus, it is best eaten lightly steamed with butter, and fittingly it makes a marvellous accompaniment to fish dishes.

Since the 17th century, Suffolk and Norfolk have been famous for rearing turkeys, geese and ducks. Huge droves of turkeys used to be driven via Colchester to London, from as far away as the Fens to the north or Ipswich to the east. Buttons of Redgrave continue to rear legions of Aylesbury ducks, and no one can be ignorant of the "bootiful" company which sells turkey in every conceivable guise. But for a really old-fashioned turkey, with an almost gamey flavour, try a bronze turkey reared and hung for a goodly time by Mr Munton of Boxted near Colchester.

Consumption of goose has certainly diminished over the years, but Norfolk Geese of Pulham Market amongst others, continue to produce fine birds. For an occasional treat, the goose's unhealthy fattiness should be overlooked and the wonderful richness of its meat relished to the full.

Suffolk, and Norfolk particularly, have also long been synonymous with game shooting, and despite the deleterious effect that modern agricultural methods have had on much wild life, there is still no shortage of pheasant and partridge in the autumn and winter months. Butchers have to be licensed to sell game, but most small towns boast at least one dealer, and at R T Harvey of Norwich it can be difficult to see inside the shop for the serried rows of feathered and furry bodies in the window.

Venison, perhaps more readily associated with Scotland than Suffolk, is now farmed widely, and one of the best producers of this healthy-for-humans meat, is the Denham Estate near Bury St Edmunds. The flavour of farmed deer may be a little less intense than wild deer, but a much tenderer texture seems to be a fair exchange.

After the Agricultural Revolution, with its links to Norfolk in the persons of Coke of Holkham and "Turnip" Townshend of Raynham, and to Suffolk by Arthur Young of Bradfield Combust, production of cereals, peas, beans, carrots, parsnips and cabbages grew tenfold. These basic foodstuffs still grow in great abundance, along with sugar beet and oil seed rape. But thankfully for those who prefer the finer things in life, delicious vegetables and fruits are also grown in East Anglia.

Still truly seasonal and very special because of its relatively short growing season from May to June, asparagus must count as one of the glories of the eastern counties. Asparagus, like sweetcorn, should ideally be eaten within an hour of cutting. So come the spring, pitch camp near Colin Goodard of Redgrave, or N Baldry and Son, near Aldeburgh, and with melted butter dripping down your chin, indulge in some of the most beautifully fresh asparagus you are ever likely to come across. Apples, pears, damsons and plums, all flourish in this dryish, windy region. Eliza Acton, one of England's most famous 19th century cookery writers and a native of Ipswich, suggested in 1845 that Norfolk biffins should be used in her recipe for Black Caps. It is doubtful if any of Norfolk's once most famous apple survive now - perhaps in a far corner of some derelict orchard - but newer varieties, grafted on smaller and more easily tended stock, as well as carefully cherished older varieties are still widely grown.

From apples, unsurprisingly, come apple juice and cider, and while Aspalls of Debenham and Copella near Stoke by Nayland are nationally famous for their excellent products, even more appealing are the three unblended juices that James White of Brandeston presses - the slightly acidic Bramley, nuttily sweetish Cox's and sumptuously rich Russet should been sought out by any discerning palate.

In 1724, at Hengrave Hall near Bury St Edmunds, Sir William Gage planted a plum tree imported from France which had lost its label. The green fruits subsequently borne became known as greengages, and from the 18th century onwards, with the proliferation of corn and wheat growing, these fruits would have been among the gooseberries, currants, damsons and plums which were turned into the pastry dominated desserts of dumplings, puddings, pies, tarts and cakes.

It should be apparent to even the most cynical gastronome, that East Anglia is not just the cereal and sugar bowl of England, but the fruit, fish, meat and vegetable bowl too. Good foodstuffs of infinite variety have always been produced here. But the particular marvel has been the burgeoning of countless small enterprises which are either marketing native produce in new and enticing forms, or just as excitingly, going back to old methods and recipes, to produce traditional foods seemingly vanished forever. Buy a 1lb of sweet-cured bacon from J R Creasey in Peasenhall, and know instantly that real food is alive and well, at least in East Anglia.

Prices are intended as a guide only and may change over the course of the year We recommend that you check details when you book. Prices do not usually include drinks with your meal. Please mention East Anglia Guide when replying to advertisements.

SUFFOLK

BURY ST EDMUNDS

The Angel Hotel, Angel Hill
Tel: (0284) 753926

If most of the houses in Bury St Edmunds look as edible as angel cake, the creeper-clad Angel Hotel must be the plum pudding. In an imposing position overlooking the Abbey Gardens, this fine hotel with its Dickensian connections is owned and run with pleasing professionalism by the Gough family. With three dining areas to choose from, the impressive Norman vaulted cellars, cosy Pickwick bar or handsome Regency restaurant, the food ranges from sandwiches made from local bread through homely brasserie dishes such as braised oxtail to an up-market, classic Chateaubriand with Bearnaise sauce. Adnams supplies the beers and the wine list is thoughtful and modestly priced. *Average price per head, without wine, £15-£20*

IPSWICH

The Marlborough Hotel, Henley Road
Tel (0473) 257677

Tucked away in a quiet residential quarter, this solid, red-brick Victorian hotel exudes a strong feeling of comfortable dependibility. A beguiling and unexpected inner garden soothes the spirit, as do classic dishes such as eggs Florentine and more adventurous combinations from the well-priced set menu. The only unrestrained note is sounded by the flambe dishes, which run the gamut from beef Stroganov to crepes Suzette, providing diners with moments of fun and high drama. An efficient young staff, led by managers David and Wendy Brooks, treat parties, businessmen and private diners alike with skill and courtesy. *Average price per head, without wine, £15-£20.*

FELIXSTOWE

Waverley Hotel and Wolsey Restaurant
Wolsey Gardens
Tel (0394) 282811

At the Waverley Hotel you have the choice of dining in the Wolsey Restaurant or the Gladstone Bar and you will be assured of a delicious choice of meals made with fresh local produce. Dramatic views of the North Sea make this a very special place to eat. Conferences, receptions and parties can be catered for. *Open: daily. Average prices: lunch £10.25, dinner £13.95. Fax (0394) 670185.*

WOODBRIDGE

Seckford Hall Hotel and Restaurant
Tel (0394) 385678

The two restaurants at this Elizabethan country manor provide a choice of style. Oak panelling, beams and tapestries form the backdrop to the main restaurant where the speciality is fresh lobster from a splendid illuminated homarium in the hall. A professional team offer full silver service in the traditional manner. The Club Restaurant overlooking the swimming pool in the old tithe barn is bistro style and serves delicious modern plated dishes: for example guacamole, lasagne, giant garlic prawns, in a relaxed, informal setting. *Open: daily. Average prices: lunch (table d'hote) £11.50, lunch and dinner (à la carte) £22 average.*

ALDEBURGH

Uplands Hotel, Victoria Road
Tel (0728) 452420

This establishment is a fitting compliment to the charming and tranquil seaside resort of Aldeburgh. The Uplands faces the beautiful 15th century parish church and stands in lovely gardens only a stone's throw from the shingle beach. The table d'hote menu features fresh local produce and is changed daily. There is an interesting wine list and an extensive range of malt whiskies. The elegant dining room overlooks the gardens and is perfect for a traditional, relaxed evening meal. *Open: daily. Average price: Table d'hote dinner £15.00.*

LAVENHAM

The Angel
Market Place
Tel: (0787) 247388

In one of the best-loved and best-known of Suffolk's mediaeval villages, the Angel is so resolutely settled into its corner site overlooking the market square that one almost feels that its strong timbers have grown straight from the soil. Two dining rooms, one informally strewn with pine tables, the other rich with mahogany tables and bric-a-brac, offer home-made fresh food: garlic mushrooms, pates, home-made soups and pies, casseroles of pork and apple or steaks and lamb chops, as well as delicious treacle tart or Suffolk apple flan, with a menu that changes daily. The atmosphere is easy, the staff delightful. *Average price per head, without wine, £10-£15.*

HAVERHILL

Mill House Restaurant
Mill Road
Tel (0440) 712123

The enthusiastic owners of this pink-washed town house, Mr and Mrs Thorpe, arrange special dining evenings, from Greek to Cajun (featuring a splendid jambalaya), as well as offering two modestly-priced set menus, of traditional English and provincial French fare. House cocktails, taken in the modern conservatory bar, are vital when trying to choose from amongst snails in garlic butter, chicken breast with prawns, or steak chasseur. The generous portions hardly leave room for the most popular pudding, RSJ, a confection of meringues, cream, raspberries and ice cream. The excellent wine list is an example of how much care goes into this restaurant. *Average price per head for 3 courses £12-£17.*

CRETINGHAM

The Cretingham Bell
The Street
Tel (0728) 685419

This cheerfully renovated village pub with its flagged floors, ubiquitous beams and open dining areas lies in the middle of a labyrinth of twisting lanes in the Suffolk countryside. The menu ranges widely through old favourites such as a pint of prawns, sausages or char-grilled steaks to zappy newcomers like deep-fried potato skins, nachos or chilli, with more than just a cursory nod to vegetarians with dishes like fruity curry and trio bean bake. Puddings tend to be American-inspired: fattening, chocolatey and delicious. Adnams supply real ales which can also be drunk in the well-kept garden, and mastermind a short but sound wine list. Average price for 3 courses £9-£15

HOLBROOK

The Compasses
Tel (0473) 328332

Holbrook is at the head of Alton Water, an ideal spot for windsurfing, walking and bird watching. The bar at the Compasses is comfortable, with a varied menu including old favourites as well as some unusual dishes. A fascinating collection of keyrings decorates the walls. The restaurant is tastefully decorated in a delicate pink. The menu offers an excellent variety of fish, meat and poultry dishes, with a vegetarian choice of spinach & mushroom lasagne and mushroom & nut fettuccini and others. Large car park, garden play area, children welcome. *Open: daily for lunch and dinner. Average prices: Restaurant £12, bar meals £4-£5, Sun lunch £9.25 (booking advised).*

STOWMARKET

Tot Hill House Restaurant
Bury Road
Tel (0449) 673375

This charming restored 16th century timber-framed house fronted with local Woolpit bricks is found on the A45 between Stowmarket and Haughley. You will receive a warm welcome and friendly efficient service from John and Jean McBain. The kitchen is under the control of their son Andrew who will offer you freshly prepared dishes made from the best of local produce such as rack of Suffolk lamb and Lowestoft plaice or more exotic delights such as Swordfish steak marinated in lemon and lime, baked with prawns and parsley. Your meal is taken in the pleasant, comfortable restaurant with views across the lawns and gardens. The fixed price 4 course Gourmet Menu is changed regularly. There is also a carefully selected wine list. *Open: Tues-Sat evenings and lunch on Sundays. Gourmet menu £14.75 also à la carte menu. Sunday lunch £8.50. Access/Visa.*

HINTLESHAM

Hintlesham Hall
Tel (047 387) 334/268

Set in 170 acres of parkland and golf course, Hintlesham Hall with 33 bedrooms and suites, is renowned for its excellent cuisine and luxurious accommodation. Hintlesham Hall is a member of Small Luxury Hotels of the World. There are 5 reception rooms, including the splendid Salon, the intimate book-lined Library, and the mellow pine-panelled Parlour. Throughout the hotel, individuality is displayed in the eclectic selection of modern and traditional works of art, and the fine antiques. The style of cooking is modern British, using local and home-grown produce for the seasonal menus. Above all, the service from the young team is unfailingly pleasant and helpful. *Open: daily, except Sat - lunch time. Average prices: House lunch (A la carte) including coffee and petits fours £21. Table d'hote menu Sun to Thurs £19.50. Full a la carte every day. £18.50 table d'hote lunch. Coffee & petits fours £2.50.*

ORFORD

King's Head Inn
Front Street
Tel (0394) 450271

The King's Head Inn lies at the heart of Orford, a delightful village by the river Alde. Relax at the bar with a drink whilst choosing from a wide selection of local fish dishes, some meat and a vegetarian choice. Meals are served either in the traditional restaurant which is cheerfully decorated in a nautical theme, or in the 'olde worlde' bar. My starter was a delicious sweet half melon, complemented with prawns, followed by halibut with a rich lobster sauce, served with a platter of fresh vegetables. Fresh local seafood and game are a speciality. *Open: daily lunch 12-2, dinner 6.30-9 (restaurant closed Sun & Thur evenings, but bar meals always available). Average price: 3 course meal £15. Lunch & bar meals £8.*

FRESSINGFIELD, Nr DISS

Fox and Goose Inn
Tel (037986) 247

In 1509 the Fox and Goose was built in the Fressingfield churchyard , parishioners up to that time having eaten and drunk in the nave of the church. Still owned by the church the Inn was taken over by Ruth Watson (ex-owner of Hintlesham Hall) in 1990 who combines the informality of a British pub with the genuine dedication to good cooking of a family-owned French restaurant. The eclectic menu, from which you can choose most dishes in either starter or main course sizes, ranges from Peking duck or Japanese tempura to local cod and chips or English lamb with rosemary sauce, finishing with sticky toffee pudding or chocolate St Emillion. The extensive wine list is reasonably marked up and has won awards from all the major guides. *Average price per head, without wine, £20.*

WOODBRIDGE

Captain's Table
Quay Street
Tel (0394) 383145

This delightful restaurant is to be found in one of Woodbridge's quaint, narrow streets between the town centre and the yacht haven. The atmosphere is warm and cosy and you will receive the personal and friendly attention of the proprietor's family and helpers. There is a pleasant patio where you can eat during the warmer months, a licensed bar and small car park. As you may have guessed, seafood is the speciality–lobster, oyster, crawfish and fresh salmon when available and there is a comprehensive wine list. *Open: Tues-Sat. Average prices: lunch £6, dinner £16.50, 3 course fixed price menu £11.50*

YOXFORD

JaCey's Charcoal Pit
High Street
Tel Yoxford (072877) 298

Friendly and enthusiastic young owners, Jackie and Colin, have just effected an up-to -the minute change of identity on this unpretentious village restaurant. As well as tried and tested favourites such as beef carbonade and the very popular vegetarian roulades, they have just installed a barbecue. Generous skewers of lamb, king prawns or the house special of salami, beef, garlic sausage and onions, are cunningly presented on iron serving stands and then lubricated with herby butter. The home-made bread is terrific, as is the fabulously rich Banoffi Pie, and Pavlova, which along with other puddings can be ordered as a take-away. The very modestly priced wine list is small and interesting. *Open for dinner Mon-Sat. Average price per head, £8-£13.*

ESSEX

HARWICH

Pier at Harwich
The Quay
Tel (0255) 241212

Nothing could be more titillating gastronomically, than the idea of eating freshly caught fish in a harbourside restaurant. The restaurant upstairs has the feel of a bridge of a jolly ship with a pianist as captain where the food ranges from the simple and familiar appeal of such things as a delicious fish pie to the distinctly luxurious suggested by crab, turbot or halibut in sophisticated sauces, as well as stunningly good lobster Thermidor. The Ha'penny Pier on the ground floor is geared to family eating and offers cheap and cheerful grub like spanking fresh fish and chips. A veritable piscatorial playground. Average prices: restaurant £15-£20, Ha'penny pier £5-£8.

ARDLEIGH, nr COLCHESTER

The Wooden Fender
Harwich Road
Tel: (0206) 230466

The Wooden Fender is easily recognised by its brightly coloured fairy lights, on the Colchester to Harwich road. It is renowned for its history as the meeting place of Matthew Hopkins, the "Witchfinder General" and his henchmen who decided the fate of 29 local witches over a pint or two of local ale. The ale is still excellent, with Adnams and Greene King as well as guest beers to be sampled. Eat either a la carte in the restaurant, or in the bar where bar snacks are good value and the choice is extensive – there are 4 different versions of lasagne alone! *Open: lunch & bar meals daily, restaurant nightly except Tues evening. Average prices: bar meals £2.60-£4. Access, Visa & Amex accepted.*

CASTLE HEDINGHAM (Nr Halstead)

The Old Moot House Restaurant
1, St James Street
Tel (0787) 60342

The Moot House (old English for meeting place) has been at the hub of village life for centuries, more recently under the ownership of Michael and Maureen Medcraft. The beautiful timbered dining room was built as a Cross Wing Hall back in 1320. A varied and interesting menu offering a good selection of fish and meat dishes, with weekly specials, coupled with a warm welcome, good service and popular pricing have been the key to 12 years continued success, with a well established following. *Mid- week and Sunday lunch set menus £11.50 to £12.95, set dinner menu £16.75, a la carte £15.50 to £16.50. Light lunches and snacks available, garden on fine days. Closed Mondays.*

ROXWELL, Nr CHELMSFORD

Farmhouse Feast
The Street
Tel (0245) 248583

The name of this restaurant conjures up an image of kitchen tables laden with nourishing and delicious country products, and indeed the feeling of plenty comes across as soon as you enter and are confronted by a table groaning under the weight of assorted hors d'oeuvres. Make your choice, but I advice restraint: save space for the rest of the meal! A tureen of home-made soup is to follow and then a choice of four main courses. For dessert there is no problem with indecision for you help yourself from the buffet and can sample a little of two or even three extravaganzas. Coffee and petits fours complete the feast. *Open for lunch Tue-Fri, dinner Tue-Sat. Average prices: lunch £12, dinner £23.*

CAMBRIDGESHIRE

MELBOURN

The Pink Geranium
Tel (0763) 260215

A real gem of a restaurant. Steven Saunders understands that eating out is as much about relaxation and enjoyment as it is about eating. He somehow manages to make all his guests feel that they are personally welcome. Cooking is of an unusually high standard. We enjoyed a delightfully light mousseline of fish and shellfish, courgette flowers with soft cheese in a light pastry tart, and then splendid crispy duck, a famous dish of the house. Puddings are light and sensational. A la carte prices are reasonable for such high standards of cooking. Sunday lunch inclusive menu is particularly good value. On a sunny day or a warm evening one can enjoy a drink in the delightful garden, surrounded, of course, by pink geraniums. *Open: Tues-Fri, lunch & dinner, Sat dinner, Sun lunch. Average prices: evening a la carte £30,set menu £24.95, Sunday lunch £16.95, weekday lunch £15.95*

KEYSTON (off A604 between Huntingdon & Thrapston)

The Pheasant Inn
Tel (08014) 241

A delightful thatched village pub, its 17th century interior decorated with farming bygones on high white walls beneath the old beams. Chef Patron Nick Steiger produces a sophisticated restaurant menu which is acclaimed in every major national guide. At the comfortable banquettes or the oak tables in the bar you can enjoy good home cooking, competitively priced and finely presented, with real ales and wine by the glass. Should the sun shine, enjoy eating outside overlooking the village green. *Open: daily. Average prices: lunch or dinner a la carte £22.30, bar food from £3.95.*

MADINGLEY (4m NW Cambridge)

Three Horseshoes
Tel (0954) 210221

Just outside Cambridge, this enchanting thatched village inn with exposed oak beams, is well worth a visit. The very pretty restaurant and conservatory is the setting for cooking of the highest standard in an informal atmospere and at sensible prices. There is a welcoming bar (which offers over ten wines by the glass) and imaginative bar snacks are available every lunchtime and evening. The large garden is beautifully maintained. *Open: daily. Average prices: lunch & dinner à la carte £22.00, bar food from £3.95.*

ELY

Steeplegate Tea Rooms
16/18 High Street
Tel (0353) 664731

Steeplegate Tea Rooms nestle next to Ely's magnificent cathedral. Upstairs, pictures line the walls of the white painted tea rooms, which are divided into areas for smokers and non-smokers. The simple menu includes delicious freshly baked quiches and flans, cakes, pies, scones and shortbread, as well as a selection of different teas. Downstairs is a craft shop and the vaulted undercroft is used for art and craft exhibitions. *Open: Mon, Wed, Thur, Fri & Sat 10-5. Average prices: lunch £2.50-£3.75*

HUNTINGDON

The Old Bridge Hotel
Tel (0480) 52681

The ultimate "country hotel in a town". The lounges extend into a really splendid conservatory with attractive and comfortable cane chairs and tables amidst lush green plants in great tubs. Here one can enjoy exceptional bar-food, with a lavish buffet including a huge range of interesting salads, Baron of rare roast beef, whole Scotch salmon and spectacular sweet trolley. Also a top-class, panelled restaurant with a wine list which won Egon Ronay's "Cellar of the Year" for 1989. *Open: daily. Average prices: 3 course meal £22.00. Hot bar food from £2.95.*

WANSFORD-IN-ENGLAND (Just off the A1)

The Haycock Hotel
Tel (0780) 782223

The Haycock is a splendid 17th century coaching inn. The atmosphere is warm and informal. Especially popular is the cold buffet, which includes whole salmon, traditional beef, moist turkeys, hams, home made pies and all manner of salads. The restaurant itself is well known for its traditional English food: roast beef, steak and kidney pies or puddings, game in season and excellent, fresh, Fenland vegetables. Do not miss the splendid riverside gardens, a winner of the Tourist Board's annual garden competition. *Open: daily. Average prices: à la carte £20,00, buffet £4.95-£9.95, bar food from £3.95.*

STAMFORD

The George of Stamford
Tel (0780) 55171

Here is a restaurant in the very best English tradition of the coaching inn. The fine oak panelled dining room is a place for serious eating. There are ribs of beef, racks of lambs and just the odd Italian dish reflecting the taste of Ivo Vannocci, Director of this small hotel group. There is an outstanding wine list. Less formal food is served in the airy Garden Lounge and in the summer the flower-decked courtyard is a most delightful place to meet and eat. Stamford provides a beautiful backdrop for this historic hotel. *Open: daily. Average prices: lunch & dinner, 3 course £28, bar snacks from £3.25*

NORFOLK

KING'S LYNN

The Garden Restaurant, Knights Hill Hotel
Knights Hill Village, South Wootton
Tel (0553) 675566

Dinner at the Garden Restaurant is a civilised and leisurely affair in stylish, elegant surroundings overlooking the walled garden. On arrival you will be invited to relax in the lobby bar while you choose your meal. The fare is light and caters for all tastes. Chicken and Stilton mousse make a delicious starter. There is a variety of mouth watering main courses including scampi with grapes, orange and pink grapefruit and Norfolk Duck. *Open: daily for dinner. Average price: £15-£20.*

KING'S LYNN

The Farmers Arms
Knights Hill Village, South Wootton
Tel (0553) 675566

When next in King's Lynn call at this popular inn. Originally a barn, the rustic atmosphere has been skilfully retained. Beams, exposed brickwork and farm implements abound. The menu is unpretentious and very reasonable in price. It features favourites like chargrilled ground burgers and jacket potatoes. A speciality of the house is Norfolk kebab-pitta bread filled with slices of roast turkey on a bed of salad topped with mayonnaise. A smooth pint of draught Bass is a perfect accompaniment. *Open: daily, both Farmers Arms Inn and Restaurant. Average price: Farmers Arms Restaurant lunch or dinner £11, Farmers Arms Inn, bar snacks £4.*

GREAT YARMOUTH

Imperial Hotel, North Drive
Tel (0493) 851113

The Rambouillet Restaurant at the Imperial Hotel has an outstanding reputation for the quality of its cuisine. In addition to the chef's table d'hote and the a la carte menus, there is usually a gastronomique menu with French regional dishes or local specialities, all prepared by the restaurant's award-winning chefs. Only the finest and freshest ingredients are used, the wine list is excellent and the service is always professional and attentive. *Open: daily, closed for Saturday lunch. Average prices: lunch (table d'hote) £10.50, dinner (table d'hote) £16.50.*

NORWICH

The Trafalgar Restaurant
Hotel Nelson, Prince of Wales Road
Tel (0603) 760260

We recommend the Trafalgar Room for your meal. At lunchtime they present a spectacular hors d'oeuvre/buffet, or you can choose from two splendid roast joints, together with puddings or cheese and coffee. In the evening the Trafalgar Room has a comfortable atmosphere with views across the river, and it serves good local produce. Good light meals and snacks at the Quarter-Deck Buttery. *Open: daily (ex Sat lunch). Average prices: lunch £10.25, table d'hote £12.50, à la carte dinner £10-£15.*

CAWSTON (10m N of Norwich)

Grey Gables Country House Hotel
and Restaurant
Tel (0603) 871259

A beautiful former rectory set in wooded grounds. In the winter there is an inviting log fire which, together with the elegant candlelit dining room, make Grey Gables the ideal settting for a relaxing, romantic meal. The cooking is traditionally prepared and cooked by Chef/Proprietor, Rosalind Snaith using fresh, local produce. There is a fine wine cellar with many French & German classics, as well as ports and wines from Italy, Spain, Australia, New Zealand, California, Chile, Hungary and Romania. The sweets are gorgeous and each customer is served with three sweets to sample-an excellent idea! *Open: daily. Average prices: lunch bookings by arrangement, dinner £17 per person.*

WELLS-NEXT-THE-SEA

Crown Hotel & Restaurant, The Buttlands
Tel (0328) 710209

Set in North Norfolk's finest coastal scenery this old coaching inn attracts people from around the world. "The sort of small hotel tired travellers dream about" as The Times said of this famous hotel in this picturesque old port. A busy popular bar with lots of local character makes this an ideal meeting place. Bar meals and snacks are always available. The food offered is freshly prepared and is of a high standard. The Restaurant under the direction of Mr Foyers and his four chefs offers both English and French cuisine and is open for both lunch and dinner. *Open: daily. Average prices: Bar snacks from £1.75, luncheon from 11.50, dinner from £16.00.*

GRIMSTON (nr King's Lynn)

THE ORANGERY RESTAURANT

Congham Hall Country House Hotel
Tel (0485) 600250

For excellent food, go to Congham Hall. Chef Murray Chapman interprets "modern English cooking" intelligently and with a fine balance of taste and decoration. The restaurant and "orangery" is delightfully decorated in the Georgian manner. On hot summer days we particularly recommend Congham's outdoor lunches-ask about the luncheon club; but eating in the dining room or on the lawn one has the feeling of being part of an English Country Home, which is what Trevor and Christine Forecast set out to achieve when they established Congham as a country house hotel and now appropriately a member of the "Pride of Britain" group. *Open: daily. Average prices: lunch table d'hote £15, Sunday lunch £15, dinner from £30.*

LONG STRATTON

Snickerdoodles Restaurant
The Street
Tel (0508) 31845

For those who like classic bistro cooking, this place is a must. Guests walk in off the pavement into a delightful little sitting room, crammed with Victoriana and the dining room too is filled with a charming collection of stripped pine, pictures and artefacts.The Gibbs (Ray cooks, Penny hosts) offer a 5-course set menu, starting with classics such as mussels, pan-fried mushrooms or melon with port. The 12 or so main courses-wild duck, fillet steak, salmon, lamb and halibut-come with sumptuous sauces. Puddings are home-made and portions, especially fresh vegetables, are very generous. *Average price per head for 5 courses, without wine, £20.*

BANHAM

Pantiles Bistro Country Restaurant
The Appleyard
Tel (095 387) 709

Set in a sympathetically restored and converted farm building, this restaurant has recently been recommended for entry into the Best Hotels and Restaurants Guide on the basis of its range of daytime menus and a unique combination of dishes available in the evening. Typical bistro cooking featuring dishes such as Fillet of Pork with a cider, apple, garlic and cream sauce (with cider from the adjacent cidery) complement the range of traditional Sunday roasts that have become a popular addition to the food on offer. *Open 7 days a week for morning coffee, lunches and afternoon teas and Friday and Saturday evenings. Full function facilities available on request. Prices for three courses without wine start at £13.*

NORWICH

Boswells RESTAURANT

Boswells Brasserie
24 Tombland
Tel (0603) 626099

Take time out to enjoy the truly continental feeling of the new Boswells. Situated along the cathedral wall in Tombland in the historic heart of the city, it is in an ideal spot to stop for lunches or afternoon tea next time you are shopping or sightseeing. The Brasserie style menu is varied and delicious, ranging from spectacular sandwiches to three course meals. The unique decor and atmosphere are further enhanced by its "all day every day" opening hours and live Jazz, tea dances, old movies, Sunday brunch and other activities. You can now enjoy all this in the open air on the fully licenced forecourt terrace. *Open: Sun 11am to 10.30pm, Mon 11am to 11pm, Tue to Sat 11am to 2am. Average price under £6 (specials for children are available).*

NORWICH

Pizza One Pancakes Too!
24 Tombland
Tel (0603) 621583

Norwich's own Pizzas, Pastas and French Crepes. A favourite haunt, where food still has that homemade taste. It's usually crowded with families, businessmen, students and tourists alike. Situated along the Cathedral wall in Tombland, the historic heart of the city, it is the perfect place to stop for lunch, afternoon pancakes or dinner. *Open daily 12 noon-11pm, Sunday 12 noon-10pm (closed 25 Dec and 1 Jan). Average price £5.45 – children's portions available.*

BUNWELL

Bunwell Manor
Tel (0953) 788304

At the end of a quiet country lane, Bunwell Manor overlooks wooded lawns, reed-fringed ponds and a terrace. The beamed restaurant with its polished wood sideboard, has a cosy upper level perfect for romantic dinners. There is a bar menu, a good value table d'hote, and an à la carte restaurant menu. Specialities include fillet steak with peppercorns, stilton, whisky and cream or steak and pheasant pie; and chocoholics will adore the chocolate mousse topped with white and dark chocolate flakes! *Open: 7 days, lunch 12-2; dinner 7-9.30. Average prices: Table d'hote £12.25, à la carte £14-£18.*

HETHERSETT (Nr Norwich)

Park Farm Hotel & Restaurant
Tel (0603) 810264 Fax (0603) 812104

Park Farm Hotel has earned a well deserved reputation for good food, a warm welcome and excellent service in this family-run hotel and restaurant. Set in beautiful surroundings, Park Farm provides both French and English cooking prepared with the best local produce. A good selection of menus, both a la carte and table d'hote, whilst the chef's speciality menus have more skilfully prepared dishes. Bar meals are also available. *Open: daily. Average prices: lunch £10 (table d'hote), dinner £14 (table d'hote), £18-£20 (à la carte).*

WEST RUNTON, Nr SHERINGHAM

The Pepperpot
Tel (0263) 837578

Tucked away down a narrow lane leading to the beach, it is only the illuminated sign that distinguises this restaurant from the other private houses. A warm welcome is offered by hostess Barbara (who with husband Ron have run the Pepperpot since March) that complements the immediate feeling of hospitality, comfort and intimacy that suggests itself upon arrival. The set menu, offering a choice of two or three courses is understated and modest, for the emphasis is on quality through dishes such as delicious breast fillets of duck in peach sauce and incredibly lean steak in a brandy and cream sauce, without forgetting quantity. Desserts are lavish and the wine list is small but thoughtful. *Price per head without wine: 2 courses £13.95, 3 courses £15.95.*

NORWICH

Adlard's
79, Upper St Giles Street
Tel: (0603) 633522

In an emerald green jewel of a restaurant a few hundred yards above the market place, chef-proprietor David Adlard and his lovely American wife Mary are responsible for some of the most serious food in East Anglia, served in a genial and unstuffy manner. Winner of a rare Michellin star, David's perfectly judged and meticulously prepared dishes utilise much seasonal and local produce including wild mushrooms from a local stud-owner. Sauces which accompany noisettes of English lamb, breast of Gressingham duck or fillets of brill are always based on excellent stocks, carefullly reduced. Pastry for a delicious apple tart surrounded by caramel sabayon is buttery and feather-light, and ice cream silky and smooth. *Average price per head, without wine, £18-£30.*

PRETTY CORNER, nr SHERINGHAM on A148

PRETTY CORNER
CONTINENTAL CAFE
& RESTAURANT
Tea Garden – Buttery

Tel: (0263) 822358

At Pretty Corner, a variety of food is available to suit different tastes and appetites. The new restaurant has continental style decor and excels in continental and Indonesian food. The Dutch-Indonesian Rice Table nights with 14-20 different dishes, are a speciality of the house. Alternatively, in the summer you can eat at the Tea Garden Buttery next door, which serves drinks and light snacks indoors or in the split level terraced gardens with pond, where dogs are welcome. Disabled facilities. *Restaurant open Thurs, Fri and sat, 7.30pm, buttery open 10am-5.30pm, all year. Booking recommended for Rice Table nights. Tea Garden Buttery open Easter-mid Oct, daily 10-5.30.*

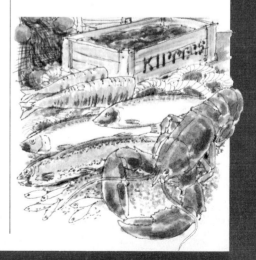

93

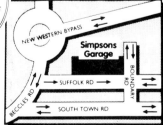
Please mention East Anglia Guide when replying to advertisements

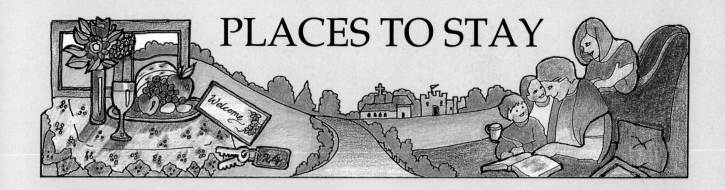

PLACES TO STAY

Essex

Cambridgeshire

Miami Hotel
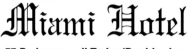

**57 Bedrooms, all Twins/Double size
with colour TV (Sky available) in all
rooms, teasmade, shower, WC, direct
dial telephone, hairdryers
WEEKEND RATES,
GROUP RATES ON REQUEST**

⚜⚜⚜⚜ APPROVED

**Restaurant
Open 7 Days for Lunch/Dinner
Table d'Hote • A la Carte • Bar
Meeting & Conference Facilities
PRINCES ROAD, CHELMSFORD
Telephone: (0245) 264848 & 269603
Telex: 995430 Fax: 0245 259860**

Roslin Hotel
**Thorpe Esplanade, Thorpe Bay, Essex
Telephone: 0702 586375**

⚜⚜⚜⚜ COMMENDED

Overlooking the sea in residential Thorpe Bay.
Offering good food and friendly informal service.
All bedrooms with private facilities, Sky TV, hairdryer, tea/coffee making facilities.
Mulberry Restaurant open to non-residents
Large car park

Ilfracombe House Hotel

Residential Proprietor: Michael Pearmain
**Wilson Road
Southend-on-Sea
Essex SS1 1HG**

Set in Southend's conservation area close to Cliff Gardens, promenade, shopping precinct, theatres, art gallery, rail links and bus/coach terminals.
13 bedrooms, 1 self-catering studio apartment. All en-suite, colour T.V., telephone, radio, tea/coffee maker.
Single room from £34 inclusive,
Double/Twin from £44 inclusive.

Southend (0702) 351000

MAJOR CREDIT CARDS ACCEPTED   Licensed

*Tel: Brentwood 225252
Telex 995182*

BRENTWOOD MOAT HOUSE HOTEL

London Road, Brentwood, Essex
Two Minutes from the M25 Intersection 28
In the warm and friendly atmosphere of this genuine Tudor house, you can enjoy the traditional comfort of open log fires in oak panelled lounges. Accommodation consists of garden suites facing onto an olde worlde garden, and three luxury period rooms with four-posters and marbled spa bathrooms. Elegant restaurant with extensive, fresh produce menu.
Twenty four hour room service.

⚜⚜⚜ HIGHLY COMMENDED

WHITEHOUSE HOLIDAY APARTMENTS
Conduit Head Road, Cambridge CB3 0EY
Tel: 0223 67110 & 0954 211361
Self catering units in most attractive location
within University Faculties with attractive gardens.   ✓✓✓

THE CROWN IS YOUR SURE SIGN
OF WHERE TO STAY

HOTELS, GUESTHOUSES, INNS, B&Bs & FARMHOUSES

Throughout Britain, the tourist boards now inspect over 17,000 hotels, guesthouses, inns, B&Bs and farmhouses, every year, to help you find the ones that suit you best.

THE CLASSIFICATIONS: 'Listed', and then ONE to FIVE CROWN, tell you the range of facilities and services you can expect. The more Crowns, the wider the range.

THE GRADES: **APPROVED, COMMENDED, HIGHLY COMMENDED and DE LUXE**, where they appear, indicate the quality standard provided. If no grade is shown, you can still expect a high standard of cleanliness.

Every classified place to stay has a Fire Certificate, where this is required under the Fire Precautions Act, and all carry Public Liability Insurance.

'Listed': Clean and comfortable accommodation, but the range of facilities and services may be limited.

ONE CROWN: Accommodation with additional facilities, including washbasins in all bedrooms, a lounge and use of a phone.

TWO CROWN: A wider range of facilities and services, including morning tea and calls, bedside lights, colour TV in lounge or bedrooms, assistance with luggage.

THREE CROWN: At least one-third of the bedrooms with ensuite WC and bath or shower, plus easy chair, full length mirror. Shoe cleaning facilities and hairdryers available. Hot evening meals available.

FOUR CROWN: At least three-quarters of the bedrooms with ensuite WC and bath/shower plus colour TV, radio and phone, 24-hour access and lounge service until midnight. Last orders for meals 8.30 pm or later.

FIVE CROWN: All bedrooms having WC, bath and shower ensuite, plus a wide range of facilities and services, including room service, all-night lounge service and laundry service. Restaurant open for breakfast, lunch and dinner.

Every Crown classified place to stay is likely to provide some of the facilities and services of a higher classification. More information available from any Tourist Information Centre.

🏵 **English Tourist Board** 👑

Please mention East Anglia Guide when replying to advertisements

Norfolk

Norwich and Norfolk Holiday Homes

REGISTERED AGENCY

Historic City – Beautiful County.
Well equipped, convenient city properties and delightful country cottages.
Visit coast, Broads and Stately Homes.
All properties personally inspected.
We offer a friendly service and will send a Free Brochure on request.
18 Keswick Road, Cringleford, Norwich Norfolk, NR4 6UG
Tel: (0603) 503389 Fax: (0603) 55123

Grey Gables
Norwich Road, Cawston, Norwich NR10 4EY
Country House Hotel and Restaurant
Tel 0603 871259
A beautiful former rectory, comfortably furnished with many antiques, in a pleasant rural setting 10 miles from Norwich, coast and the Broads. 7 en suite bedrooms. £18-£44 single, £48-£56 double. Special Breaks 2 nights or more

Le' Strange Arms Hotel

**Golf Course Road
Old Hunstanton
Norfolk**

This fine Country House hotel standing in its own grounds, with lawns sweeping down to the beach. A wide range of bedrooms including Family Suites are available, whilst the hotels restaurant and Ancient Mariner Bar are known for their standard of food and quality of service.

Telephone: 0485 534411 Fax: 0485 534724
RAC ★ ★ ★

Congham Hall
COUNTRY HOUSE HOTEL & RESTAURANT

**GRIMSTON,
KING'S LYNN, NORFOLK**
Luxurious Georgian Manor, 40 acres
6 miles King's Lynn   5 miles Sandringham
A superb hotel created from a Georgian Manor House and acclaimed by many leading guides. Offering peaceful relaxation and high quality accommodation and cuisine. Under persoanl supervision of the owners. RAC Blue Ribbon, AA 3 red star and two Rosettes. Egon Ronay.

HIGHLY COMMENDED

'A Pride of Britain Hotel'
**Dining and Hotel Reservations:
(0485) 600250**

CROSSKEYS RIVERSIDE HOTEL
Hilgay, Nr. Downham Market, Norfolk, PE38 0LN.   Tel. No. (0366) 387777

A small country hotel beside the tranquil River Wissey. Formerly a coaching inn carefully renovated to retain its original character, our oak beamed dining room with inglenook fireplace offers à la carte, table d'hôte and vegetarian menus complemented by a selection from the rustic bar. Bedrooms with ensuite bathrooms have colour T.V., tea/coffee making facilities three have four-poster beds. Special breaks available.

B&B (Double) £48 to 31 Mar 93; £53 from 1 Apr 93. Special breaks for 2 (half board) £59.50 per person to 31 Mar 93; £66.50 per person from 1 Apr 93.
Family suite and longer breaks available.
APPROVED

Elm Farm Chalet Hotel
**ST. FAITHS,
NORWICH NR10 3HH**
Tel. Norwich (0603) 898366
Fax. (0603) 897129

Attractive 17th C farmhouse and chalet accommodation in charming village, 4 miles north of Norwich. Ideal for touring Norfolk & Suffolk. Rooms mainly en-suite, all have colour television, room telephone, hair dryers, facilities for tea & coffee making.
Ample Parking.

Cliftonville Hotel
Cromer, Norfolk NR27 9AS
Tel: (0263) 512543 (3 lines)
Fax (0263) 511764
✳ Fully licensed – Free House ✳ Most rooms facing the sea ✳ Open to non-residents for all meals ✳ Buttery Bar ✳ Bargain Breaks available ✳ Lift to all floors ✳ Some non-smoking bedrooms ✳ T.V. Radio & Direct-Dial Telephone in all rooms.
Brochure and Tariff on Request
Propietor T.A.Bolton

THE OLD COURT HOUSE
ROLLESBY, Nr GT. YARMOUTH

Peaceful country hotel, set in 4 acres of grounds with an outdoor swimming pool, heated during the summer. 7 comfortable bedrooms including 2 ground floor suites and 2 family suites with colour TV and tea/coffee making facilities. Cosy bar for residents only. Delicious home cooking. Games room. Bicycles for hire. Fishing, tennis, boating and seaside nearby. **Tel: Gt. Yarmouth (0493) 369665**
COMMENDED

Spindrift
AA
APPROVED
PRIVATE HOTEL

Adjacent sea front, bowling greens, tennis courts, waterways. Front bedrooms have sea views. All bedrooms have colour TV, tea/coffee, central heating. Some en-suites. Payphone. Open all year from £14 per night
**36 Wellesley Road, Gt. Yarmouth, NR30 1EU
Tel: 0493 858674**

FIRST CHOICE FOR KING'S LYNN

A sympathetically restored farm complex with well appointed accommodation, choice of restaurant style, a traditional country pub, and featuring an extensive Health and Leisure club with indoor pool, spa bath, steam room, sauna, solarium, snooker and tennis courts. A unique venue and ideal location to enjoy the beauty of West Norfolk
Further details and reservations:

*Knights Hill Hotel
South Wootton, King's Lynn,
Norfolk, PE30 3HQ
Telephone King's Lynn (0553) 675566
Telex 818118 Knight G : Fax (0553) 675568*

COMMENDED   RAC ★ ★ ★ AA

PARK·FARM·HOTEL
Hethersett, Norwich, NR9 3DL.
**Tel: Norwich (0603) 810264
Fax (0603) 812104**
Attractive family-run hotel set in beautiful landscaped gardens off the A11. 38 individually designed bedrooms all with private bath or shower, colour tv, telephone and teamaking facilities. Some with trouser press. 12 rooms have 4-poster beds and whirlpool bath en suite - ideal for honeymooners. First class restaurant. Superb leisure complex with sauna, swimming pool, solarium, jacuzzi, steam room, and gym. Hard tennis court, croquet and putting on lawns Special weekend rates. Open all year.
Egon Ronay
AA ★★★   COMMENDED

BED & BREAKFAST
Glavenside Guest House
Country house on River Glaven which flows through 4 acres of gardens. Beaches and places of interest nearby. Colour T.V. Tea & coffee in all rooms.
**Open all year from £10 per night
Letheringsett, Holt,
Norfolk NR25 7AR
Tel. Holt (0263) 713181**
Listed

The Historical Thomas Paine Hotel and Restaurant
Tel: Thetford (0842) 755631

Reputed birthplace of Thomas Paine, Thetford's most famous son, and author of "The Rights of Man". Small, privately owned, family run hotel. Warm welcome, fine food and superb service assured. All bedrooms are tastefully furnished with bathrooms en suite, colour TV, and tea/coffee facilities. Getaway weekend breaks available all year.
APPROVED

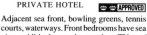

The Old Rectory
Gissing, Diss, Norfolk. IP22 3XB
Tel: Tivetshall (037 977) 575
Elegant decor in a lovely Victorian house 5m north of Diss. All bedrooms with private and ensuite facilities and every comfort. Indoor pool, beautiful grounds of 3 acres. Central for touring East Anglia and within easy reach of Norwich. Candlelit dinner by arrangement
HIGHLY COMMENDED

THE MAIDS HEAD HOTEL

TOMBLAND, NORWICH NR3 1LB
Tel: Norwich (0603) 761111
Fax: (0603) 613688 Telex: 975080
This 700 year old former coaching inn is situated opposite the Norman Cathedral in the old part of the City. Surrounded by cobbled streets and specialist shops, the Hotel is steeped in atmosphere and tradition and is a 'must' for visitors to the City.
Special weekend rates available.

Tel: Bunwell (0953) 788304
Fully Licensed AA ★★ RAC ★★
Just 12 miles south of Norwich, off the B1113. Our country house hotel dates originally from the 16th century. 2 acres of lovely grounds and 10 bedrooms all en-suite. Carefully prepared à la carte and table d'hôte menus. Ideally peaceful base for touring Norfolk, Suffolk and Cambridgeshire. Full Central heating and welcoming log fire in winter. Children and dogs welcome. Special Breaks available all year.
**Bunwell Manor
Bunwell, Norfolk, NR16 1QU**
COMMENDED

The Georgian House Hotel
32/34 Unthank Road, Norwich
Tel. (0603) 615655 (4 Lines)
Fax 765689   APPROVED
Friendly proprietor operated hotel, centrally heated. Ample parking. A few minutes walk from the city centre. Restaurant. Lounge Bar. Colour Television. Telephones. Radios. Tea/Coffee in all rooms. All bedrooms equipped with en-suite facilties.   **Licensed**

Please mention East Anglia Guide when replying to advertisements

Suffolk

The Crown & Castle COMMENDED
Orford, Nr. Woodbridge,
Suffolk IP12 2LJ
Tel: Orford (0394) 450205 Fax: (0394) 450176
The hotel is an attractive timbered building situated opposite the Castle. There are 20 bedrooms, most ensuite, all with telephone, television & coffee/tea making facilities. The table d'hôte menu features fresh local produce & is changed daily. Bar snacks are available in our cosy bar, open to non-residents. A very relaxed, friendly atmosphere.

The Cedars Hotel and Restaurant

A delightful 16th cent. farmhouse which has been extended and modernised to offer character and comfort. Weekend rates from £35 per person.

Needham Road, Stowmarket.
(0449) 612668

SWYNFORD PADDOCKS
HOTEL AND RESTAURANT

HIGHLY COMMENDED

Weekend Breaks available

Six Mile Bottom, Newmarket CB8 0UE, England.
Telephone: (063-870) 234 Facsimile: (063-870) 283

Swynford Paddock stands in 60 acres just 6 miles from Newmarket and 8 from Cambridge.

Once the country retreat of Poet Lord Byron, it is now a deluxe country-house hotel with 15 large and individually decorated bedrooms.

All rooms have private bathroom with WC & shower, colour TV, clock radio/alarm, tea and coffee facilities, direct-dial telephone, mini-bar, trouser-press and hair-drier.

A warm welcome, log fires and a sumptuous lounge, friendly attentive staff, and a first class restaurant combine to make Swynford Paddocks the ideal base for exploring East Anglia.

SECKFORD HALL
HOTEL & RESTAURANT

Nr. Woodbridge, Suffolk IP13 6NU
A warm and inviting hotel, personally supervised by the owners, ensures a high standard of service and food. Dating from Elizabethan times the Hall is tastefully furnished with antiques, yet includes every modern comfort. The grounds are quite lovely, the terrace overlooking a willow-fringed lake. Recently opened is The Courtyard, a group of ten luxury suites; indoor Swimming pool with leisure facilties and another restaurant in the Tudor Tithe-barn.
Tel: (0394) 385678

HIGHLY COMMENDED

ORWELL MEADOWS LEISURE PARK

Superb location, just off A45, in country setting. Luxury holiday homes to hire or buy. Spacious touring pitches swimming and toddlers pools. Play area.
Newly opened bar / restaurant and family games room.
For brochure: 0473 726666
Priory Lane, Nacton,
Ipswich IP10 0JS. ✓✓✓✓

The Wentworth Hotel stands of the edge of the Suffolk coast at the old fishing town of Aldeburgh and has the comfort and style of a country house with open fires and antique furniture. All indvidually decorated bedrooms have colour television, radio, telephone, hairdryers and optional tea facilities. The restaurant serves a wide range of dishes using fresh produce and the lunch time bar menu can be enjoyed in the sunken terrace garden.

Aldeburgh has quality shops, two excellent golf courses and nearby are long walks, Minsmere bird reserve, Snape Maltings concert hall and of course, miles of beach to sit upon and watch the sea.

Selection of breaks available throughout the year.

WENTWORTH HOTEL, HIGHLY COMMENDED
Wentworth Road, Aldeburgh, Suffolk IP15 5BD Telephone: (0728) 452312

THE DOLPHIN HOTEL

41 Beach Station Road
Felixstowe, Suffolk
Near to Beach and Passenger Terminal and Town Centre, Bars, meals, functions, TV in all bedrooms.
Proprietor: H. Hoffacker
Tel. (0394) 282261

The Waverley Hotel

The Waverley Hotel, Wolsey Gardens,
Felixstowe, Suffolk IP11 7DF
Telephone: Felixstowe (0394) 282811
Fax: (0394) 670185

All bedrooms have en suite bathrooms, trouser presses, colour television, tea and coffee making facilities, and direct dial telephones. Our Wolsey Restaurant features a high standard of a la carte cuisine featuring fresh local produce.
Please contact us for details of weekend breaks, colour brochure and tariff.

THE GRANGE HOTEL

Barton Road, Thurston,
Nr. Bury St. Edmunds, Suffolk IP31 3PQ
Telephone: Pakenham 31260

The Grange Hotel is a family-owned country house set in two acres of grounds, only four miles from Bury St. Edmunds. There are fifteen bedrooms, most with facilities. There are two golf courses within five miles, also riding, fishing and shooting within easy distance. We are also just two miles from main roads to Cambridge, Norwich and Ipswich and 30 minutes from the coast at Felixstowe. Bargain break week ends available all year round. APPROVED

APPROVED

The Bell Hotel

Clare, Sudbury, West Suffolk,
England CO10 8NN
Telephone Clare (0787) 27 7741
16c. posting house with beams, restaurant and wine bar. Within easy reach of ports, yet only 60 miles to London.

Ipswich Moat House

COPDOCK, IPSWICH, SUFFOLK IP8 3JD
Tel: Copdock (047386) 444 Telex: 987207

Queens Moat Houses

INTERNATIONAL HOTELIERS

Delightful modern hotel set in 5 acres of landscaped gardens, rurally located close to the heart of Constable Country, 3 miles south of Ipswich, just off the A12. 75 bedrooms with private bathrooms and colour TV. Leisure Centre. Special weekend and summer rates, family rooms available.

THE ANGEL

Market Place, Lavenham CO10 9QZ
Tel: 0787 247388

This family-run inn overlooks the market place and offers relaxation in a calm and quiet environment. Dating from 1420, it retains a wealth of period features and is ideal for exploring the area which is of great historic interest. The 7 en suite bedrooms all have telephone, colour TV and tea/coffee making facilities. The restaurant menu changes daily and features fresh local ingredients. Amenities include good music, attractive gardens and free parking. Les Routiers. Logis of Great Britain. HIGHLY COMMENDED

Special Breaks: 3 nights for the price of 2.
Also available half board with menu choice.
November to March.

THE HOUSE IN THE CLOUDS
THORPENESS·Near LEISTON·SUFFOLK

AVAILABLE FOR HOLIDAYS AND SHORT BREAKS
A FANTASY UNMATCHED IN ENGLAND
Sleeps 10 in 2 double bedded rooms, 3 twin bedded rooms, and for the extra 2 guests an additionial double sofa bed. 3 bathrooms, drawing room, kitchen, dining rooms and 'The Room at the Top' with the finest views in Suffolk.
Situated in 1 acre of grounds overlooking Thorpeness Golf Course, Thorpeness Mere and the sea. Close to Snape Maltings, home of Aldeburgh Festival and to Minsmere and other bird and nature reserves.
For further information and bookings please telephone: 071-252 0743 COMMENDED

Please mention East Anglia Guide when replying to advertisements

Please mention East Anglia Guide when replying to advertisements

Please mention East Anglia Guide when replying to advertisements

TOURIST INFORMATION CENTRES

Pay a visit to your nearest Tourist Information Centre and you may be surprised by the range of services they offer both for visitors and for local people. Things to do, places to eat, how to get there, what to do if it's raining, places suitable for young children, or for the elderly and disabled ... the Tourist Information Centres are expert in answering these kinds of questions. Information covering the whole country can be found at most offices, to help you plan your next destination, or for locals to help you choose your next British holiday. Tourist Information Centres will book accommodation for you, whether in their own area, or furhter afield using the "Book A Bed Ahead Scheme". If you are looking for a local souvenir or a gift, you may find that you need look no further as many Tourist Information Centres specialise in locally produced crafts or goods and in a wide range of local interest or British travel books. Make the Tourist Information Centre your first stop in every town!

Entries marked * are not open all year.

Aldeburgh, Suffolk

* The Cinema, High Street, *tel (0728) 453637. 29 Mar-24 Oct, Mon-Fri 9-5.15, Sat, Sun & Bank Hol 10-5.15.*

Ampthill, Bedfordshire

12 Dunstable Street, *tel (0525) 402051. All year Mon-Thur 8.45-5; Fri 8.45-4. Closed Bank Hols.*

Beccles, Suffolk

* The Quay, Fen Lane, *tel (0502) 713196. 19 Apr-30 Sept, daily, 9-1, 2-5. Oct, Sat, Sun & half term week, 9-1, 2-5*

Bedford, Bedfordshire

10 St Pauls Square, *tel (0234) 215226. All year Mon-Sat 9.30-5, Sun 1-5.*

Berkhamsted, Hertfordshire

The Library, Kings Road, *tel (0442) 877638. All year, Mon & Fri 10-5.30; Tue & Thur 10-8; Sat 9.30-1. Closed Wed & Bank Hol Mons.*

Bishop's Stortford, Hertfordshire

2 The Causeway, *tel (0279) 655261 x 251. All year, Mon-Fri 9-5. Closed Bank Hol Mons.*

Borehamwood, Hertfordshire

Civic Offices, Elstree Way, *tel 081 207 2277. All year, Mon-Fri 8.30-5.*

Braintree, Essex

Town Hall Centre, Market Square, *tel (0376) 550066. 1 Apr-30 Sept, Mon-Fri 10-5, Sat 10-4, 1 Oct-31 Mar, Mon-Fri, 10-3.30.*

Brentwood, Essex

Old House, 5 Shenfield Road, Brentwood, *tel (0277) 200300. All year, Mon-Sat, 9.30-5.*

Bury St Edmunds, Suffolk

6, Angel Hill, Bury St Edmunds, *tel (0284) 764667. 1 Jan-9 Apr Mon-Fri, 10-4, Sat 10-1; 10 Apr-30 Sept Mon-Fri 9.15-5.45, Sat 10-3, Sun (Jun- Aug only) 10-3. Bank Hol Mons 10-4.*

Cambridge, Cambridgeshire

Wheeeler Street, *tel (0223) 322640. Jan-Easter & Nov-Dec, Mon-Fri, 9-5.30; Easter-June and Sept-Oct, Mon-Fri, 9-6; Jul-Aug, Mon-Fri, 9-7; all year Sats, 9-5; Easter-Sept, Suns & Bank Hols, 10.30-3.30. Wed (all year) opens 9.30. Closed Xmas, New Year.*

Chelmsford, Essex

County Hall, Market Road, *tel (0245) 283400. All year, Mon-Fri, 9.30-5. Sat, 9.30-4. 24hr leisure link service (0898) 345386.*

Clacton-on-Sea, Essex

23 Pier Avenue, *tel (0255) 423400. Jan-22 May, Mon-Sat 9-5; 24 May-5 Sept, daily, 9-5; 6 Sept-end Dec, Mon-Sat, 9-5.*

Colchester, *Essex*

1 Queen Street, Colchester. *tel (0206) 712920. 1 Jan-30 Apr & 1 Oct-31 Dec, Mon-Fri 9-5, Sat 10-1; 1-31 May Mon-Fri 9-5, Sat 10-5, Sun 10-2; 1 June-30 Sept, Mon-Fri 9-5, Sat & Sun 10-5.*

Cromer, Norfolk

Bus Station, Prince of Wales Road, *tel (0263) 512497. Jan-28 Mar, Mon-Sat 10-4; 29 Mar-18 Jul, Mon-Sat, 10-5, Sun 10-4; 19 Jul-5 Sept, Mon-Sat 9.30-7, Sun 9.30-6; 6 Sept-31 Oct, Mon-Sat 10-5, Sun 10-4; 1 Nov-31 Dec, Mon-Sat 10-4.*

Diss, Norfolk

Meres Mouth, Mere St, *tel (0379) 650523. 1 Jan-31 Mar & 1 Nov-31 Dec, Mon-Thur 10.30-2.30, Fri & Sat 10-4; 1 Apr-31 Oct, Mon-Sat 10-4.*

Dunstable, Bedfordshire

Vernon Place, *tel (0582) 471012. All year, Mon, Tue, Wed, Fri 9.30-7; Thurs 9.30-5, Sat 9.30-4, closed Bank Hols.*

Ely, Cambridgeshire

Oliver Cromwell's House, 29 St Mary's Street, *tel (0353) 662062. Jan-Apr & Oct-Dec, Mon-Sat 10-5; 1 May-30 Sept, daily 10-6. Bank Hols 10-5.*

Fakenham, Norfolk

* Red Lion House, Market Place, *tel (0328) 851981. 29 Mar-18 Apr Mon- Sat 10-5, Sun 10-4; 19 Apr-24 May, Mon-Sun 10-2; 24 May-26 Sept, Mon- Sat 10-5, Sun 10-4; 27 Sept-31 Oct, Mon-Sun 10-2.*

Felixstowe, Suffolk

Sea Front, *tel (0394) 276770. Jan-Mar & Oct-Dec, Mon-Fri 8.45-5.15, Sat 10-5, Sun 10-1; Apr-Sept, Mon-Fri 9.30, Sat and Sun 9.30-5.*

Great Yarmouth, Norfolk

Town Hall, *tel (0493) 846345. All year ex Bank Hols and the Tues following Easter, Spring and August Bank Hols. Mon-Thur, 8.30-5.30, Fri, 9-5.*

* Marine Parade (between Britannia Pier and Marina Centre), tel (0493) 842195. *9-13 Apr, 1-28 May & 20 Sept-10 Oct, 10-1, 2-5; 29 May-19 Sept, Mon-Sat 9.30-5.30, Sun 10-5.*

Hadleigh, Suffolk

Toppesfield Hall, Hadleigh, *tel 0473 822922. All year, Mon-Fri, 9-5.15.*

Harwich, Essex

Parkeston Quay, *tel (0255) 506139, fax (0255) 240570. Jan-Mar & Oct-Dec, Tue-Fri 12-7, Sat 10-4. 1 Apr-30 Sept, daily inc Bank Hols, 6.45am-7pm. Closed Christmas week.*

Hemel Hempstead, Hertfordshire

Pavilion Box Office, Marlowes, tel (0442) 64451. *All year, Mon-Fri 10.30-5, Sat 10-1.*

Hertford, Hertfordshire

The Castle, *tel (0992) 584322. All year, Mon-Fri 9-5.30; 1 Jan-3 Apr, Sat 10-2; 10 Apr-30 Oct, Sat 10-4; 6 Nov-18 Dec, Sat 10-2; Bank Hols 10-4.*

Hitchin, Hertfordshire

The Library, Paynes Park, tel (0462)434738. *All year, Mon-Fri, (closed Wed) 9.30-8, Sat 9.30-1.*

Hoveton, Norfolk

* Station Road, *tel (0603) 782281. Easter-end Sept, daily, 9-1, 2-5 (mid Jul-end Aug open 1-2). Oct, Sat-Sun & half-term week, 9-1, 2-5. Books, maps, postcards, souvenirs and information on the Broads.*

Hunstanton, Norfolk

The Green, *tel (0485) 532610. Jan-Mar & Oct-Dec, Mon-Thu 9-5.15, Fri 9-4.45, Sun 9-4, closed for lunch 1-2; Apr-Sept, daily 9-5.45. Closed 25 Dec-1 Jan inclusive.*

Huntingdon, Cambs

The Library, Princes St, *tel (0480) 425831. All year, Mon-Fri, 9.30-5.30. Sat, 9-5. Closed Bank Hol Mons.*

Ipswich, Suffolk

Town Hall, Princes Street, *tel (0473) 258070. Mon-Thur 9-5, Fri 9-4.30; Apr-Aug, Sats 10-4; Sept-Mar, Sats 9.30-12.30. Closed Bank Hols. From May moving to St Stephen's Church, St Stephen's Lane.*

King's Lynn, Norfolk

The Old Gaol House, Saturday Market Place, *tel (0553) 763044. All year, Mon-Thu 9.15-5, Fri 9.15-5.30, Sat 9.15-5. 30 May-26 Sept, also Suns 10-3.*

Lavenham, Suffolk

* Lady Street, *tel (0787) 248207. 5 Apr-1 Oct, daily 10-4.45.*

Lowestoft, Suffolk

* The Esplanade, *tel (0502) 523000/565989. 29 May-end Sept, daily, 9-6; 1 Oct-Easter, Tue-Sun, 11-5.*

Luton, Bedfordshire

65-67 Bute Street, tel (0582) 401579. *All year, Mon-Fri 9.30-4.30; Sat 9.30-4. (TIC located at 45/47A Alma Street until 29 Jan 1993).*

Luton Airport, Bedfordshire

Information Desk, London Luton Airport, tel 0582 405100. *All year, daily, 24 hours.*

Booking accommodation at the King's Lynn office

Maldon, Essex

The Hythe, *tel (0621) 856503. All year, Mon-Sat, 10-4.*

Mundesley, Norfolk

* 2a Station Road, *tel (0263) 721070. 29 Mar-18 Apr Mon- Sat 10-5, Sun 10-4; 19 Apr-24 May, Mon-Sun 10-2; 24 May-26 Sept, Mon- Sat 10-5, Sun 10-4; 27 Sept-31 Oct, Mon-Sun 10-2.*

Norwich, Norfolk

The Guildhall, Gaol Hill, Norwich, NR2 1NF. *tel (0603) 666071, fax (0603) 765389. 1 Jan-31 May, Mon-Sat 9.30-5.30, Bank Hols 9.30-1; 1 Jun-30 Sept, Mon-Sat 9.30-6, Suns & Bank Hols 9.30-1; 1 Oct-31 Dec Mon-Sat 9.30-5.30 & Bank Hols 9.30-1. Closed Christmas & New Year.*

Peterborough, Cambridgeshire

45 Bridge Street, *tel (0733) 317336. All year, Mon-Fri 9-5, Sats 10-4 & Bank Hol Mons from May 10-4.*

Ranworth, Norfolk

* The Staithe, *tel (060549) 453. 9 Apr-31 Oct, daily 9-1, 2-5.*

Rickmansworth, Herts

Three Rivers House, Northway, *tel (0923) 776611 (ext 1381). All year, Mon-Thur 9-5, Fri 9-4.30, closed 1-2.*

Saffron Walden, Essex

1 Market Place, *tel (0799) 524282. All year ex Bank Hols. Mon-Sat, 9.30-5.30 (1 Nov-31 Mar, Mon-Sat, 10-5).*

St Albans, Hertfordshire

Town Hall, *tel (0727) 864511. All year Mon-Fri 10-5, Sat & Bank Hols 10-4.*

Sheringham, Norfolk

* Station Approach, *tel (0263) 824329. 29 Mar-18 Jul Mon-Sat, 10-5, Sun 10-4; 19 Jul-5 Sept Mon-Sat 9.30-7, Sun 9.30-6; 6 Sept-31 Oct Mon-Sat 10-5, Sun 10-4.*

Southend-on-Sea, Essex

Information Bureau, High Street Precinct, *tel (0702) 355120. All year, Mon-Sat, 9.30-5.*

Civic Centre, Victoria Avenue, *tel (0702) 355122. All year, (closed Bank Hols) Mon-Thurs 9-5, Fri 9-4.45.*

South Mimms, Hertfordshire

M25 Welcome Break, Bignalls Corner, *tel (0707) 43233 ext 2. All year, Mon-Sat 9.30-5.30, Sun 9.30-4.30.*

Stevenage, Hertfordshire

The Library, Southgate, *tel (0438) 369441. All year, Mon-Thur 9.30-8, Fri 9.30-5, Sat 9.30-4. Closed Sun & Bank Hols.*

Southwold, Suffolk

* Town Hall, *tel (0502) 724729. 1 May-26 Sept, Mon-Sat, 10-5.30.*

Stowmarket, Suffolk

Wilkes Way, *tel (0449) 676800. 4 Jan-8 Apr, Mon-Fri 9-5, Sat 9-1; 9 Apr-2 Nov, Mon-Fri 9-5.30, Sat 9-4.30 (from 3 Nov Mon-Fri closes 5).*

Sudbury, Suffolk

* Town Hall, Market Hill, *tel (0787) 881320. 5 Apr-1 Oct, Mon-Sat, 10-4.45.*

Thurrock, Essex

Granada Motorway Service Area, M25 Thurrock, Grays, *tel (0708)863733. All year, Mon-Sun, 9-5 (July & Aug closes 6).*

Walsingham, Norfolk

* Shirehall Museum, Common Place, *tel (0328) 820510. 8 Apr-30 Sept, daily; Mon 10-1, 2-5, Tue-Sat 10-5, Sun 2-5; Oct, Sats 10-5, Suns 2- 5.*

Wells, Norfolk

* Wells Centre, Staithe St, *tel (0328) 710885. 29 Mar-18 Jul, Mon-Sat 10-5, Sun 10-4; 19 Jul-5 Sept Mon-Sat 9.30-7; 6 Sept-31 Oct, Mon-Sat 10-5, Sun 10-4.*

Welwyn Garden City, Hertfordshire

Campus West, The Campus, *tel (0707) 390653. All year, Mon-Fri 9-5.15 (Thur closes 1); Sat 10-12.30.*

Wisbech, Cambridgeshire

District Library, Ely Place, *tel (0945) 583263. All year. Tue & Wed, 10-6; Thur & Fri, 10-7; Sat, 9.30-5. Closed Bank Hols.* **Telephone enquiries only Mon,** *9-4.*

TOURIST INFORMATION POINTS

Limited information is also available from the following information points:

* **Aylsham,** Bure Valley Railway, Station, Norwich Road *Tel: (0263) 733858. Apr-Oct.*

Beccles, Public Library, Blyburgate *Tel: (0502) 714073. All year, Tue-Sat.*

***Santon Downham,** High Lodge Visitor Centre. *Tel (0842)810271. Apr-Oct, daily*

***Dedham,** Duchy Barn *Tel: (0206) 323447. Easter-mid Oct, daily.*

Downham Market, Town Hall, Bridge Street *Tel: (0366) 387440 All year, Mon-Sat (closes Mon Nov-end Mar).*

East Bergholt, Pot Hole, Church Plain, *Easter-end Sept, daily ex Fri. Personal callers only.*

Holt, Sanders Coaches, Market Place. *Tel 0263 713100. All year, Mon-Sat*

***Halstead,** Lodge Gate, Townsford Mill. *Tel: (0787) 477411. Apr-Sept, Tue-Sat*

Needham Market, Council Offices. *Tel: (0449) 720711. All year, Mon-Fri*

Newmarket, Public Library, The Rookery.*Tel: (0638) 661216.*

***Swaffham,** Market Place *tel: (0760) 22255. Apr-Oct, Mon-Sat*

Thetford, Ancient House Museum, 21 White Hart Street *tel: (0842) 752599. All year Mon-Sat, also Suns June-Sept.*

***Walton on the Naze,** Princess Esplanade, *tel (0255) 675542. May-Sept, daily 9-5.*

***Watton,** The Clock Tower, High Street. *tel: (0953) 881440. May-Sept, Wed, Fri, Sat, Sun.*

***Woburn Heritage Centre,** Old St Mary's Church, *tel (0525) 290631. Apr-Oct, daily.*

Woodbridge, Public Library, New Street. *tel: (0394) 384457. All year, Tue-Sat.*

***Wymondham,** Market Cross, Market Place. *Tel: (0953) 604721. Easter-end Aug, Mon-Sat*

East Anglia's newest centre at Thurrock on the M25

London Stansted Airport. The perfect gateway for Great Britain and Europe.

London

Cambridge

Constable Country

Scotland

Ireland

France

Germany

Italy

The new London Stansted airport gives you the best of both worlds.

It's on the doorstep of the Capital and perfect for onward flights to Ireland, Scotland and Europe.

Yet the enchanting East Anglian countryside (the source of inspiration for John Constable's famous paintings) and the historic cities of Cambridge and Norwich are all within easy reach.

It is also one of the newest and most up-to-date airports in Europe.

High on the list of its many features is a train station built directly under the Terminal. The train ride takes just 41 minutes to London. And there are also direct trains to Cambridge, Birmingham and the North.

For details of flights to London Stansted from the USA telephone American Airlines on 800 624 6262.

B·A·A

London Stansted
The World-Class Airport.

TRAVEL

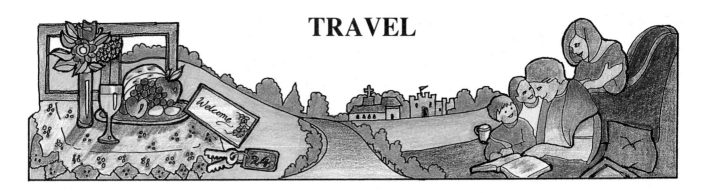

RAIL

Bedford	0234 269686
Bury St Edmunds	0473 693396
Cambridge	0223 311999
Chelmsford	0245 252111
Clacton-on-Sea	0206 564777
Colchester	0206 564777
Great Yarmouth	0603 632055
Harwich/Dovercourt	0206 564777
Hitchin	0582 27612
Huntingdon	0480 454468
Ipswich	0473 693396
King's Lynn	0553 772021
Lowestoft	0603 632055
Luton	0582 27612
Milton Keynes	0908 370883
Norwich	0603 632055
Peterborough	0733 68181
Southend-on-Sea	0702 611811
Stevenage	0582 27612
Watford	0923 245001

British Rail, Anglia Region, 112/114 Prince of Wales Road, Norwich, NR1 1NZ. Tel: (0603) 622255.

CAR HIRE

Avis
Head Office, Tel: 081 848 8765. Cambridge (0223) 212551, Colchester (0206) 41133, Great Yarmouth (0493) 851050, Norwich (0603) 416719, Peterborough (0733) 349489, Stansted (0279) 663030, Bedford (0908) 281334, Hemel Hempstead (0442) 230092.

Budget Rent-A-Car
Offices at: Bury St Edmunds (0284) 701345, Clacton (0255) 222444, Ipswich (0473) 216149, Cambridge (0223) 323838, Hitchin (0462) 431151, Luton (0582) 503101.

Candor Motors Ltd
Tel: Braintree (0376) 321202, Colchester (0206) 571171.

Europcar
Tel: 081 950 4080 (Head Office). Offices at Cambridge (0223) 233644, Ipswich (0473) 211067, Norwich (0603) 400280, Lowestoft (0502) 516982, Welwyn Garden City (0483) 715179, Hemel Hempstead (0923) 260026, Luton (0582) 413438.

Hertz Rent-A-Car
Offices at Cambridge (0223) 414600, Colchester (0206) 866559, Ipswich (0473) 218506, Great Yarmouth (0493) 857086, Norwich Airport (0603) 404010, Mildenhall (0638) 717354 Peterborough [station] (0733) 65252, [Fengate] (0733) 340493, Luton (0582) 450333, Welwyn Garden City (0707) 331433.

Willhire Ltd
Offices at Mildenhall (0638) 717505, Beck Row (0638) 712080, Bury St Edmunds (0284) 762888, Cambridge (0223) 414600, Chelmsford (0245) 265853, Colchester (0206) 867888, Ipswich (0473) 213344, Norwich (0603) 416411, Norwich Airport (0603) 404010, Great Yarmouth (0493) 857130, Southend (0702) 546666, Newmarket (0638) 669209, Thetford (0842) 761578 and Peterborough (0733) 896955.

AIRPORTS

Cambridge Airport Teversham Tel: (02205) 3621/2651/3622

Norwich Airport Tel: (0603) 411923

Southend Airport Tel: (0702) 340201. Destinations to Jersey, Guernsey and Malta.

Stansted Airport Bishop's Stortford Tel: (0279) 680500. Information desk Tel: (0279) 662379/662520.

Luton Airport Tel: (0582) 405100

Airlines:
Suckling Airways Reservations Tel: (02205) 3393. Destinations from Cambridge to Amsterdam and Cambridge to Manchester.

Air UK Tel: (0603) 424288. Destinations from Norwich: Aberdeen, Amsterdam, Bergen, Edinburgh, Humberside, Jersey, Guernsey, Stavanger, Tees-side. Tel: (0279) 680146 Destinations from Stansted: Aberdeen, Amsterdam, Bergen, Edinburgh, Florence, Humberside, Jersey, Guernsey, Nice, Paris, Tees-side,

Britannia Airways Tel: (0582) 424155. Destinations from Luton: Scheduled flights to Belfast only.

Premier Holidays, Cambridge Tel: (0223) 66122, Channel Islands.

FERRY COMPANIES

Stena Line Harwich Tel: (0255) 243333. Head office Kent (0233) 647047. Hook of Holland-Harwich: twice daily.

Scandinavian Seaways Harwich Tel: (0255) 240240.

Harwich-Esbjerg: 3 times a week (Mon, Thur, Sat), every other day in summer. Harwich-Hamburg: Nov & Dec (Tue, Thur, Sat). Rest of year every other day. Harwich-Gothenburg: Nov-Feb (Fri & Sun). Mar, Apr, May (Wed, Fri, Sun). Jun-Sep (Mon, Wed, Fri).

P & O European Ferries: Felixstowe Tel: (0394) 604100. Zeebrugge-Felixstowe: 2 daily

BUS and COACH SERVICES

There are many bus service operators throughout the region and each county council has an enquiry number as follows:

Bedfordshire	0234 228337
Cambridgeshire	0223 317740
Essex	0245 492211
Hertfordshire Traveline:	
Hertford	0992 556765
Hitchin	0462 438138
Watford	0923 684784
Norfolk	0603 613613
Suffolk	0473 265676

LOCAL EXCURSIONS

Beestons, Hadleigh (Suffolk) Tel: (0473) 823243. Dep Hadleigh and district.

Cedric Coaches International, Wivenhoe Tel:(0206) 824363.

Premier Travel, Cambridge Tel: (0480) 434909. Dep Cambridge.

Kenzies Coaches Ltd., Royston Tel: (0763) 260288.

Ipswich Coach Travel, Tel: (0473) 252895. Dep Ipswich, Stowmarket, Felixstowe and district.

United Counties Bus Co., Bedford Tel: (0234) 262151.

Cedar Coaches, Bedford Tel: (0234) 354054.

Barfordian Coaches, Bedford Tel: (0234) 870235.

Buffalo Travel, Flitwick Tel: (0525) 712132.

Luton & District Transport Tel: (0582) 400040.

Seamarks Coaches, Luton Tel: (0582) 574191

TML Tours, Ware Tel: (0920) 487999.

Reg's Coaches, Hertford Tel: (0992) 586302.

Golden Boy Coaches, Hoddesdon Tel: (0992) 467984.

County Bus & Coach Co., Hertford Tel: (0992) 444444.

St. Albans Tricolour, Welwyn Garden City Tel: (0707) 326263.

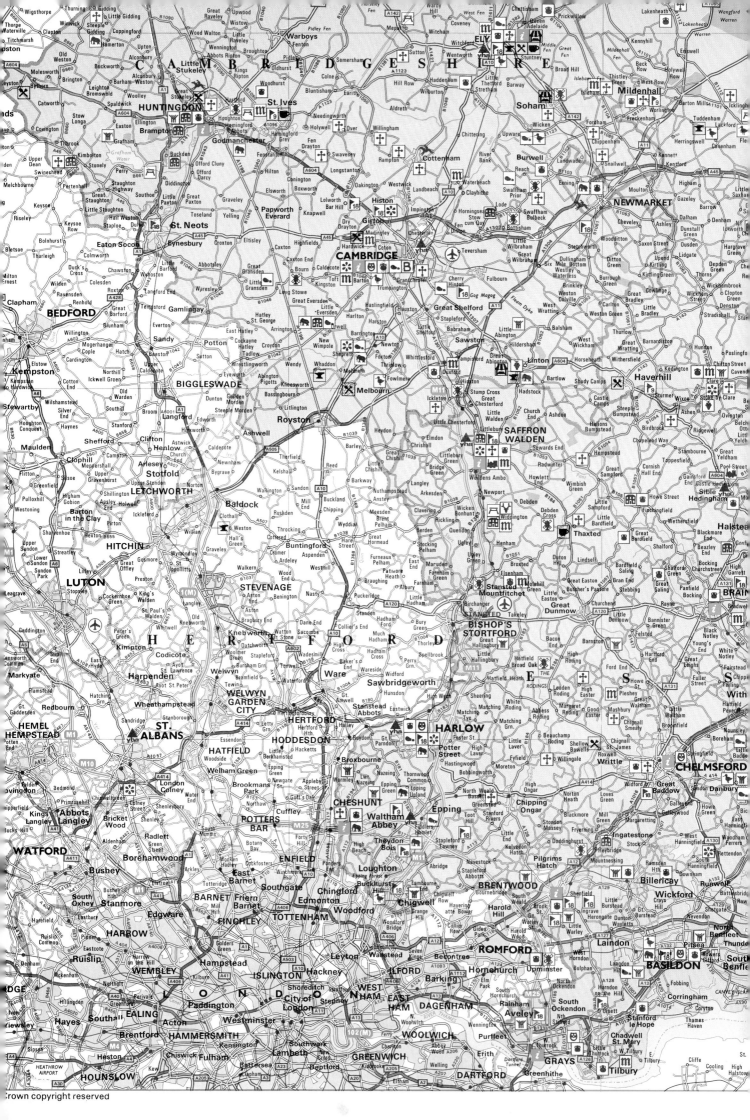

INDEX